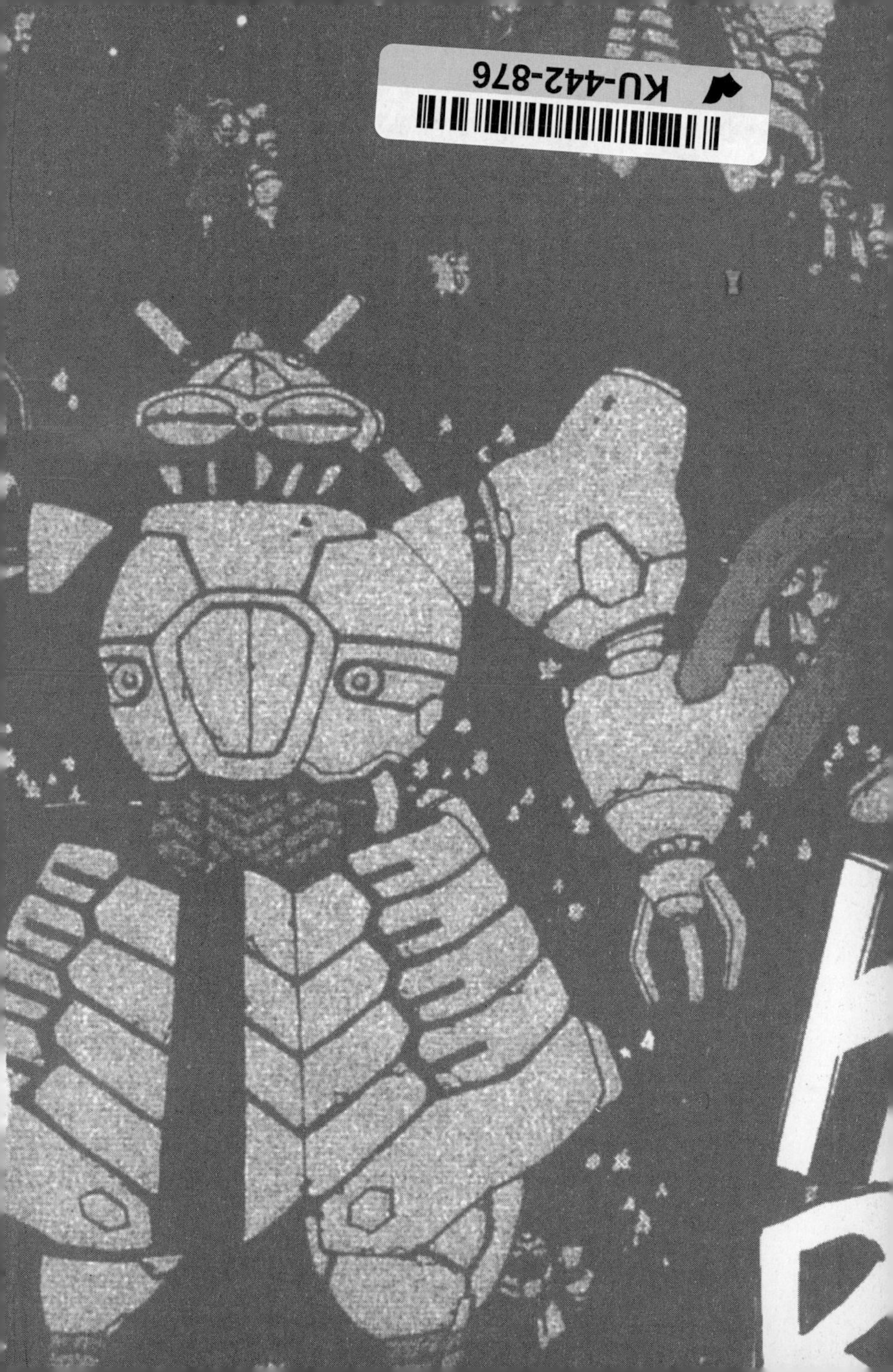

C.B. Cebulski and **Noriko Furuhata**
Translation

Dan Nakrosis and **Dano Ink Studios**
Retouch and Lettering

Vanessa Satone
Designer

Eve Grandt and **Luben Damianov**
Production Assistants

Stephen Pakula
Production Manager

Mike Lackey
Director of Print Production

Stephanie Shalofsky
Vice President, Production

John O'Donnell
Publisher

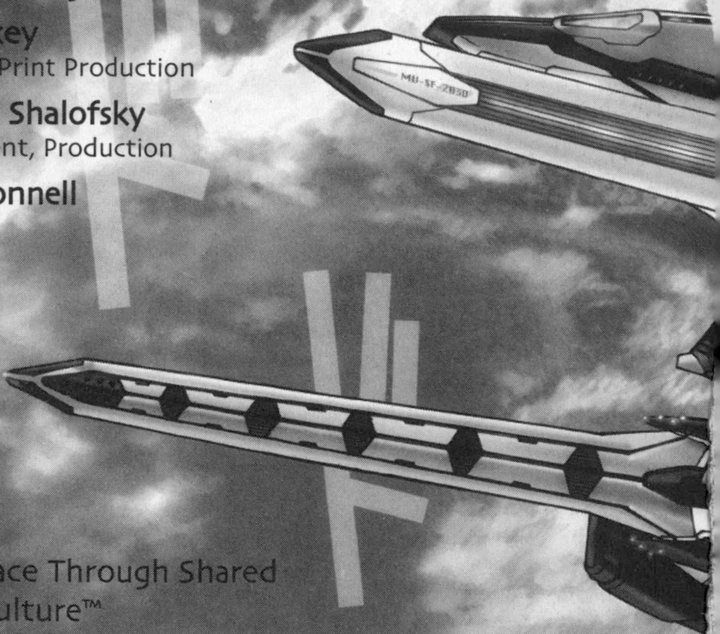
MU-SF-2830

World Peace Through Shared Popular Culture™

CentralParkMedia.com

CpmPress.com

Nadesico Book Three. Published by CPM Manga, a division of Central Park Media Corporation. Office of Publication – 250 West 57th Street, Suite 317, New York, NY 10107. Original Japanese Version "Meteor Schlachtschiff NADESICO Volume 3" © KIA ASAMIYA 1997. Originally published in Japan in 1997 by KADOKAWA SHOTEN PUBLISHING Co., Ltd., Tokyo. English version © 1999, 2000, 2004 Central Park Media Corporation. CPM Manga and logo are registered trademarks of Central Park Media Corporation. All rights reserved. Price per copy $9.99, price in Canada may vary. ISBN: 1-58664-940-X. Catalog number CMX 62403MM. UPC: 7-19987-00624-9-00311. Printed in Canada

NADESICO

Book Three

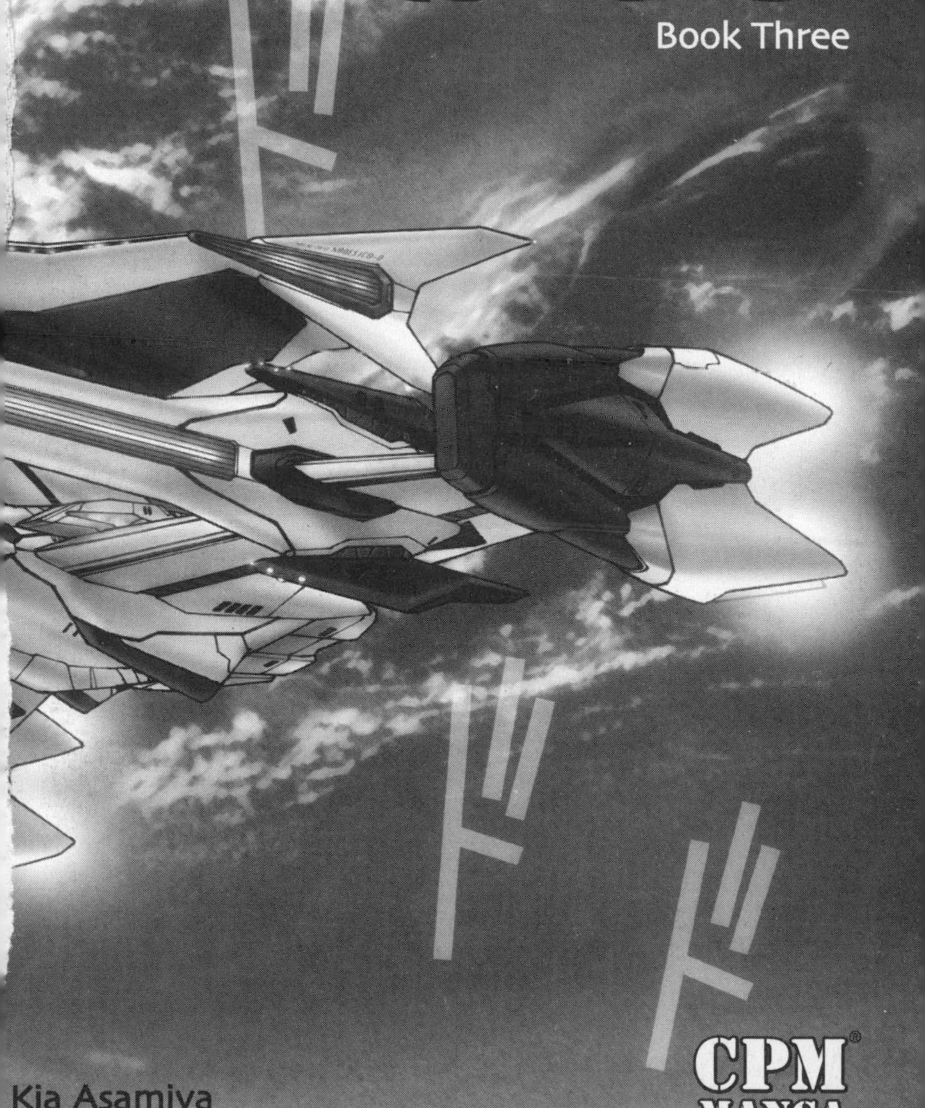

Kia Asamiya
Writer and Artist

CPM MANGA
New York, New York

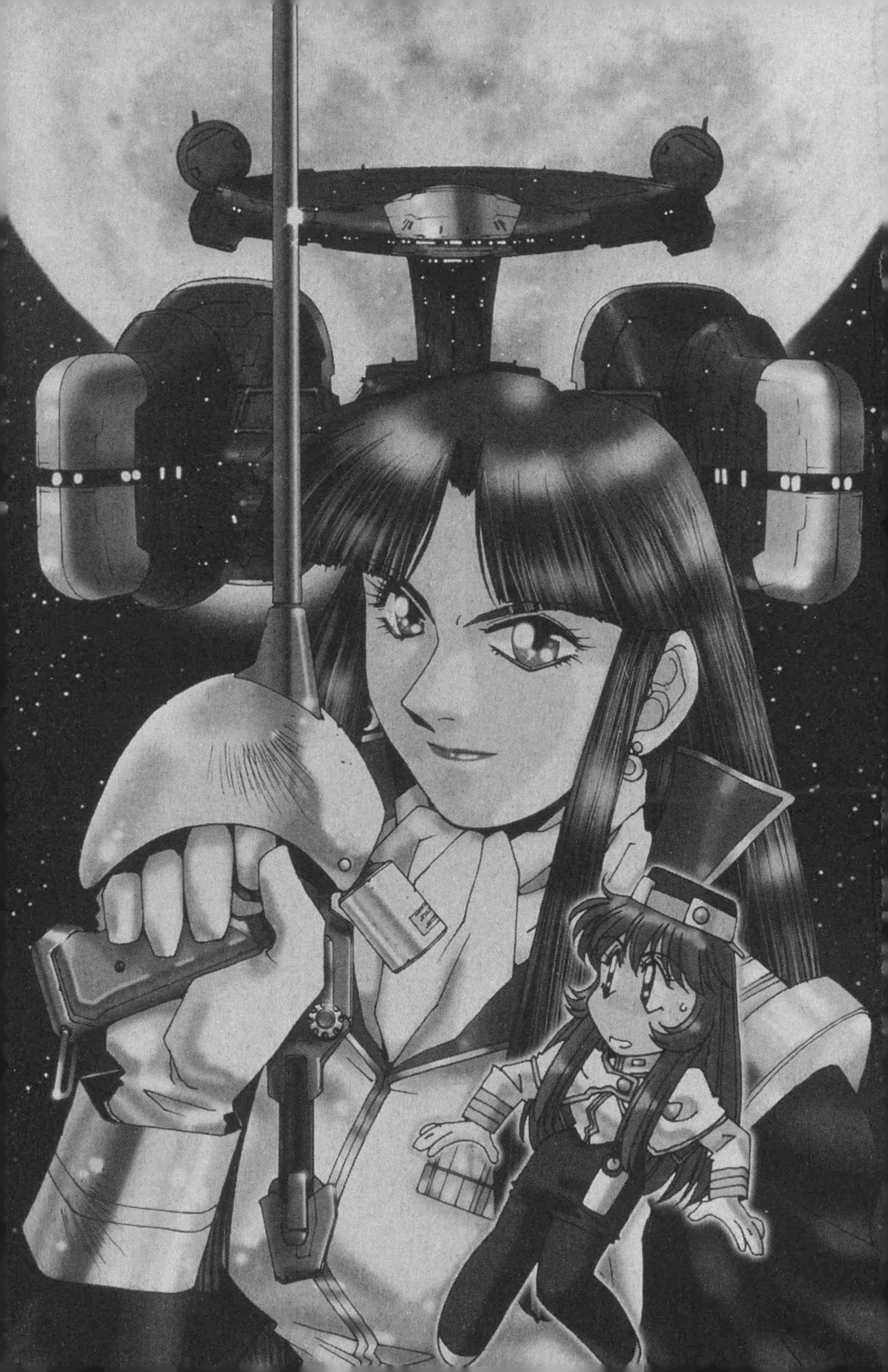

Contents

Character Profiles

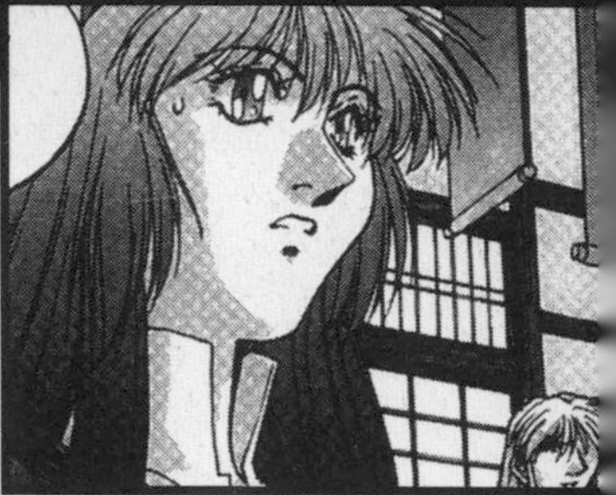

Yurika Misumaru
The headstrong captain of the *Space Battleship Nadesico*. Badly wounded during the Jupiterian attack, Captain Yurika has time to reevaluate her life as well as her career. Her decisions will change the lives of her crewmembers forever.

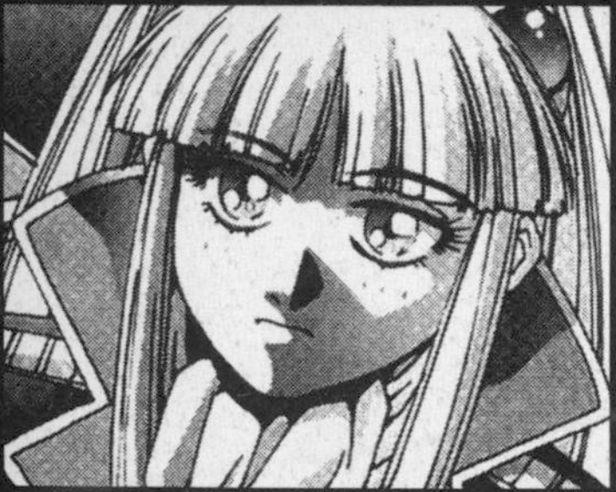

Ruri Hoshino
This cold and calculating youth is a genius, and is given command of the *Yamato-Nadesico* after crash landing on Mars. Everyone else seems to think she has what it takes to be a great leader…now if she could only convince herself.

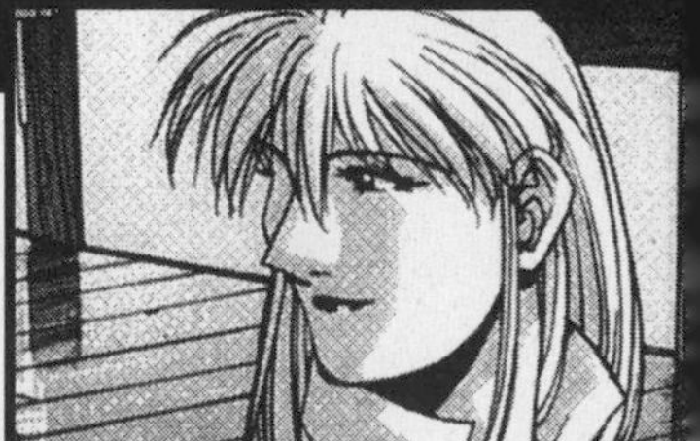

Ines Fresanjeu
The *Nadesico's* in-house doctor has a secret…one that will shake the *Nadesico* to its very foundation.

Story So Far...

The *Space Battleship Nadesico*, gravely damaged in an attack by the Jupiterians, crash-landed on Mars, causing irreparable damage and badly injuring Captain Yurika in the process. Luckily, the *Nadesico* landed close to a research facility where parts from the long lost ship *Yamato* were being stored.

Rebuilt and more powerful than ever, the newly renamed *Yamato-Nadesico* launched into space, blasting through a Jupiterian fortress under the leadership of acting-Captain Ruri Hoshino. So impressed was she by Ruri's skills, Captain Yurika handed over control of the *Nadesico* to Ruri.

After returning to Earth for a debriefing, Captain Yurika visited the ship's doctor, Ines Fresanjeu, who promptly announced that Captain Yurika was to lead all the gods of the *Yamato* pantheon, and proceeded to kidnap her.

What does it all mean? And how will the rest of the crew react to this shocking turn of events?

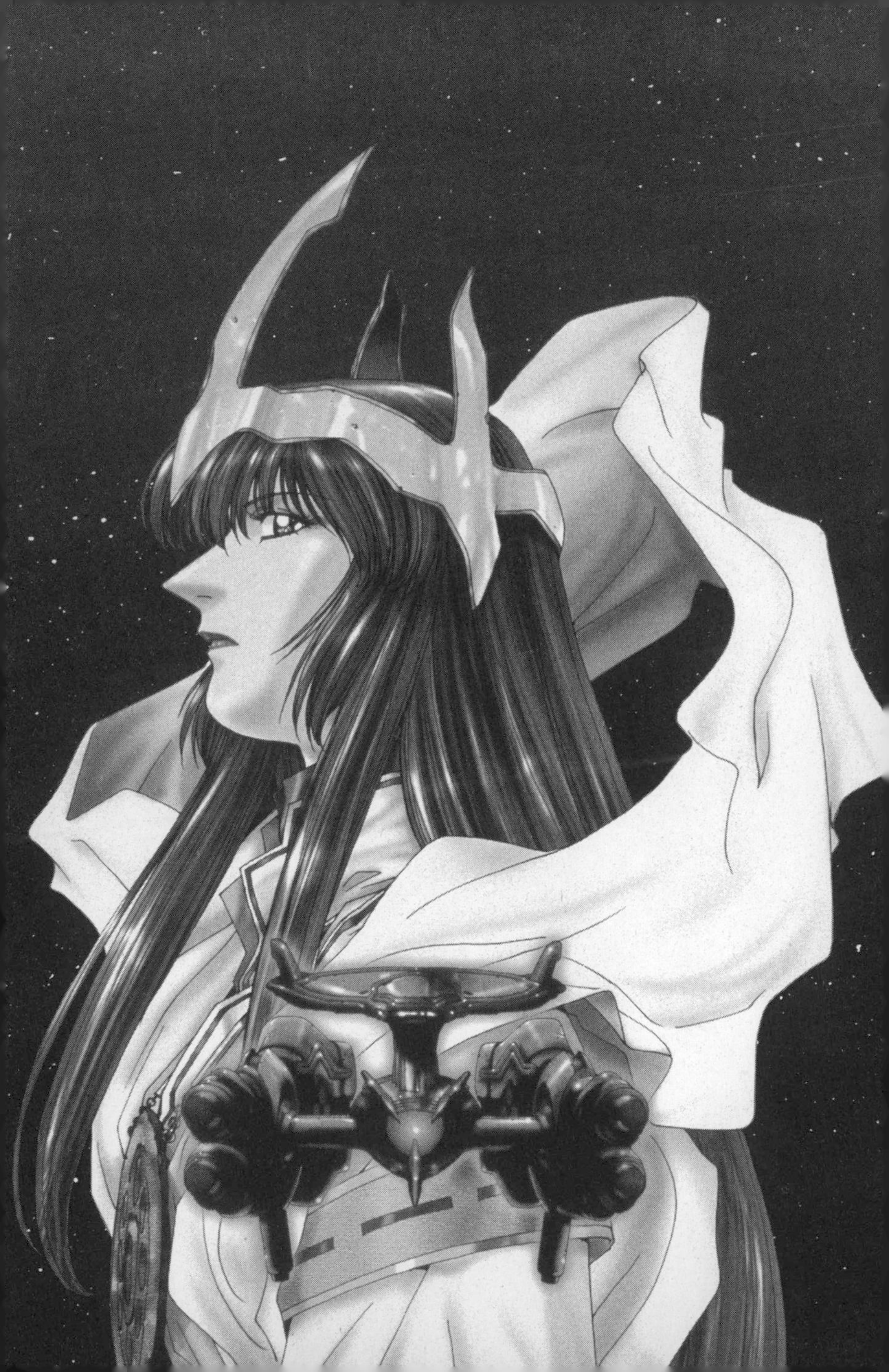

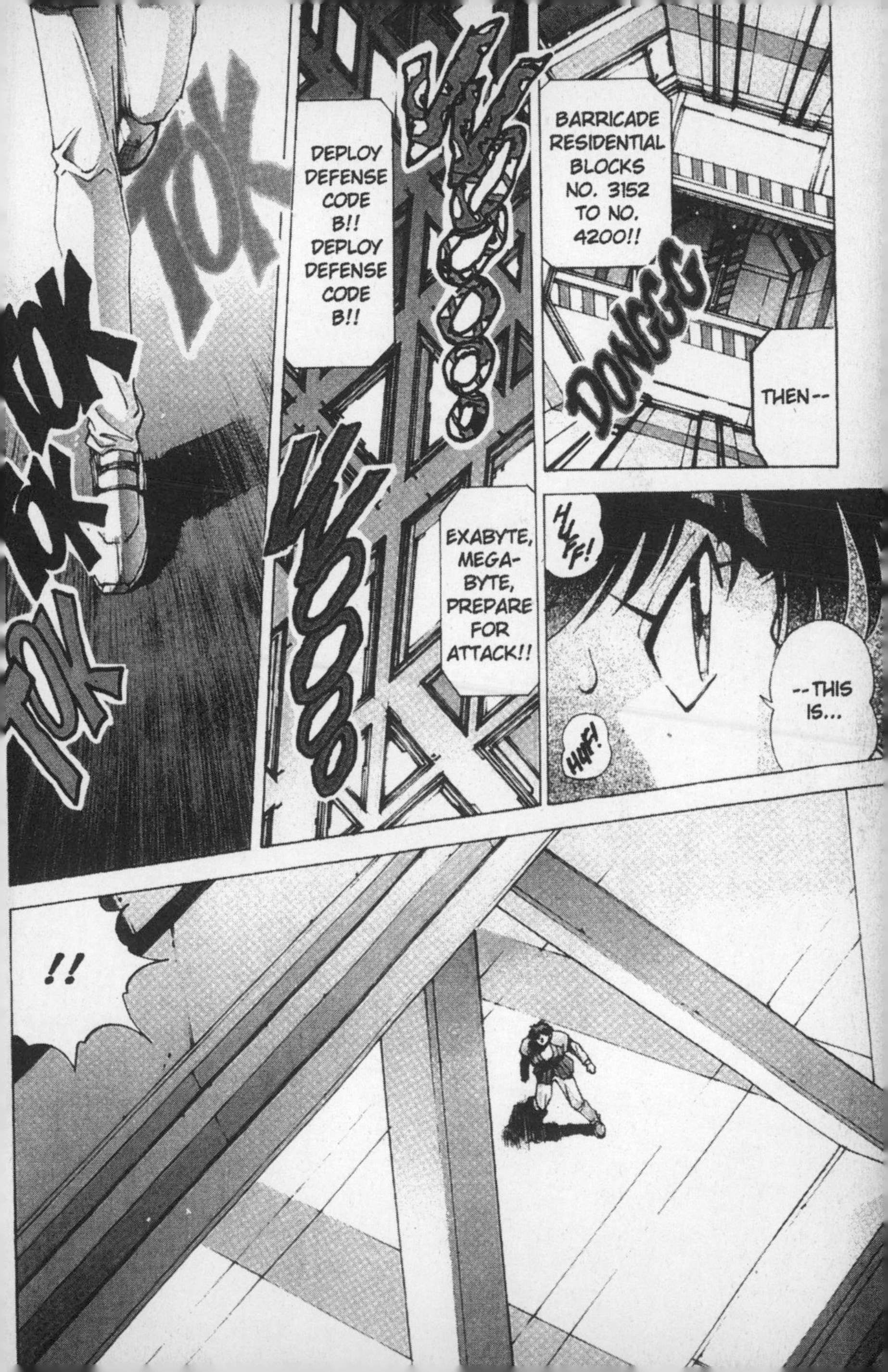

TOK TOK
TOK TOK
DEPLOY DEFENSE CODE B!! DEPLOY DEFENSE CODE B!!
WOOOOO
EXABYTE, MEGA-BYTE, PREPARE FOR ATTACK!!
BARRICADE RESIDENTIAL BLOCKS NO. 3152 TO NO. 4200!!
DONGGG
THEN--
HUFF!
--THIS IS...
HUF!
!!

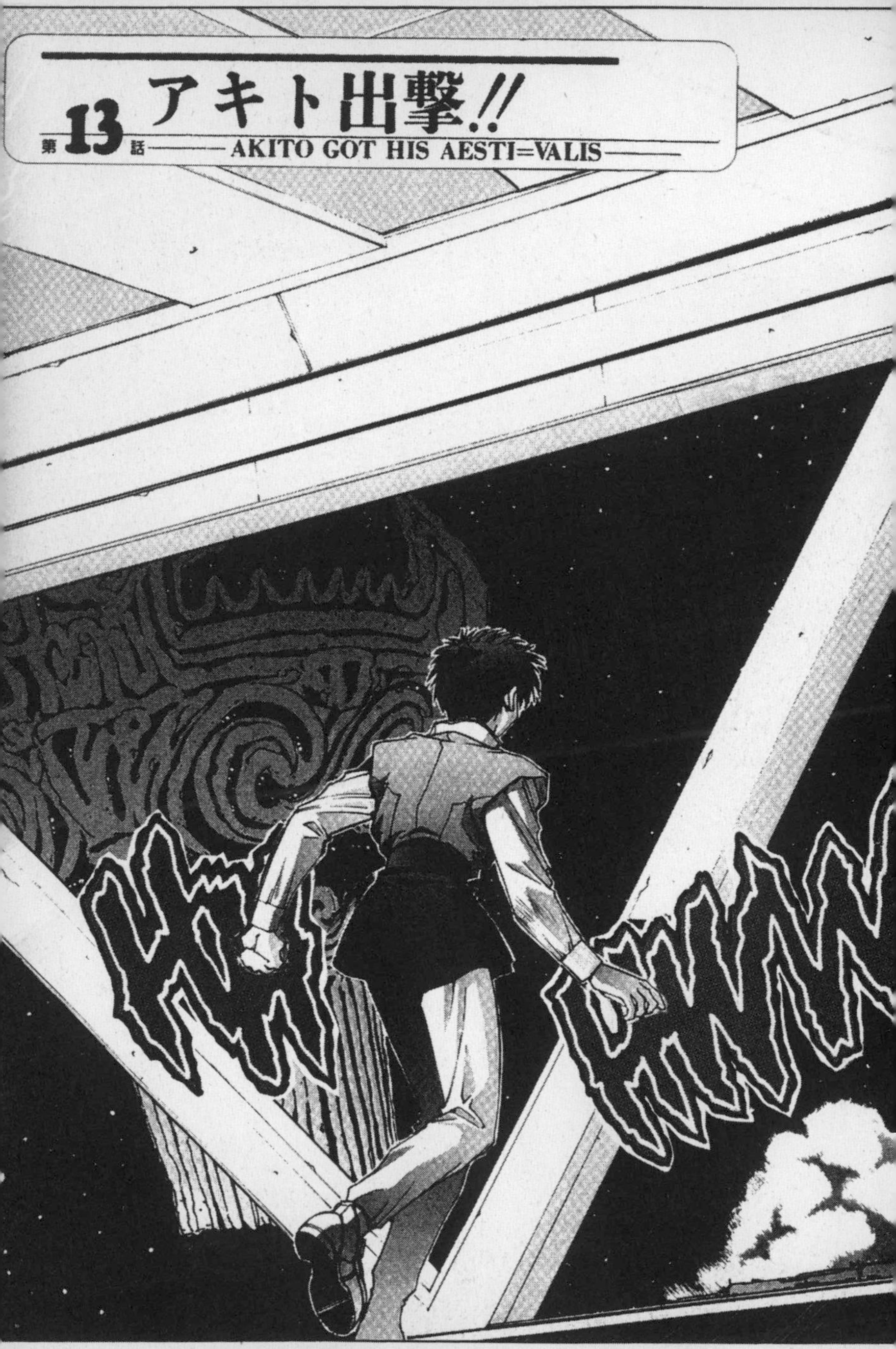
第13話 アキト出撃!!
AKITO GOT HIS AESTI=VALIS

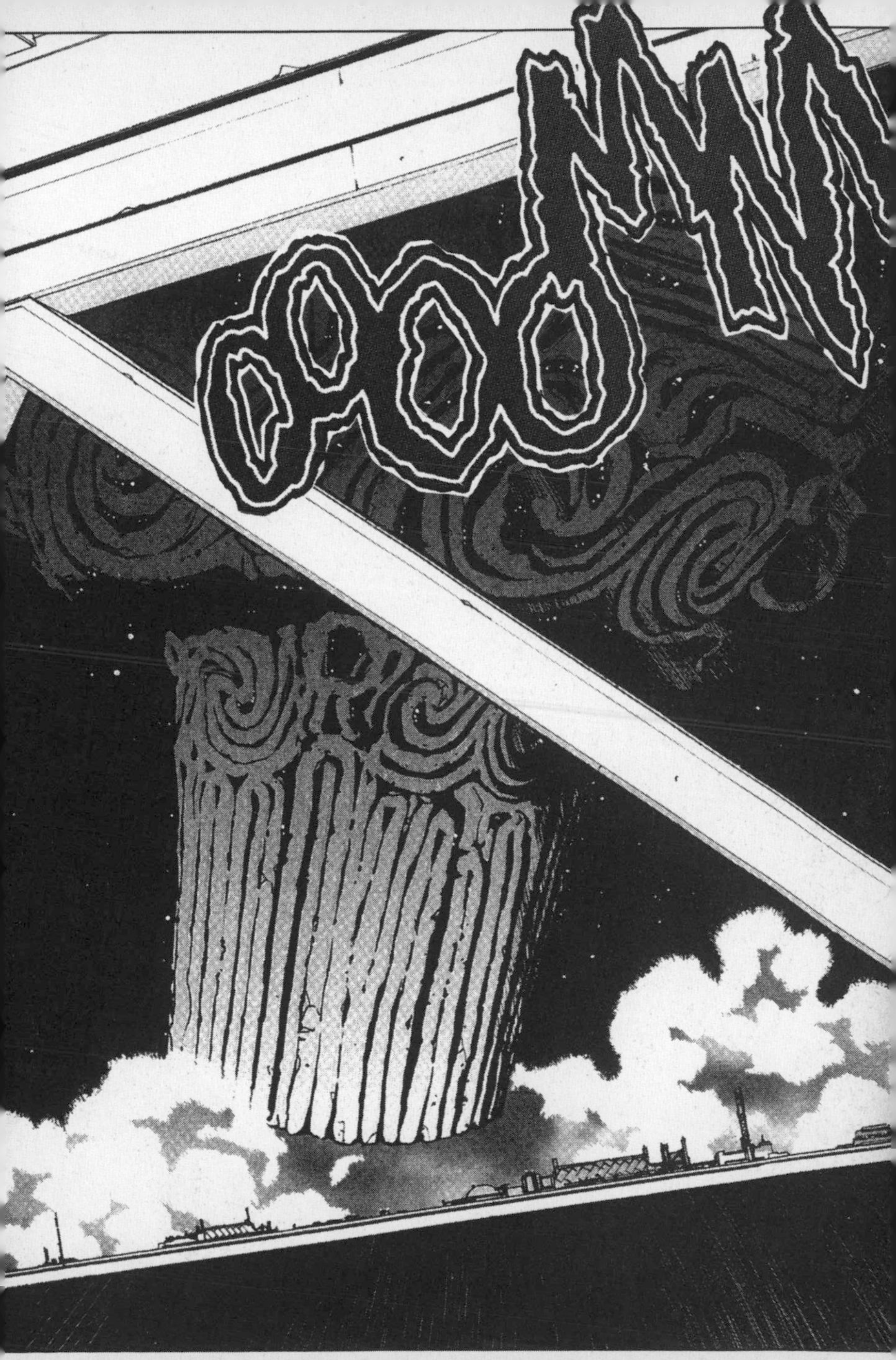

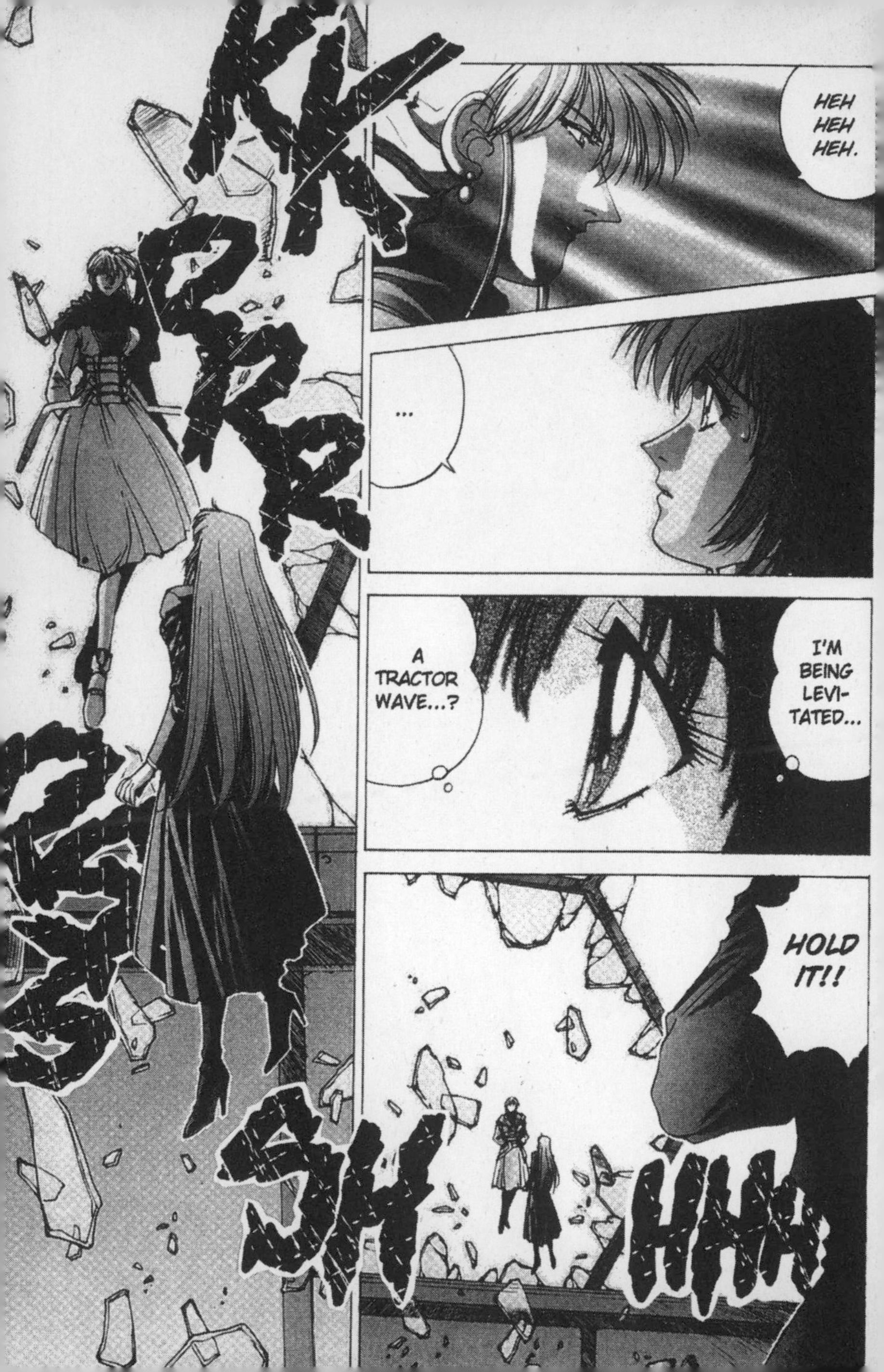
HEH HEH HEH.
...
A TRACTOR WAVE...?
I'M BEING LEVI-TATED...
HOLD IT!!

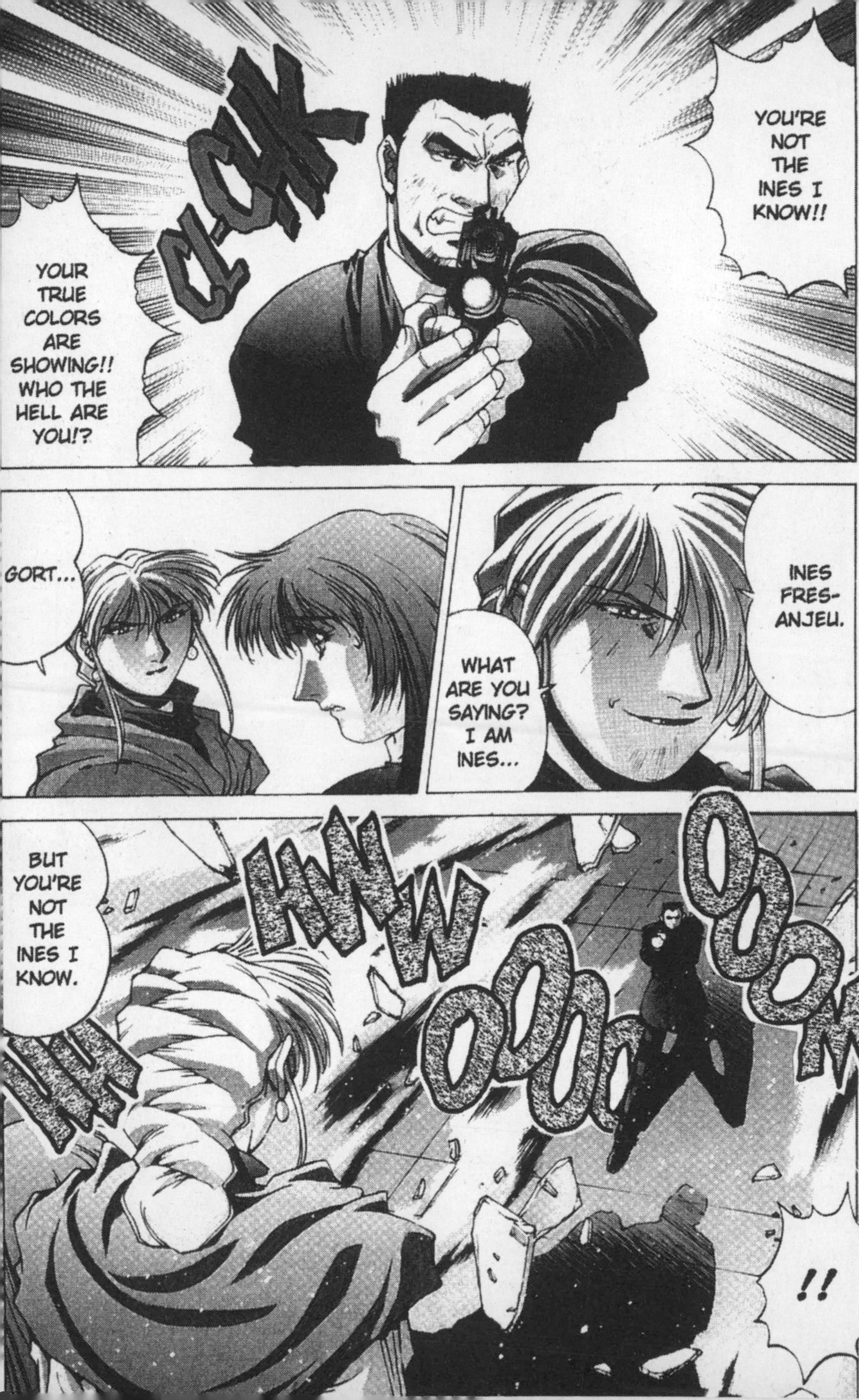
CL-CLIK
YOUR TRUE COLORS ARE SHOWING!! WHO THE HELL ARE YOU!?
YOU'RE NOT THE INES I KNOW!!
GORT...
WHAT ARE YOU SAYING? I AM INES...
INES FRES-ANJEU.
BUT YOU'RE NOT THE INES I KNOW.
HWWOOOOOOM
!!

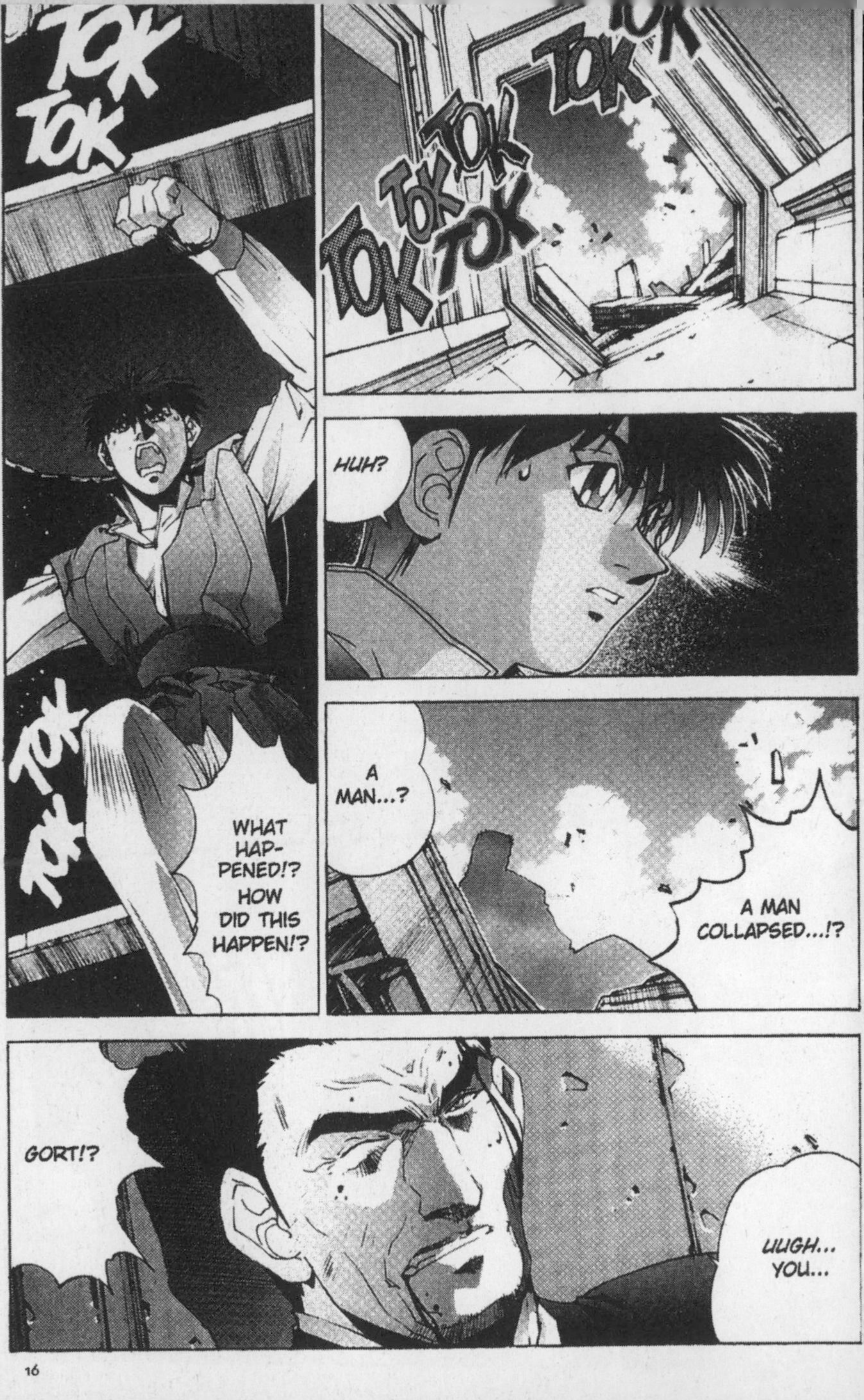
TOK TOK
TOK TOK
WHAT HAP-PENED!? HOW DID THIS HAPPEN!?
TOK TOK TOK TOK TOK TOK
HUH?
A MAN...?
A MAN COLLAPSED...!?
GORT!?
UUGH... YOU...

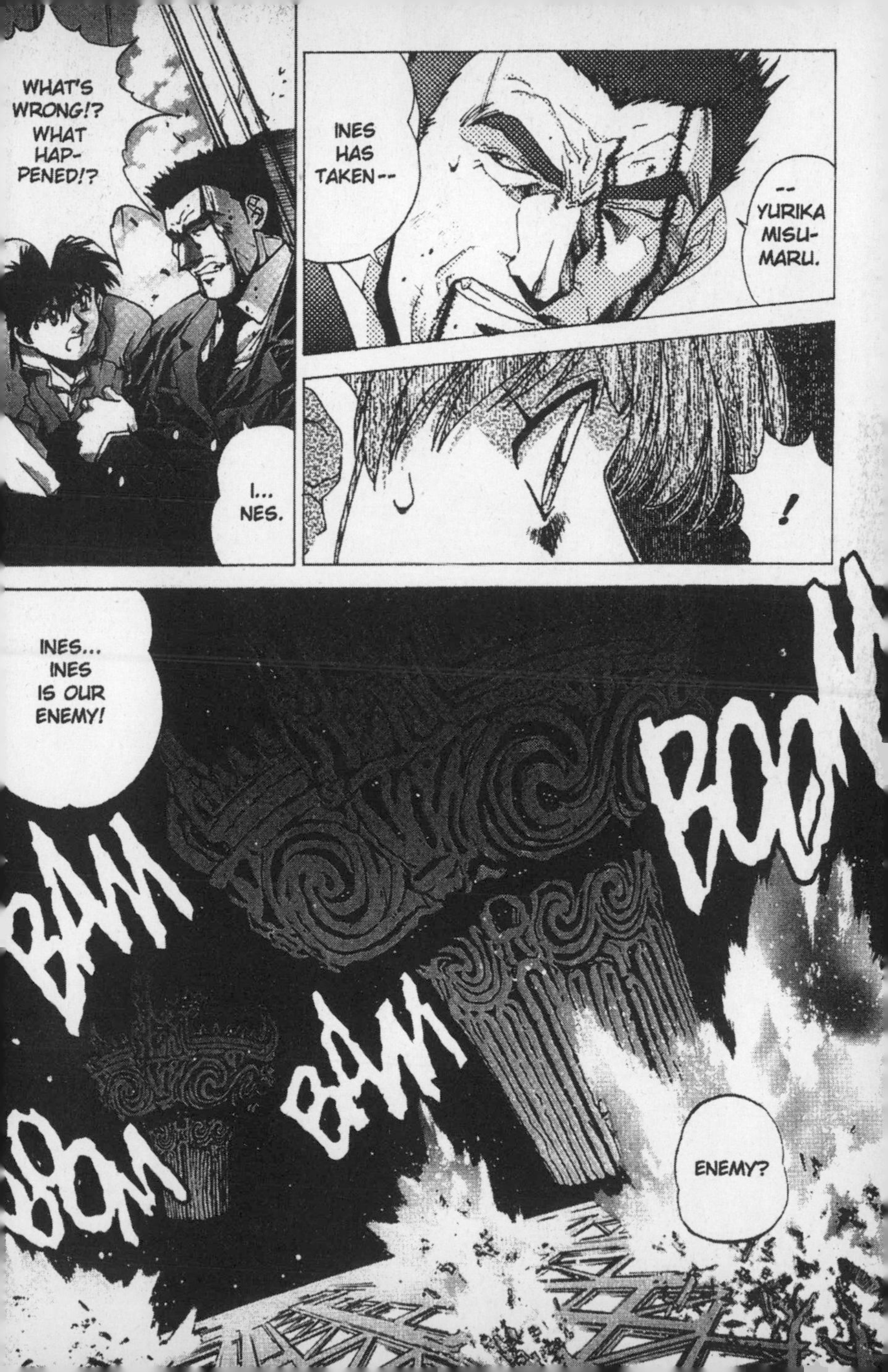

WHAT'S WRONG!? WHAT HAP- PENED!?
I... NES.
INES HAS TAKEN--
--YURIKA MISU- MARU.
!
INES... INES IS OUR ENEMY!
BAM
BOOM
BAM
BOO
ENEMY?

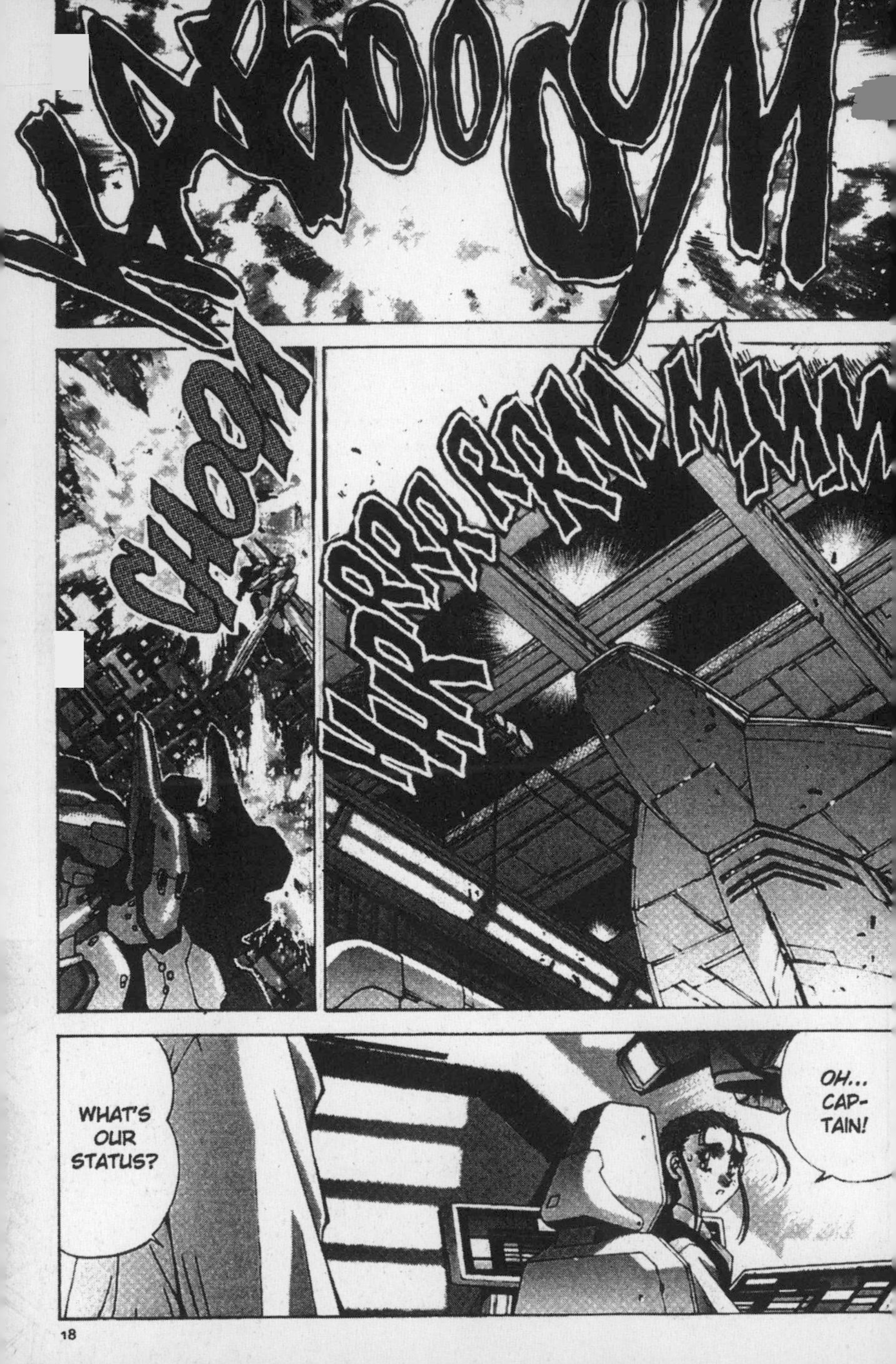
WHAT'S OUR STATUS?
OH... CAP-TAIN!

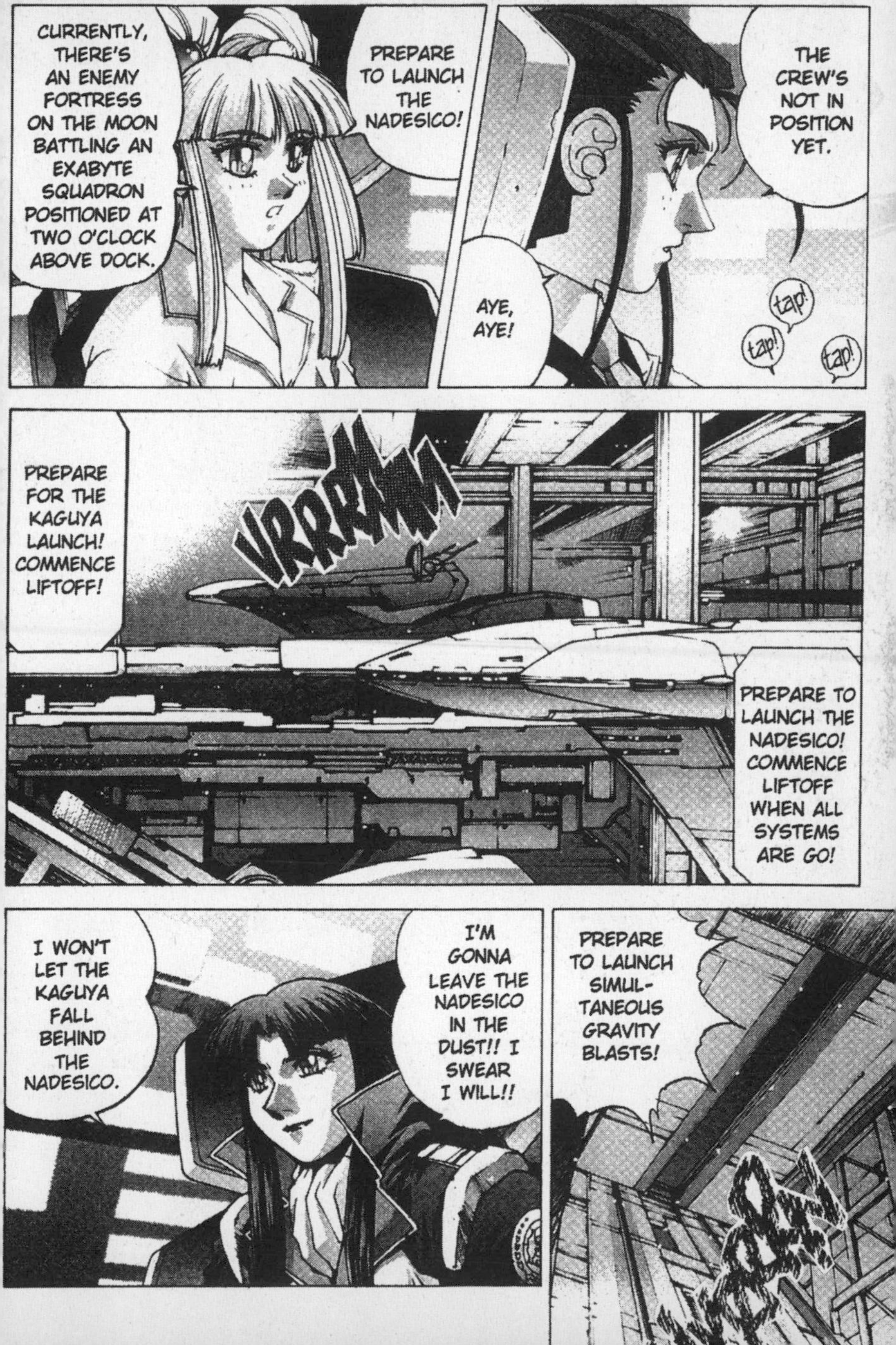
CURRENTLY, THERE'S AN ENEMY FORTRESS ON THE MOON BATTLING AN EXABYTE SQUADRON POSITIONED AT TWO O'CLOCK ABOVE DOCK.
PREPARE TO LAUNCH THE NADESICO!
THE CREW'S NOT IN POSITION YET.
AYE, AYE!
tap!
tap!
tap!
PREPARE FOR THE KAGUYA LAUNCH! COMMENCE LIFTOFF!
PREPARE TO LAUNCH THE NADESICO! COMMENCE LIFTOFF WHEN ALL SYSTEMS ARE GO!
I WON'T LET THE KAGUYA FALL BEHIND THE NADESICO.
I'M GONNA LEAVE THE NADESICO IN THE DUST!! I SWEAR I WILL!!
PREPARE TO LAUNCH SIMUL-TANEOUS GRAVITY BLASTS!

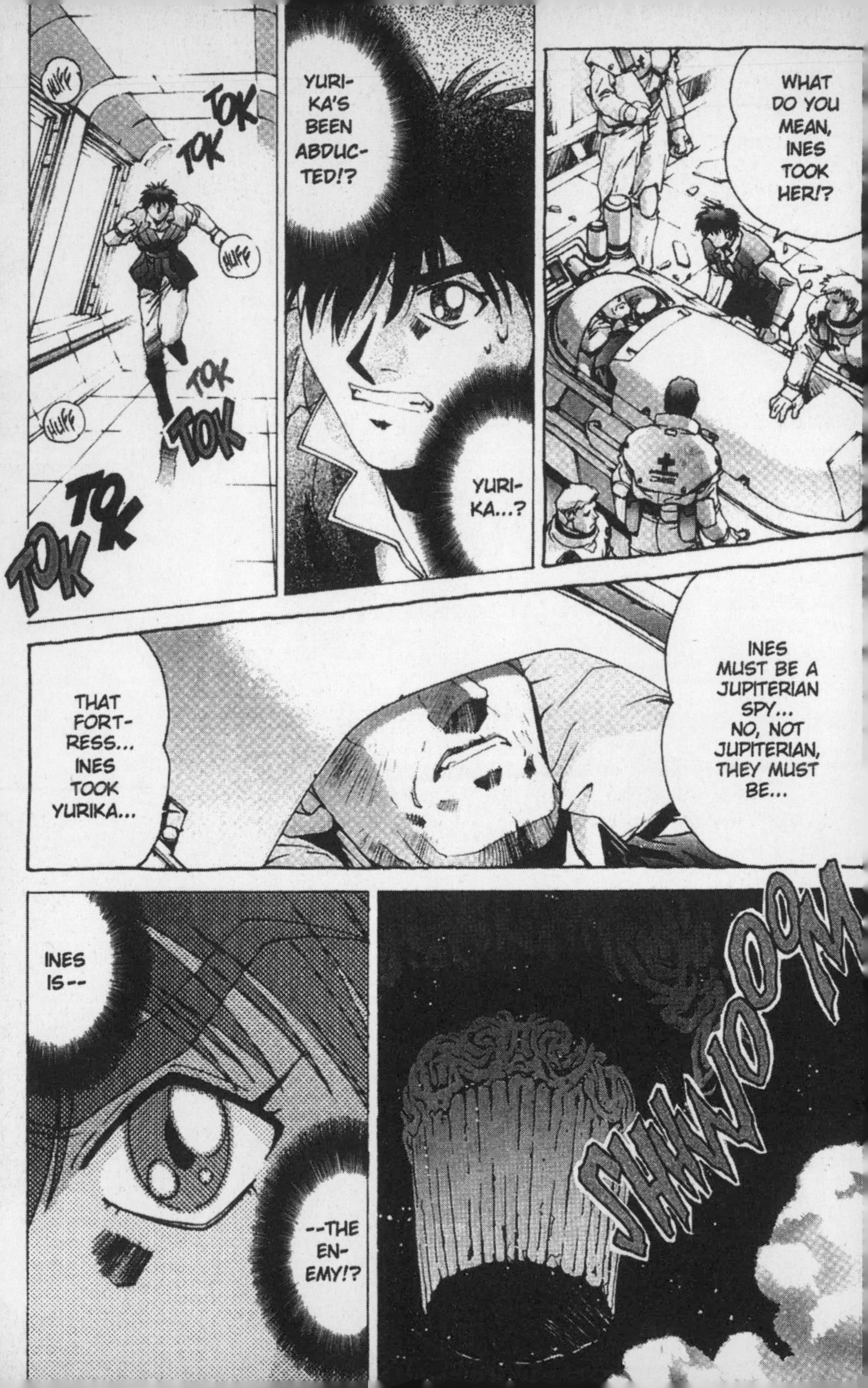
HUFF
TOK TOK
HUFF
TOK TOK
HUFF
TOK TOK
YURI-KA'S BEEN ABDUC-TED!?
YURI-KA...?
WHAT DO YOU MEAN, INES TOOK HER!?
THAT FORT-RESS... INES TOOK YURIKA...
INES MUST BE A JUPITERIAN SPY... NO, NOT JUPITERIAN, THEY MUST BE...
INES IS--
--THE EN-EMY!?
SHWOOOOM

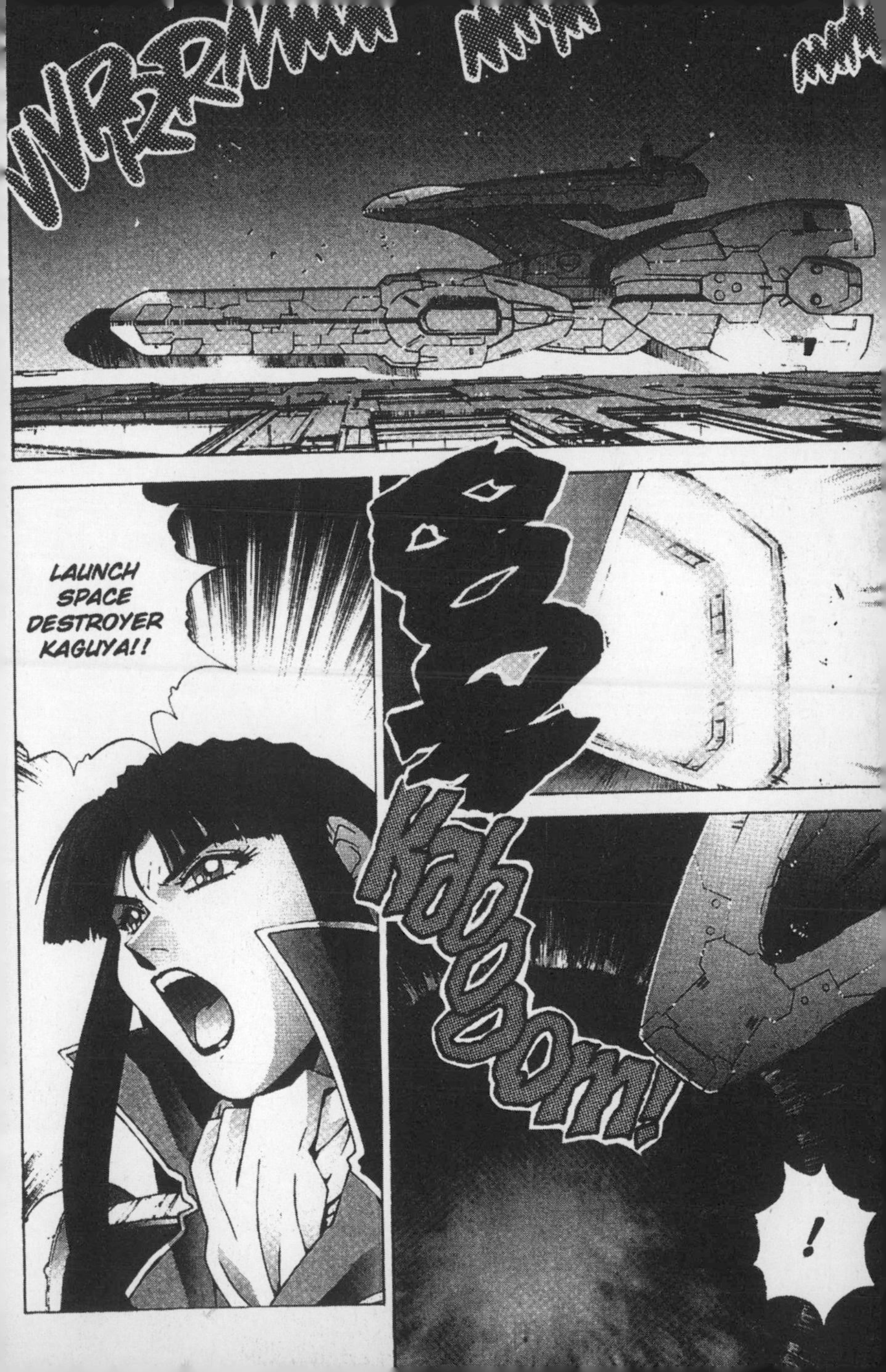
VWRRRMMMM MMM MMM
LAUNCH SPACE DESTROYER KAGUYA!!
KABOOOM!
!

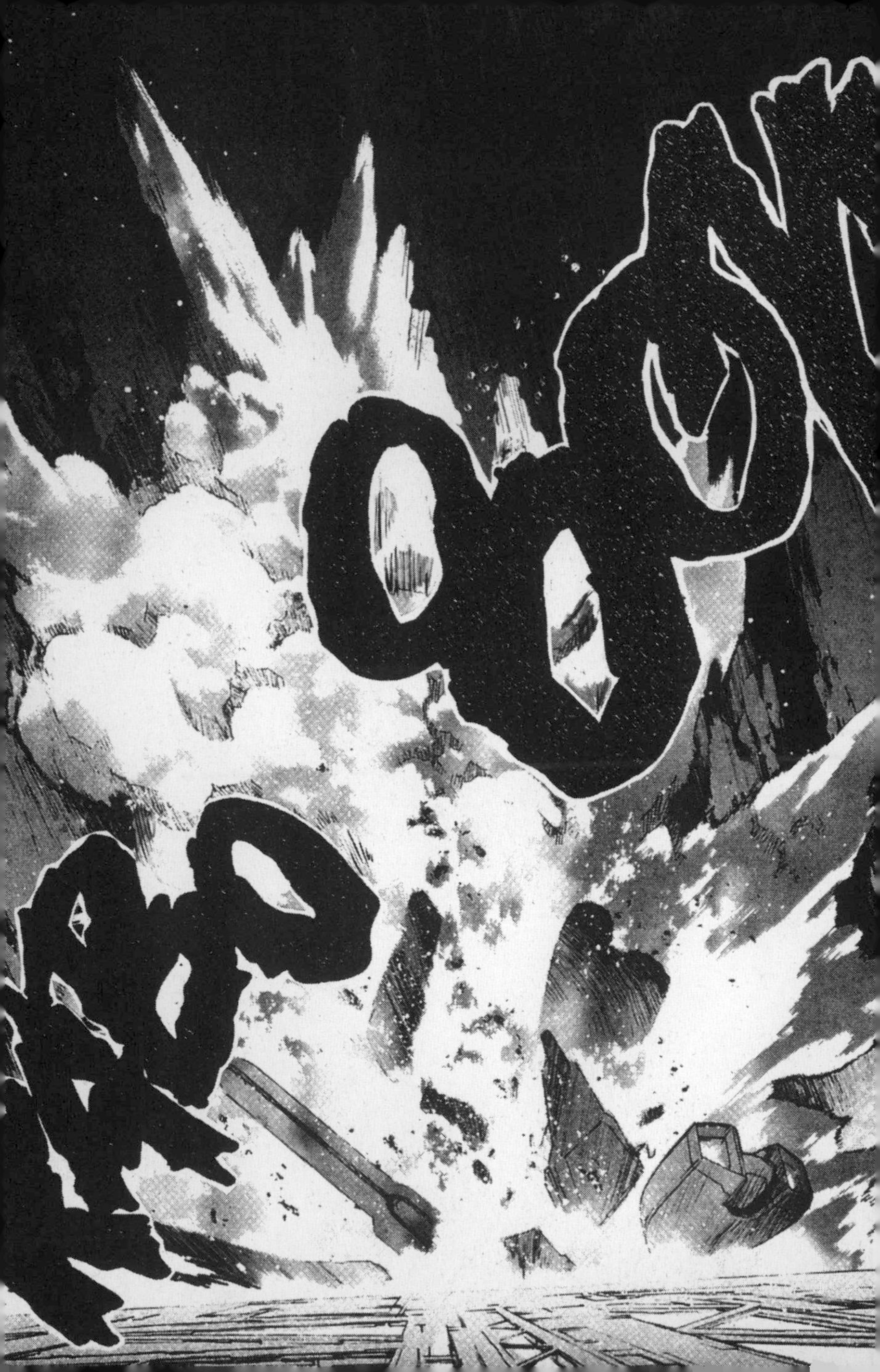

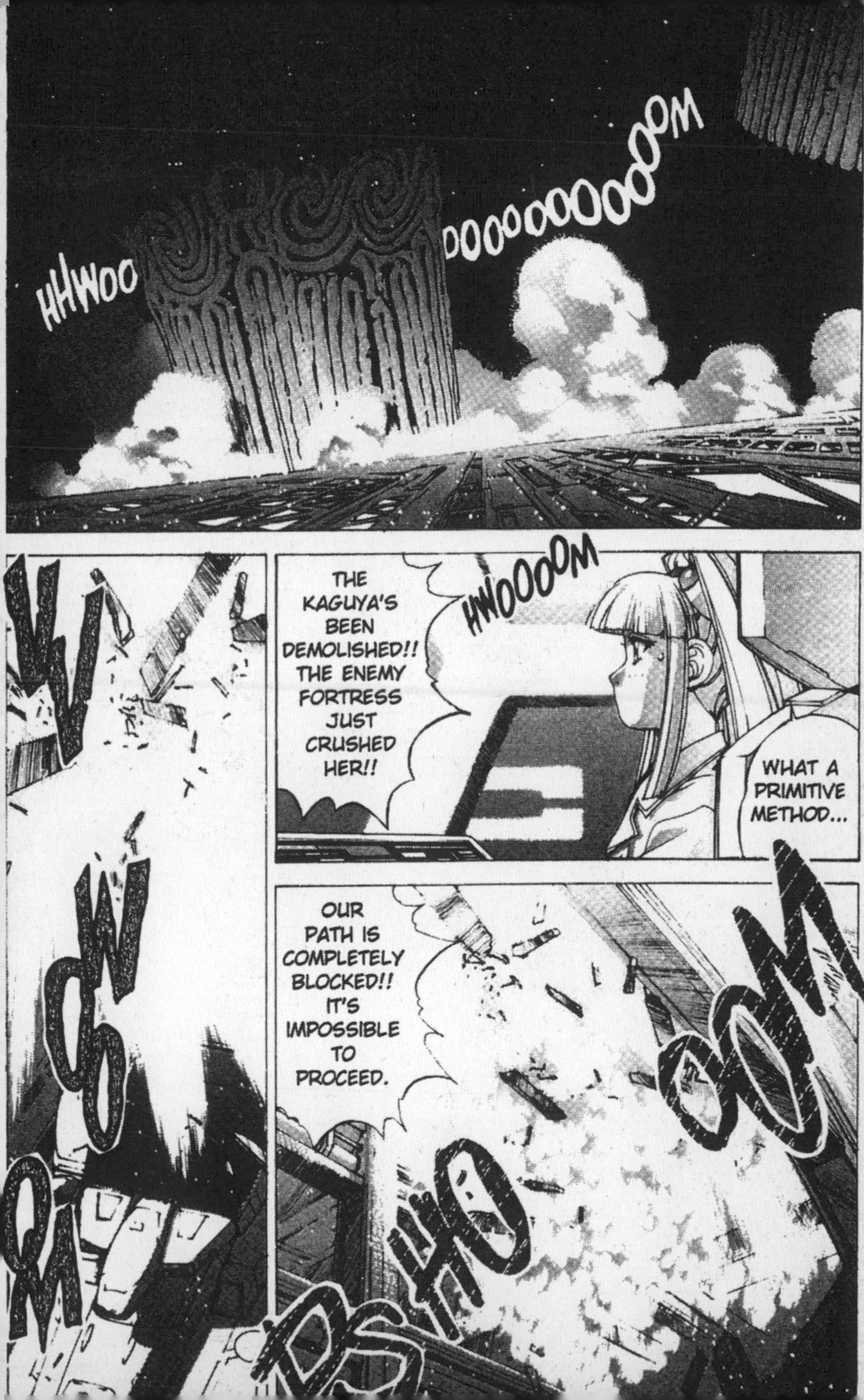
HHWOO
DOOOOOOOOOOM
HWOOOOM
THE KAGUYA'S BEEN DEMOLISHED!! THE ENEMY FORTRESS JUST CRUSHED HER!!
WHAT A PRIMITIVE METHOD...
OUR PATH IS COMPLETELY BLOCKED!! IT'S IMPOSSIBLE TO PROCEED.

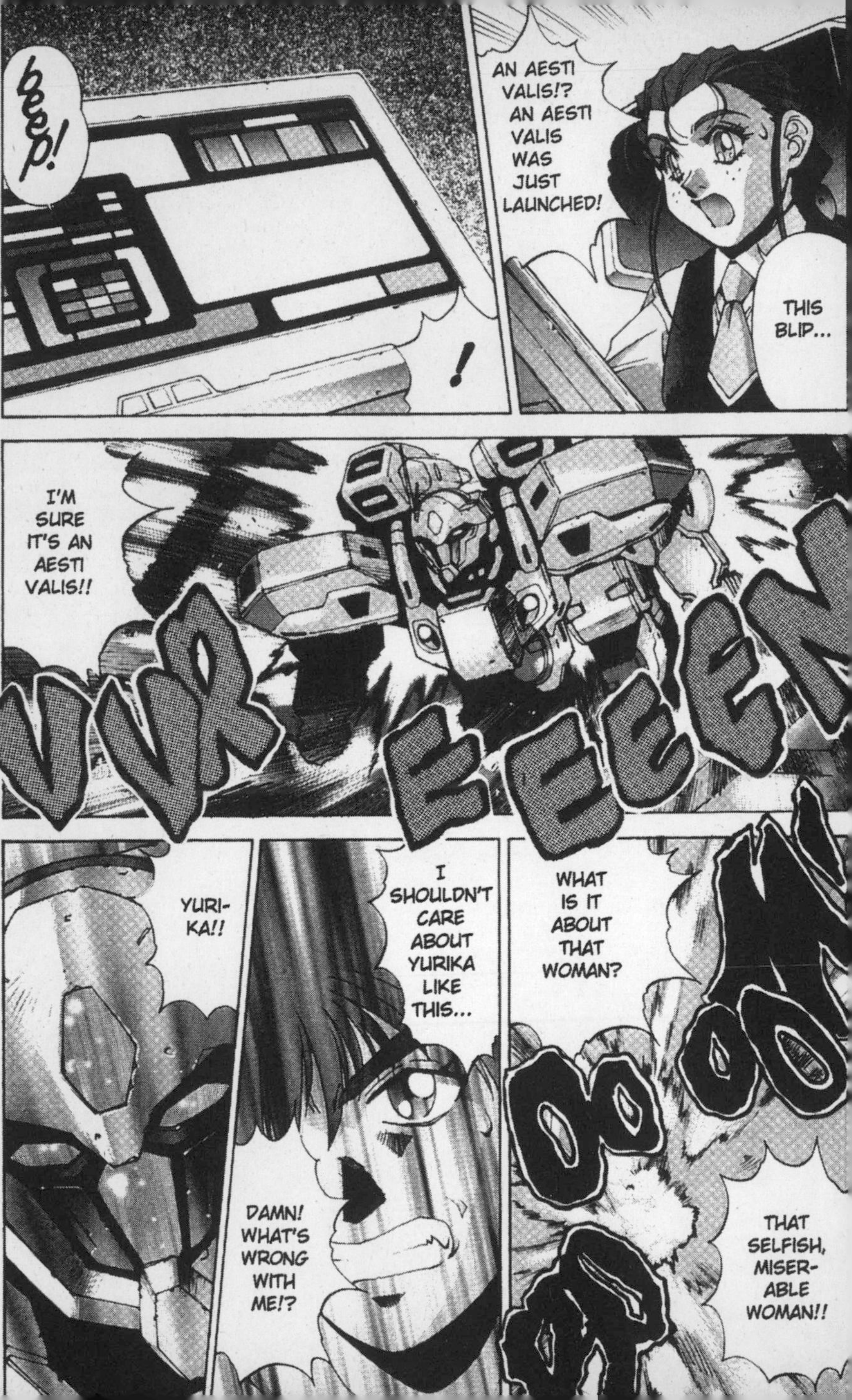
beep!
!
AN AESTI VALIS!? AN AESTI VALIS WAS JUST LAUNCHED!
THIS BLIP...
I'M SURE IT'S AN AESTI VALIS!!
YURI-KA!!
I SHOULDN'T CARE ABOUT YURIKA LIKE THIS...
DAMN! WHAT'S WRONG WITH ME!?
WHAT IS IT ABOUT THAT WOMAN?
THAT SELFISH, MISER-ABLE WOMAN!!

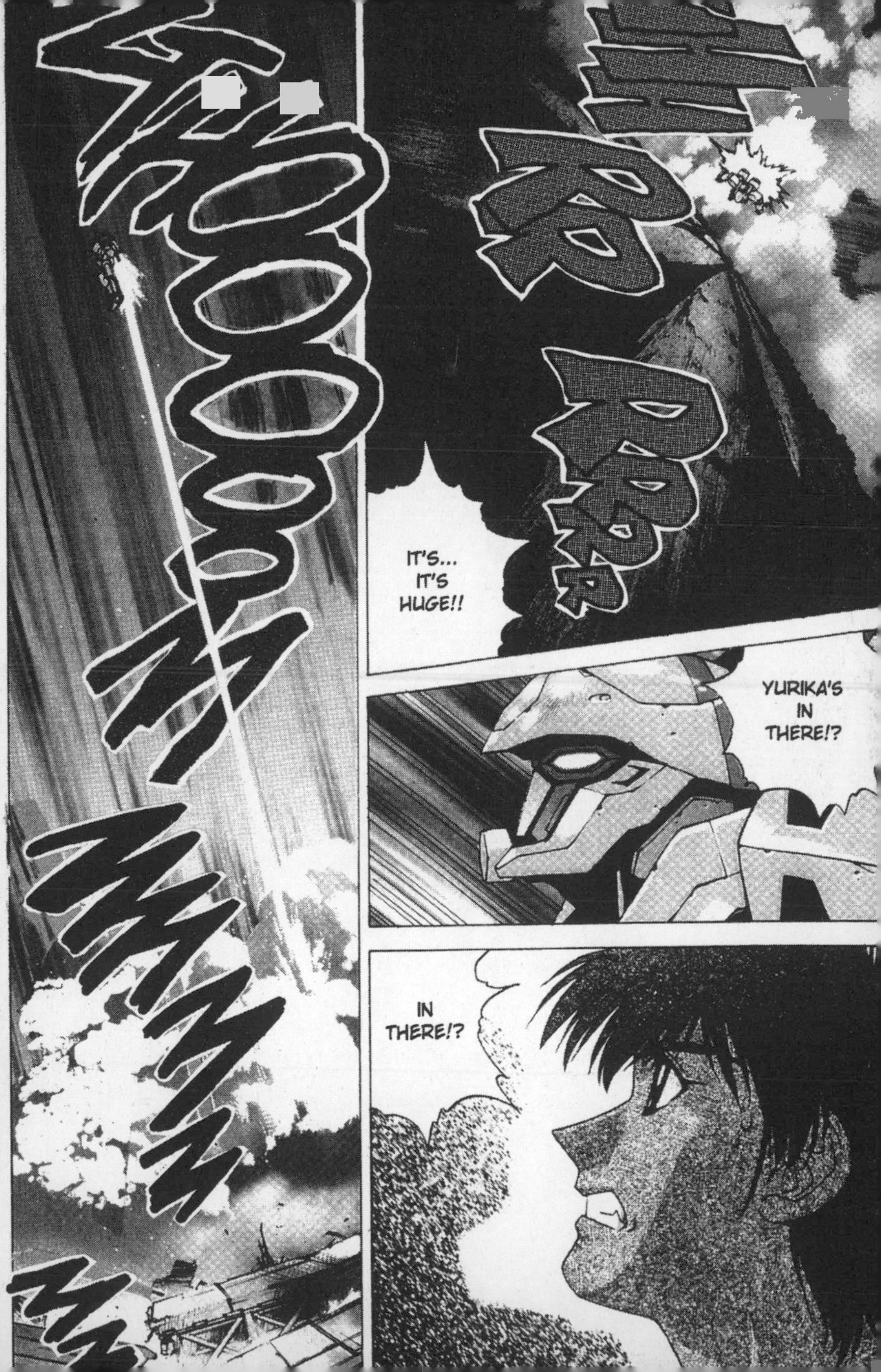
IT'S... IT'S HUGE!!
YURIKA'S IN THERE!?
IN THERE!?

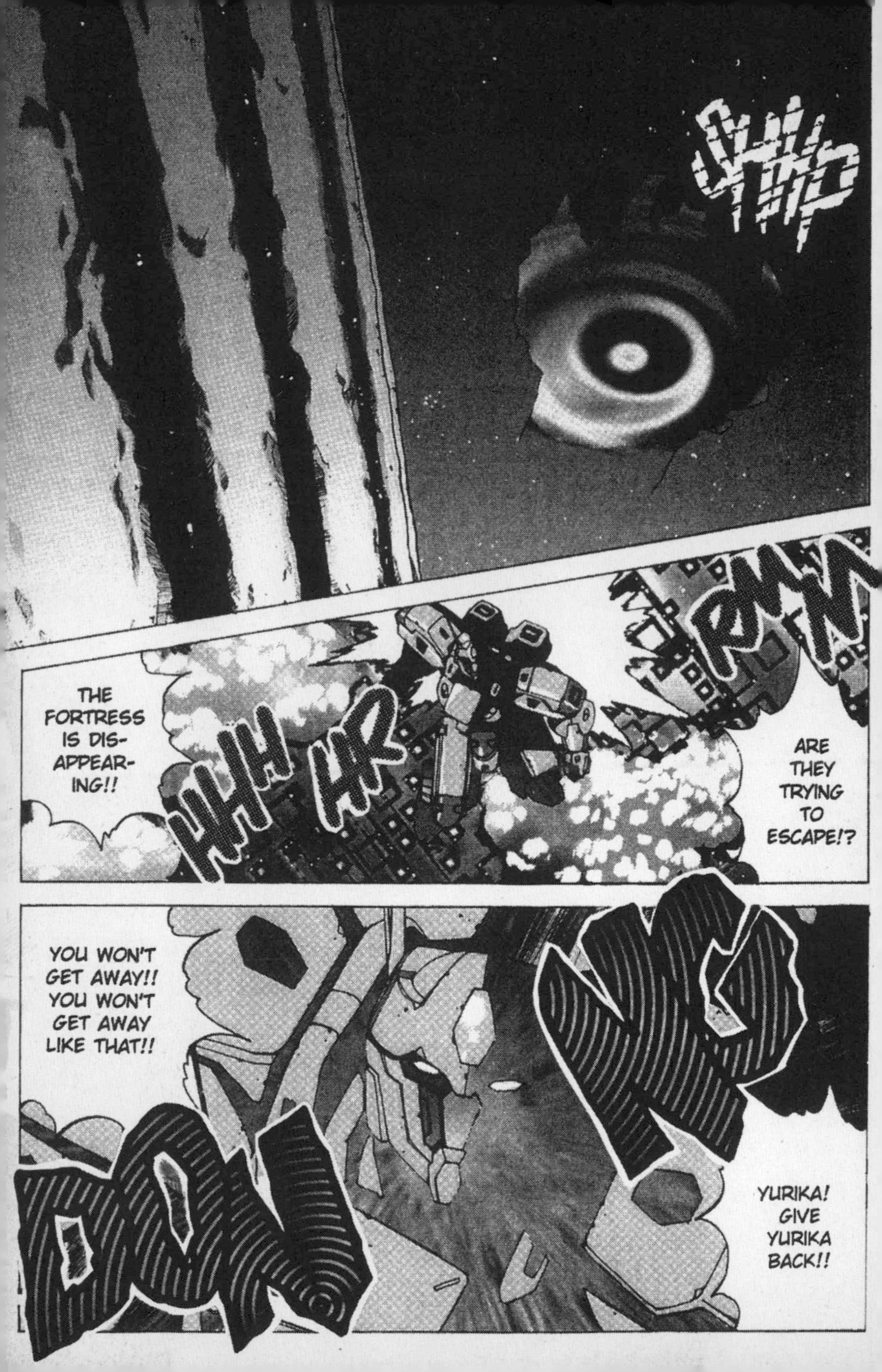
THE FORTRESS IS DIS-APPEARING!!
ARE THEY TRYING TO ESCAPE!?
YOU WON'T GET AWAY!! YOU WON'T GET AWAY LIKE THAT!!
YURIKA! GIVE YURIKA BACK!!

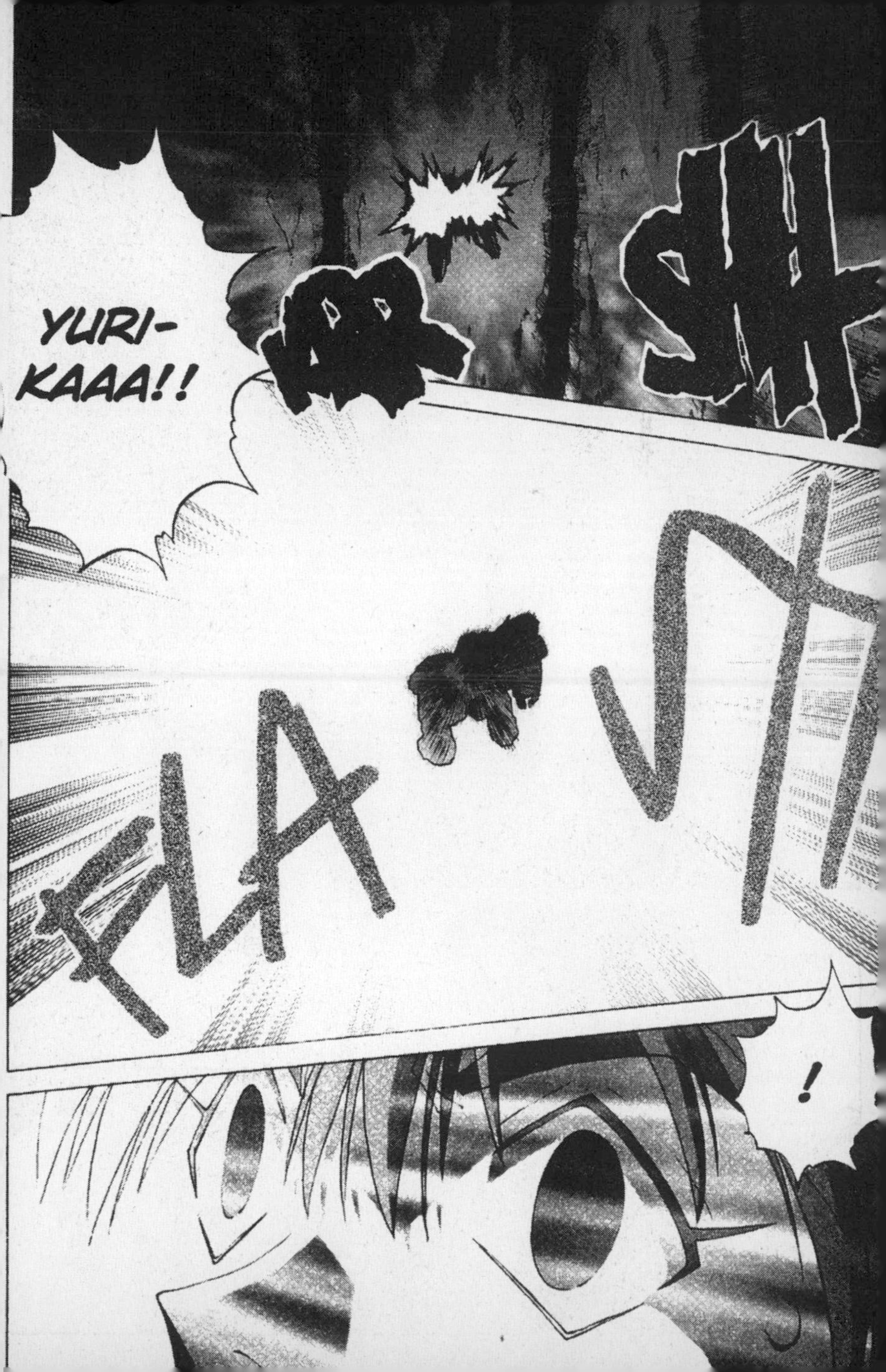
YURI-
KAAA!!
!

HUH...?

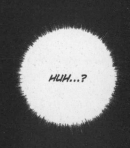

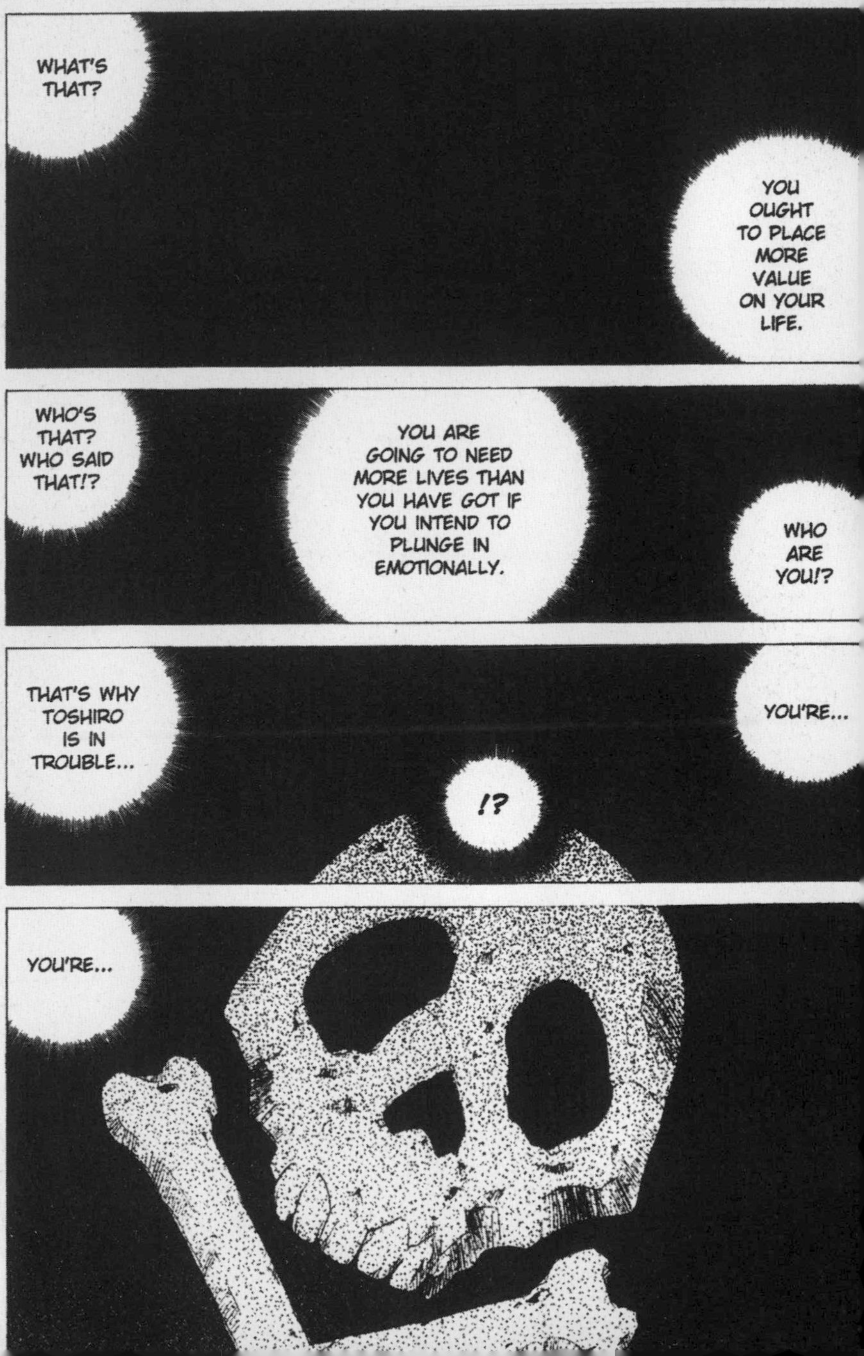
WHAT'S THAT?
YOU OUGHT TO PLACE MORE VALUE ON YOUR LIFE.
WHO'S THAT? WHO SAID THAT!?
YOU ARE GOING TO NEED MORE LIVES THAN YOU HAVE GOT IF YOU INTEND TO PLUNGE IN EMOTIONALLY.
WHO ARE YOU!?
THAT'S WHY TOSHIRO IS IN TROUBLE...
!?
YOU'RE...
YOU'RE...

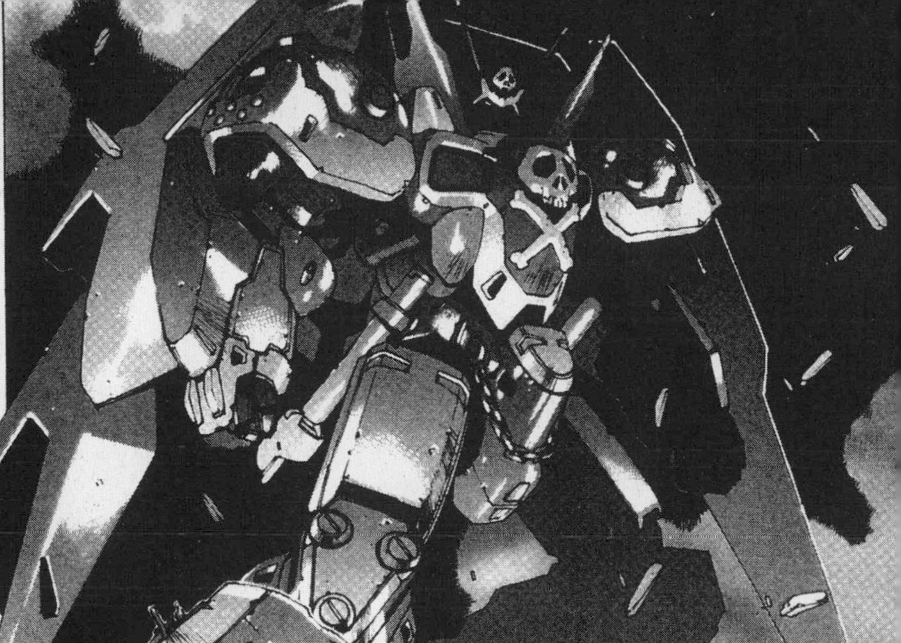
A SKULL AND CROSS-BONES!?

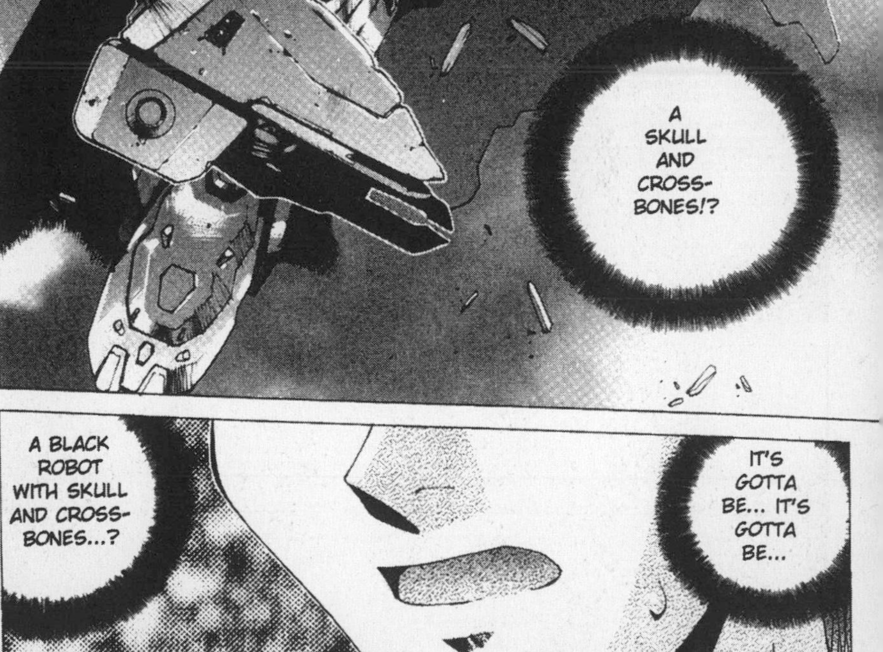
A BLACK ROBOT WITH SKULL AND CROSS-BONES...?
IT'S GOTTA BE... IT'S GOTTA BE...

CAPTAIN GOVERN-MENT!
AH!

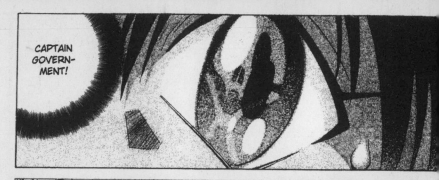

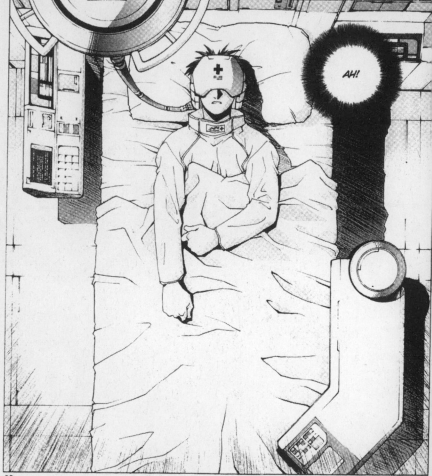

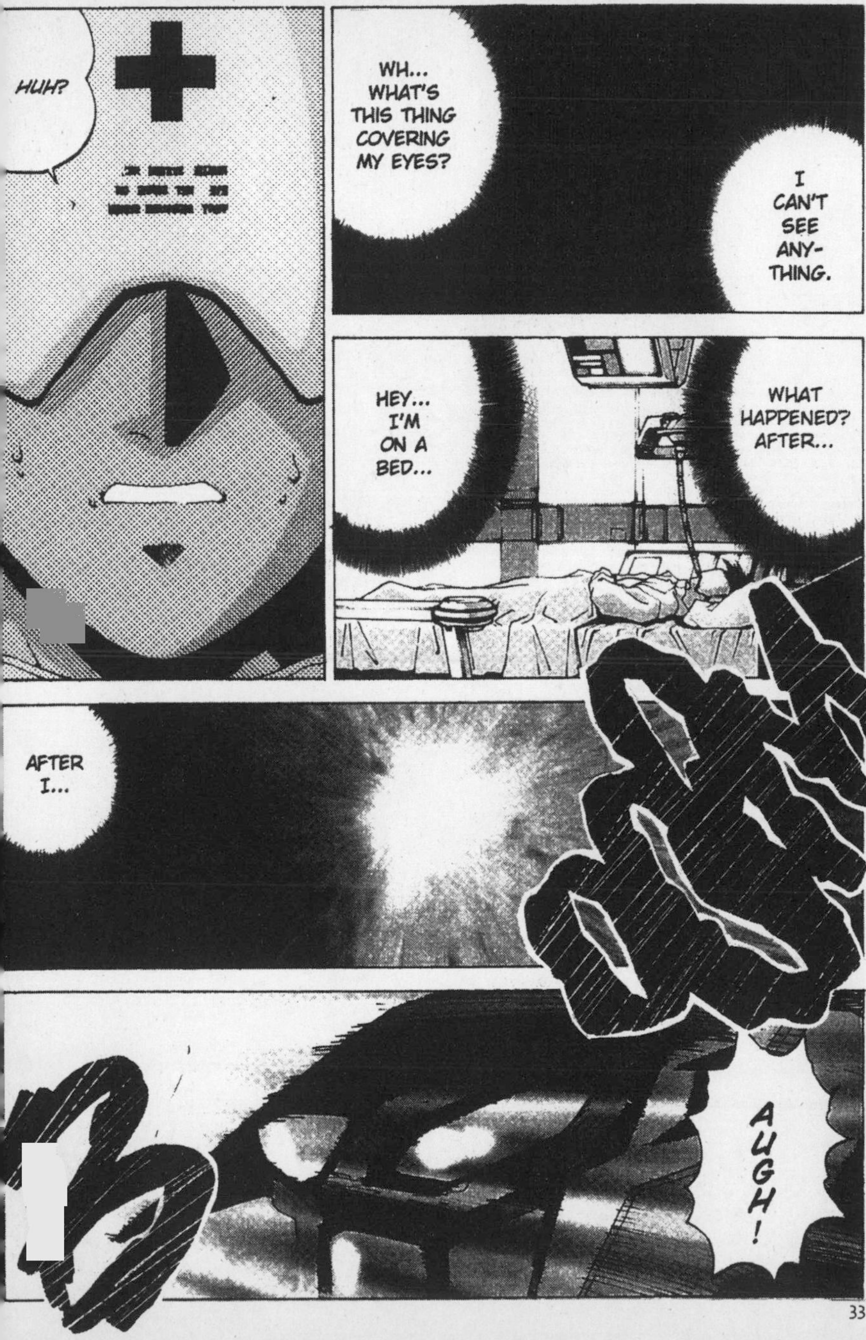
HUH?
WH... WHAT'S THIS THING COVERING MY EYES?
I CAN'T SEE ANY-THING.
HEY... I'M ON A BED...
WHAT HAPPENED? AFTER...
AFTER I...
AUGH!

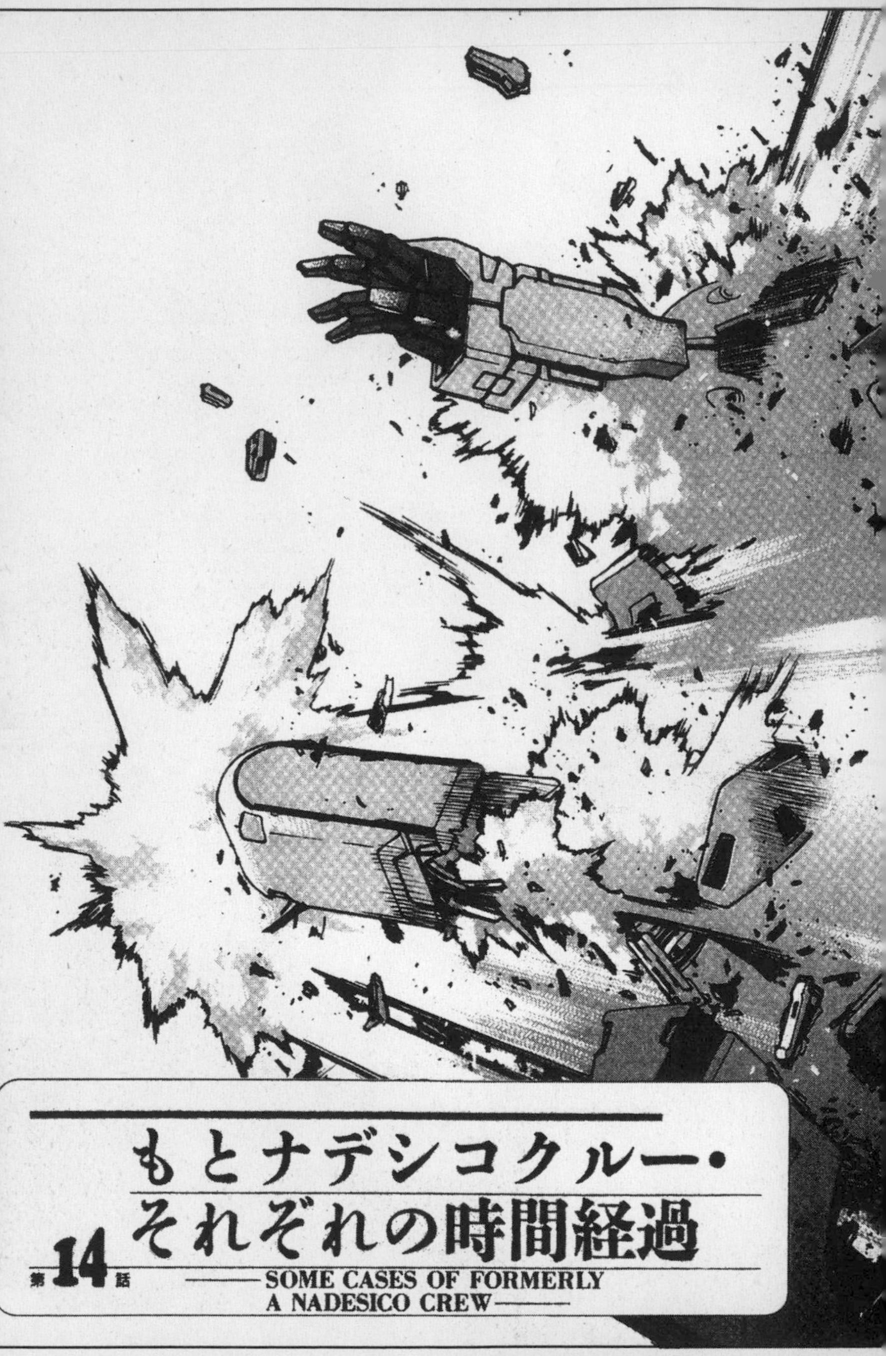

第**14**話

もとナデシコクルー・それぞれの時間経過

——SOME CASES OF FORMERLY A NADESICO CREW——

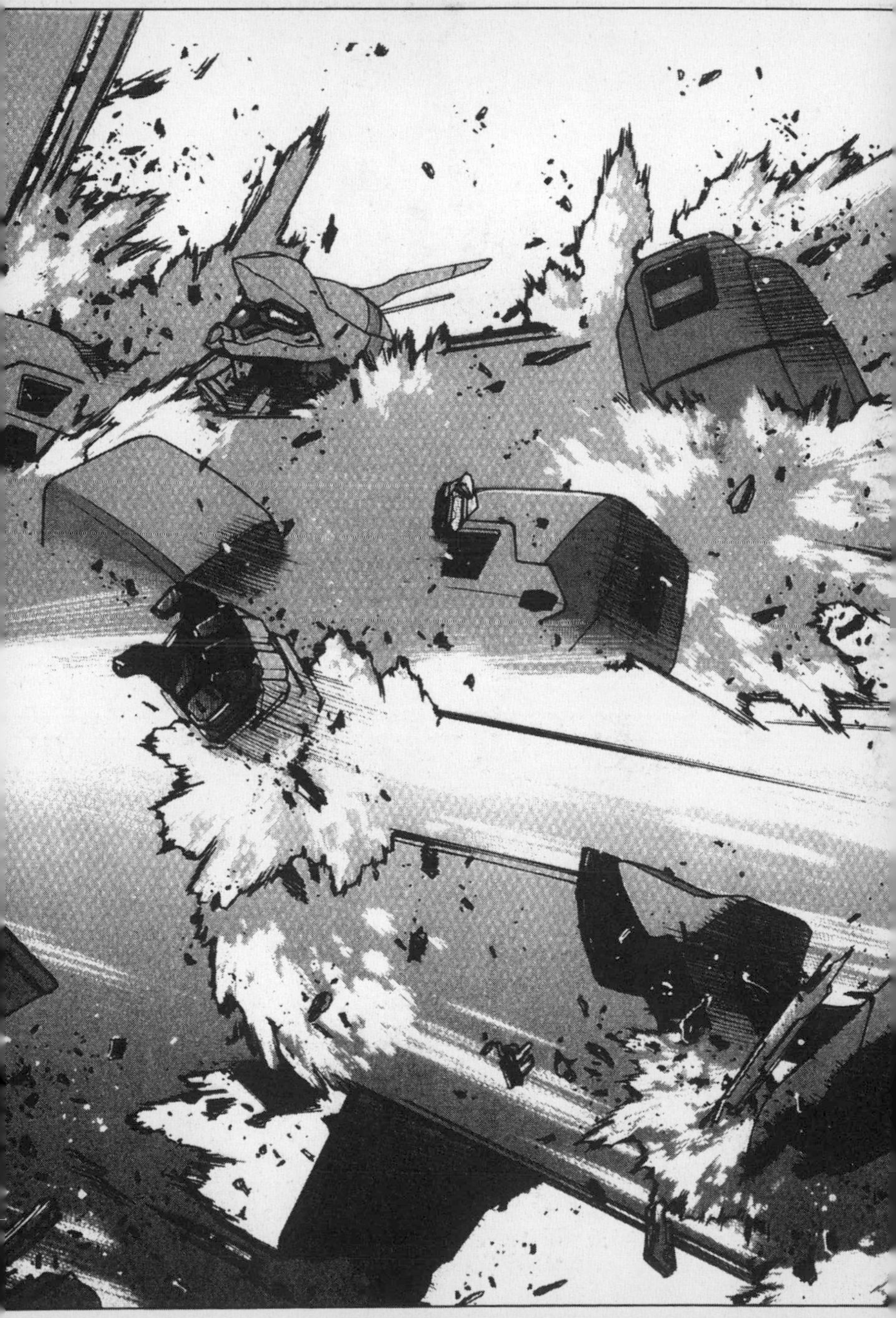

THAT WAS...

THAT WAS CAPTAIN GOVERNMENT'S FAVORITE TOY!!

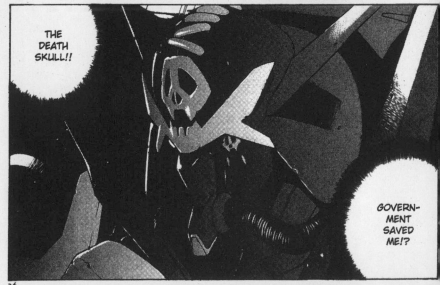

THE DEATH SKULL!!

GOVERNMENT SAVED ME!?

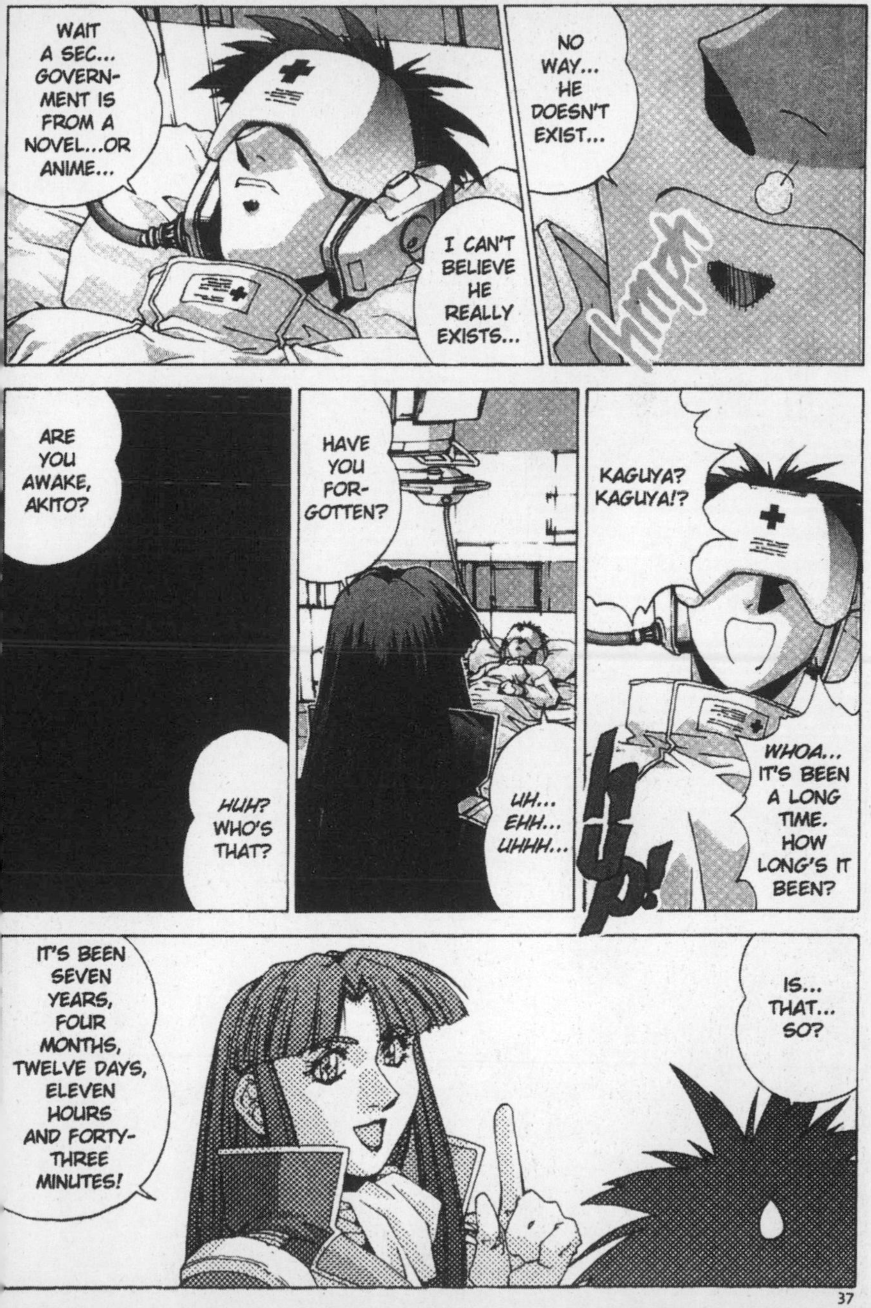
WAIT A SEC... GOVERNMENT IS FROM A NOVEL...OR ANIME...
NO WAY... HE DOESN'T EXIST...
I CAN'T BELIEVE HE REALLY EXISTS...
hmph
ARE YOU AWAKE, AKITO?
HUH? WHO'S THAT?
HAVE YOU FORGOTTEN?
UH... EHH... UHHH...
KAGUYA? KAGUYA!?
WHOA... IT'S BEEN A LONG TIME. HOW LONG'S IT BEEN?
IT'S BEEN SEVEN YEARS, FOUR MONTHS, TWELVE DAYS, ELEVEN HOURS AND FORTY-THREE MINUTES!
IS... THAT... SO?

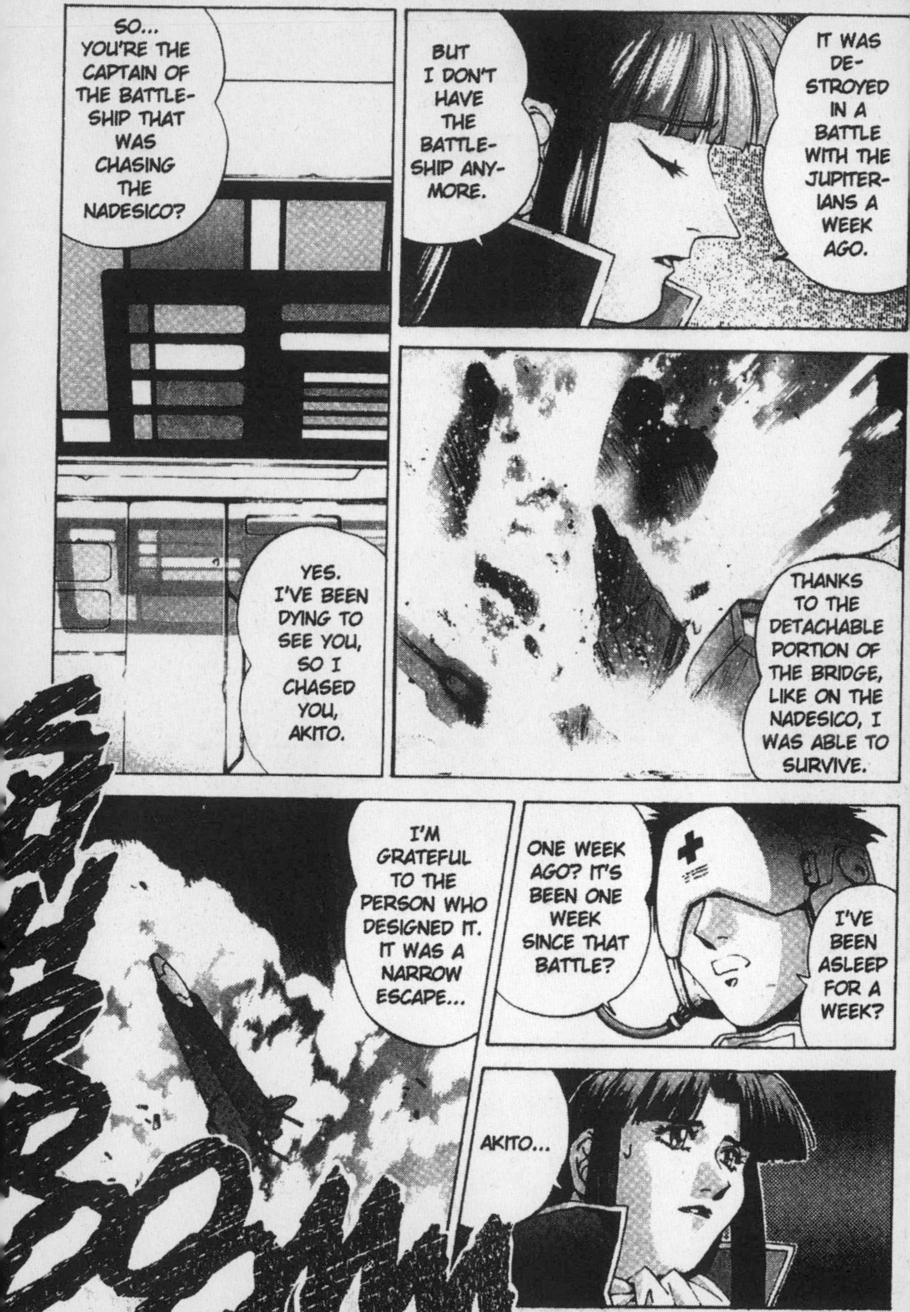
SO... YOU'RE THE CAPTAIN OF THE BATTLE-SHIP THAT WAS CHASING THE NADESICO?
YES. I'VE BEEN DYING TO SEE YOU, SO I CHASED YOU, AKITO.
BUT I DON'T HAVE THE BATTLE-SHIP ANY-MORE.
IT WAS DE-STROYED IN A BATTLE WITH THE JUPITER-IANS A WEEK AGO.
THANKS TO THE DETACHABLE PORTION OF THE BRIDGE, LIKE ON THE NADESICO, I WAS ABLE TO SURVIVE.
I'M GRATEFUL TO THE PERSON WHO DESIGNED IT. IT WAS A NARROW ESCAPE...
ONE WEEK AGO? IT'S BEEN ONE WEEK SINCE THAT BATTLE?
I'VE BEEN ASLEEP FOR A WEEK?
AKITO...

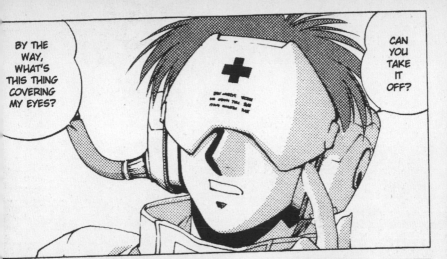

BY THE WAY, WHAT'S THIS THING COVERING MY EYES?

CAN YOU TAKE IT OFF?

AKITO...

THE FACT IS...

39

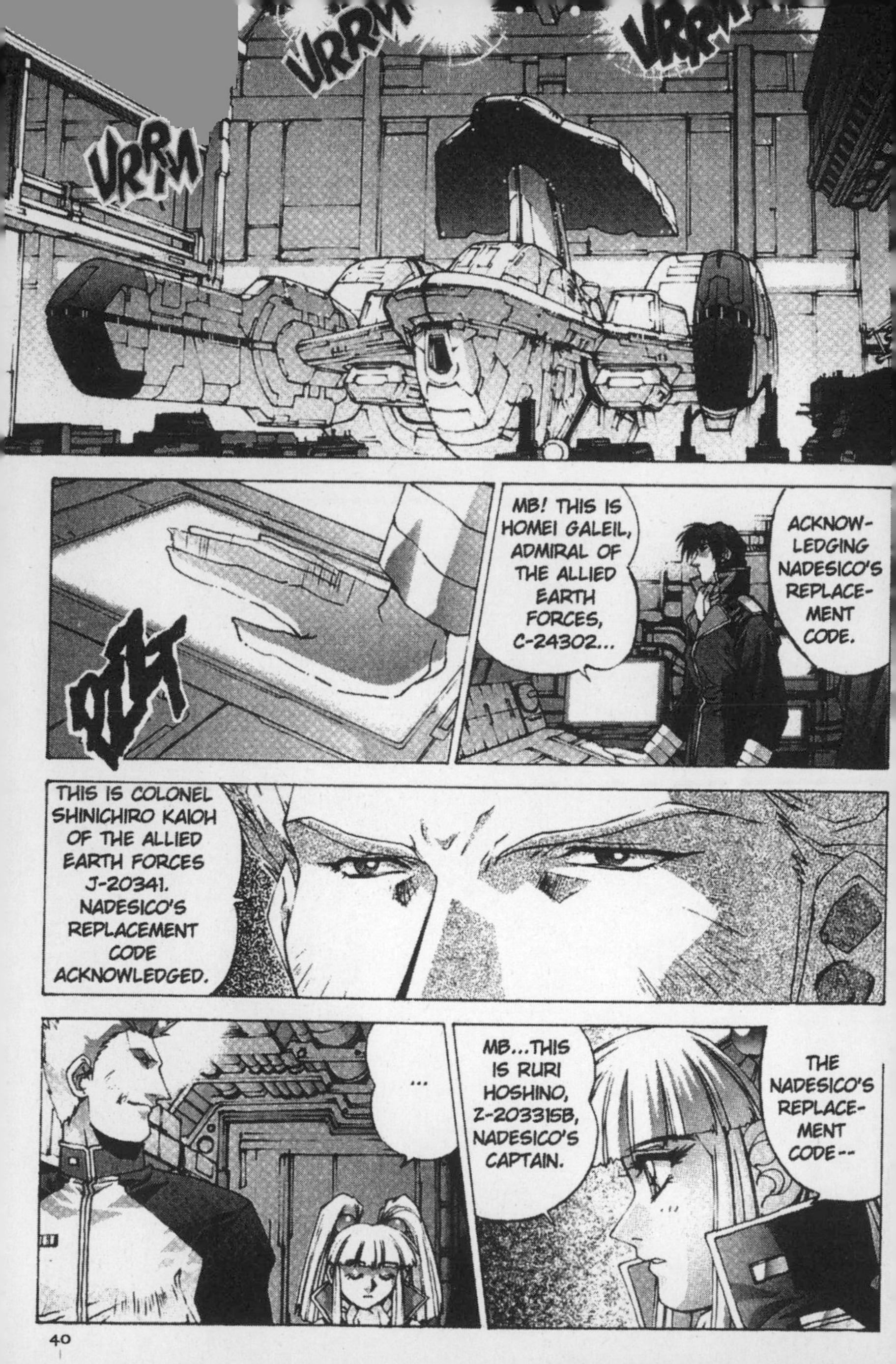
VRRM
VRRM
VRRM
MB! THIS IS HOMEI GALEIL, ADMIRAL OF THE ALLIED EARTH FORCES, C-24302...
ACKNOWLEDGING NADESICO'S REPLACEMENT CODE.
THIS IS COLONEL SHINICHIRO KAIOH OF THE ALLIED EARTH FORCES J-20341. NADESICO'S REPLACEMENT CODE ACKNOWLEDGED.
...
MB...THIS IS RURI HOSHINO, Z-203315B, NADESICO'S CAPTAIN.
THE NADESICO'S REPLACEMENT CODE--

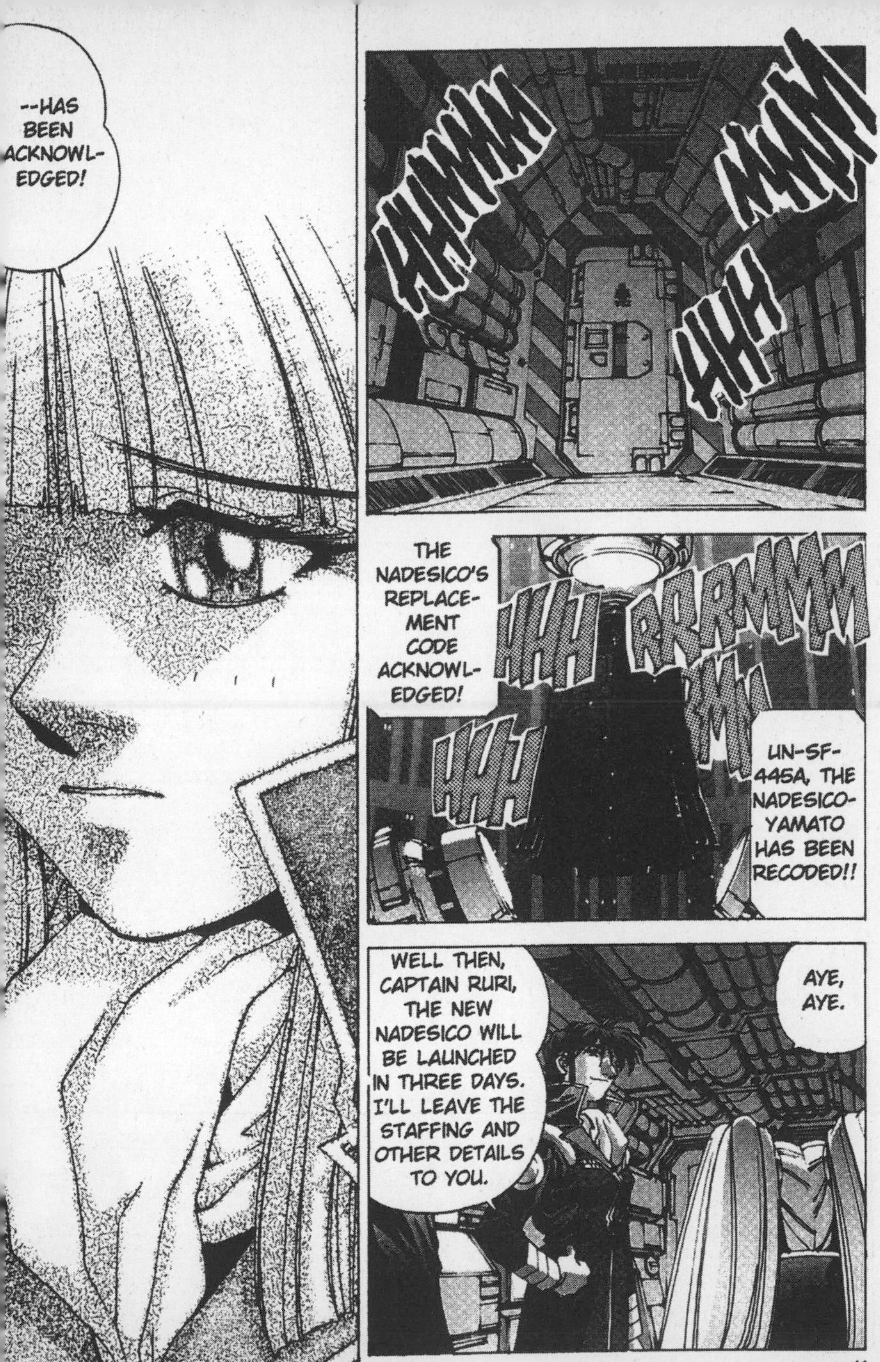
--HAS BEEN ACKNOWL-EDGED!
THE NADESICO'S REPLACE-MENT CODE ACKNOWL-EDGED!
HHH RRRMMMM
HHH
UN-SF-445A, THE NADESICO-YAMATO HAS BEEN RECODED!!
WELL THEN, CAPTAIN RURI, THE NEW NADESICO WILL BE LAUNCHED IN THREE DAYS. I'LL LEAVE THE STAFFING AND OTHER DETAILS TO YOU.
AYE, AYE.

WE'LL WIPE OUT THE JUPITERIANS AT THE FRONT LINE OF THE ASTEROID BELT.

I'M COUNTING ON THE NADESICO.

AFTER THAT IT'LL BE ALL-OUT WAR WITH THE JUPITERIANS.

WE'VE GOT TO SUCCEED TO SURVIVE!

YES, SIR. WE'LL BE READY TO LAUNCH IN THREE DAYS.

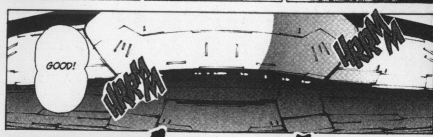

GOOD!

HRRM

HRRM

OOON

NGGG

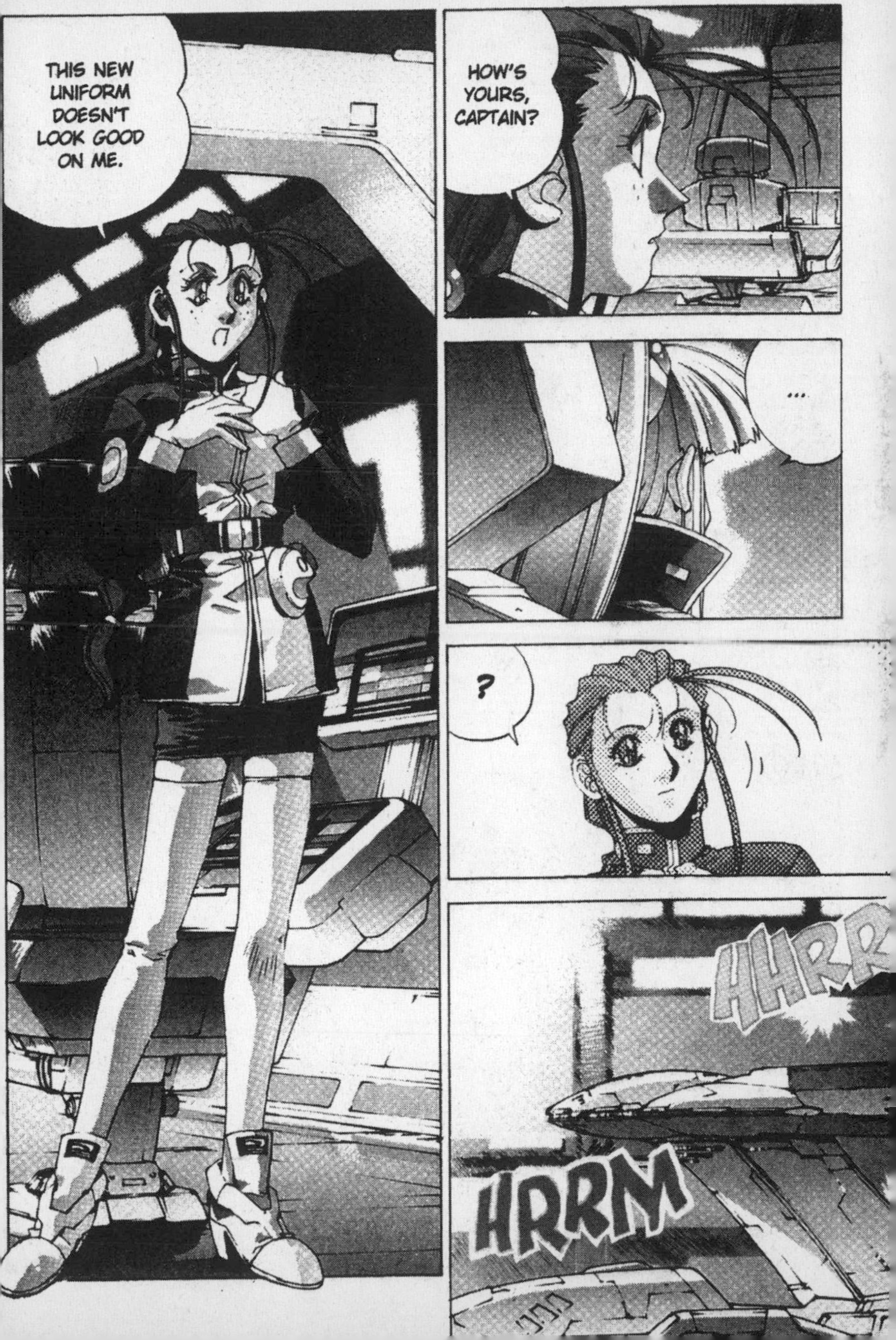
THIS NEW UNIFORM DOESN'T LOOK GOOD ON ME.
HOW'S YOURS, CAPTAIN?
...
?
HHRR
HRRM

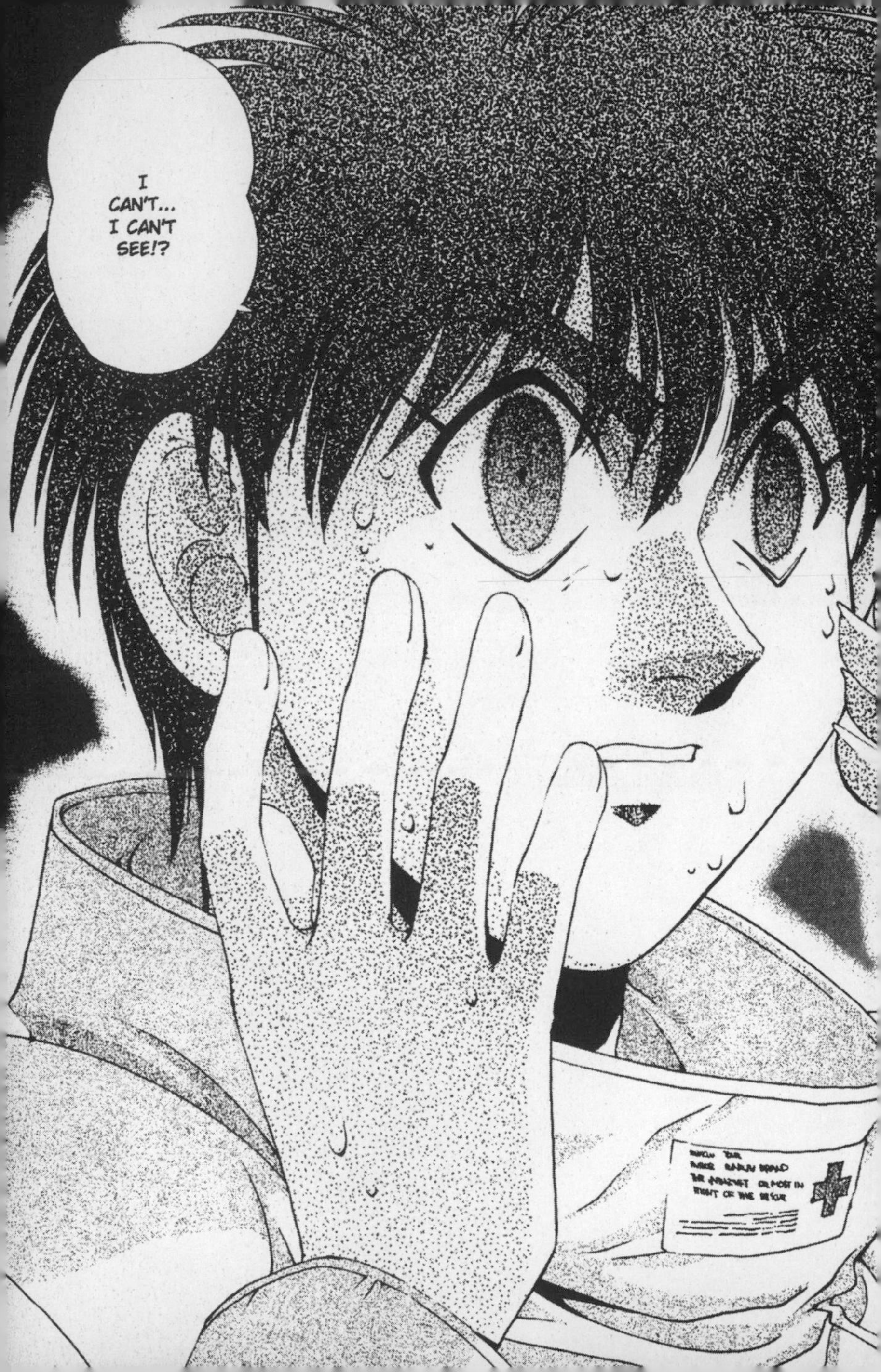
I CAN'T... I CAN'T SEE!?

NOOO...

NO, YOU HAVEN'T LOST YOUR SIGHT COMPLETELY--

--BUT YOUR VISION IS WORSENING. IT WILL TAKE SOME TIME, BUT EVENTUALLY IT SHOULD BE RESTORED.

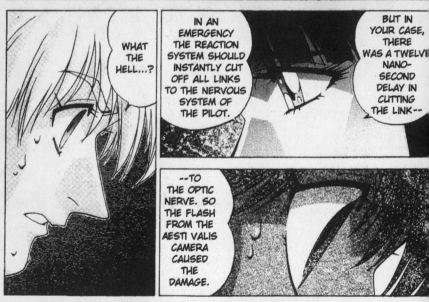

WHAT THE HELL...?

IN AN EMERGENCY THE REACTION SYSTEM SHOULD INSTANTLY CUT OFF ALL LINKS TO THE NERVOUS SYSTEM OF THE PILOT.

BUT IN YOUR CASE, THERE WAS A TWELVE NANO-SECOND DELAY IN CUTTING THE LINK--

--TO THE OPTIC NERVE. SO THE FLASH FROM THE AESTI VALIS CAMERA CAUSED THE DAMAGE.

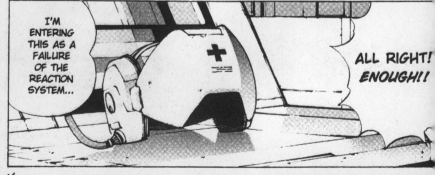

I'M ENTERING THIS AS A FAILURE OF THE REACTION SYSTEM...

ALL RIGHT! *ENOUGH!!*

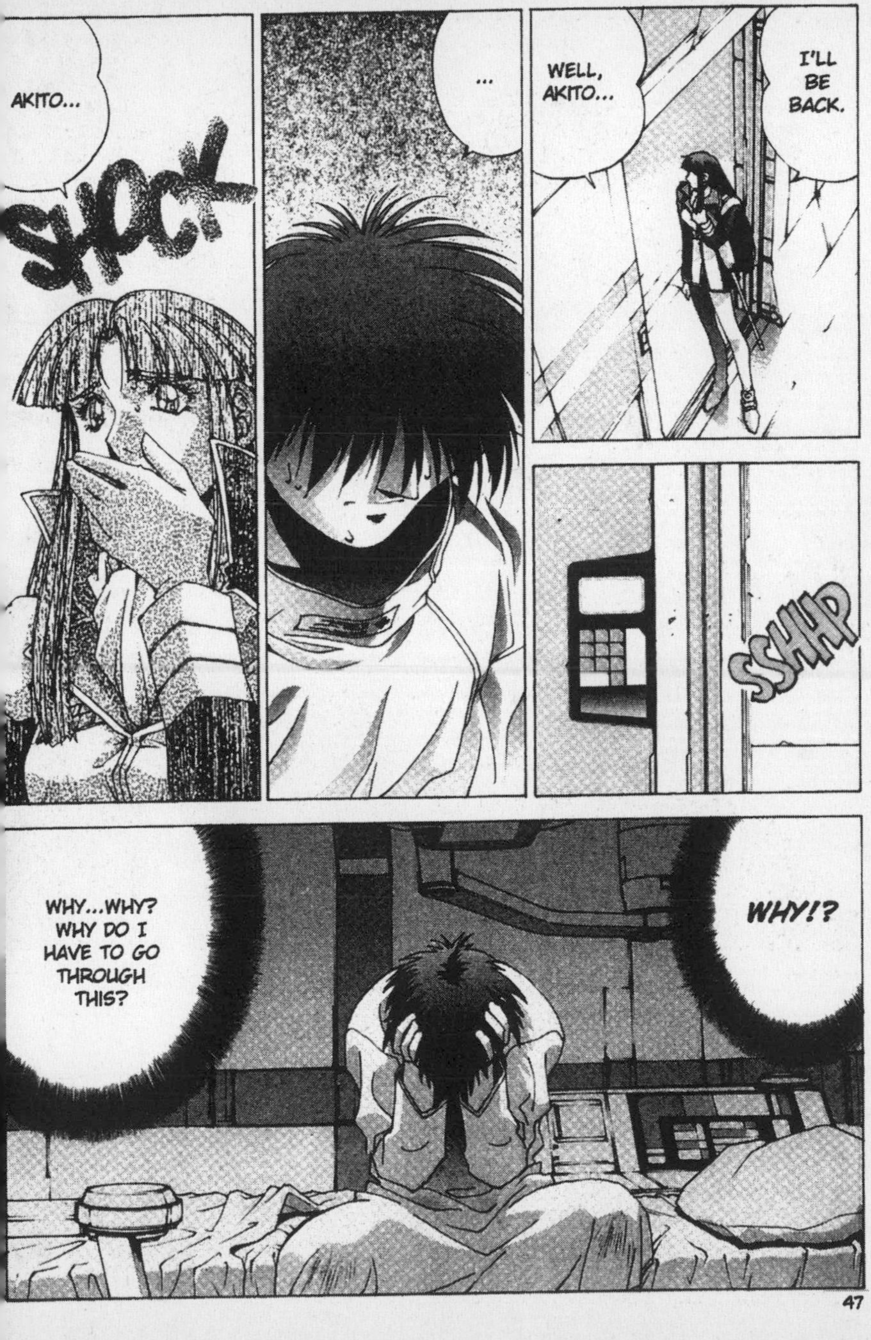
AKITO...
SHOCK
...
WELL, AKITO...
I'LL BE BACK.
SSHP
WHY...WHY? WHY DO I HAVE TO GO THROUGH THIS?
WHY!?

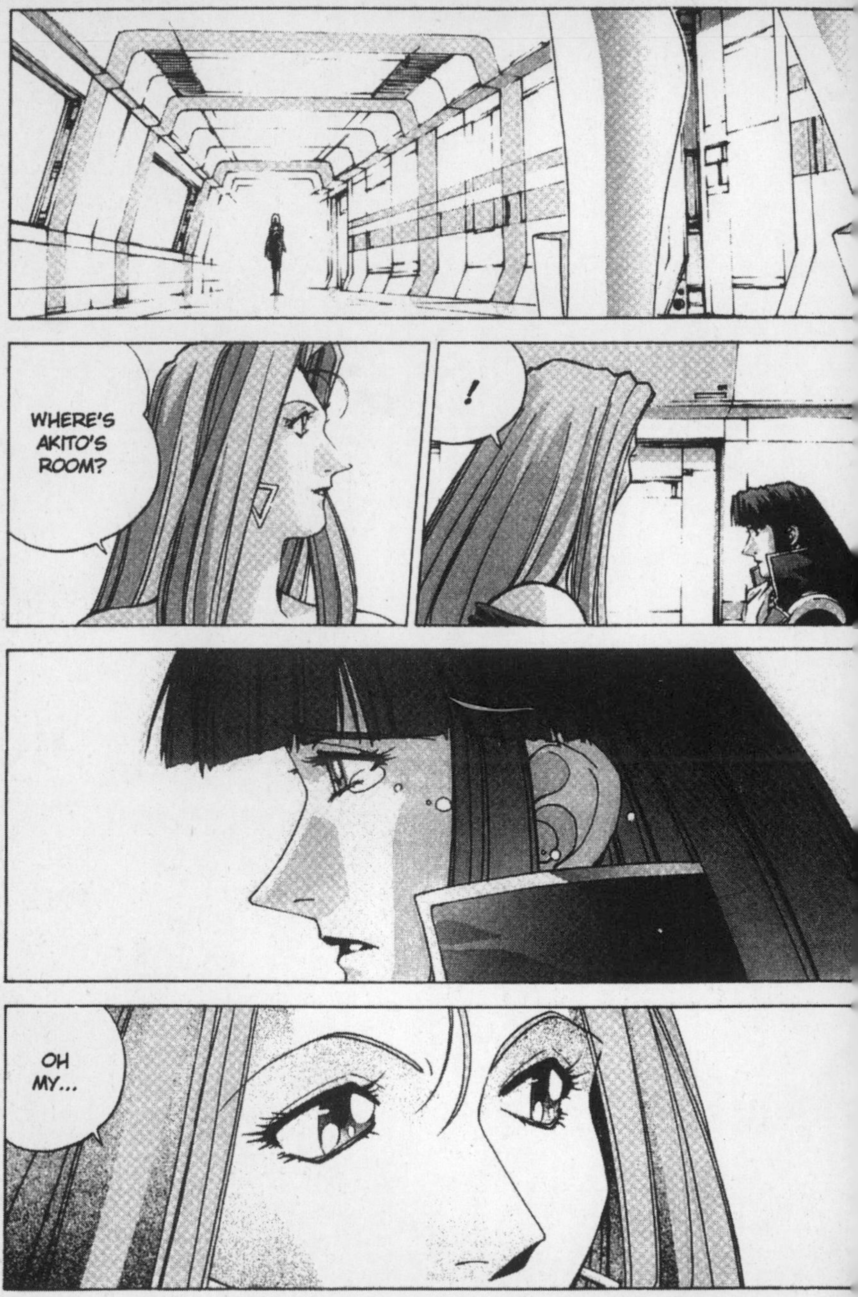
WHERE'S AKITO'S ROOM?
!
OH MY...

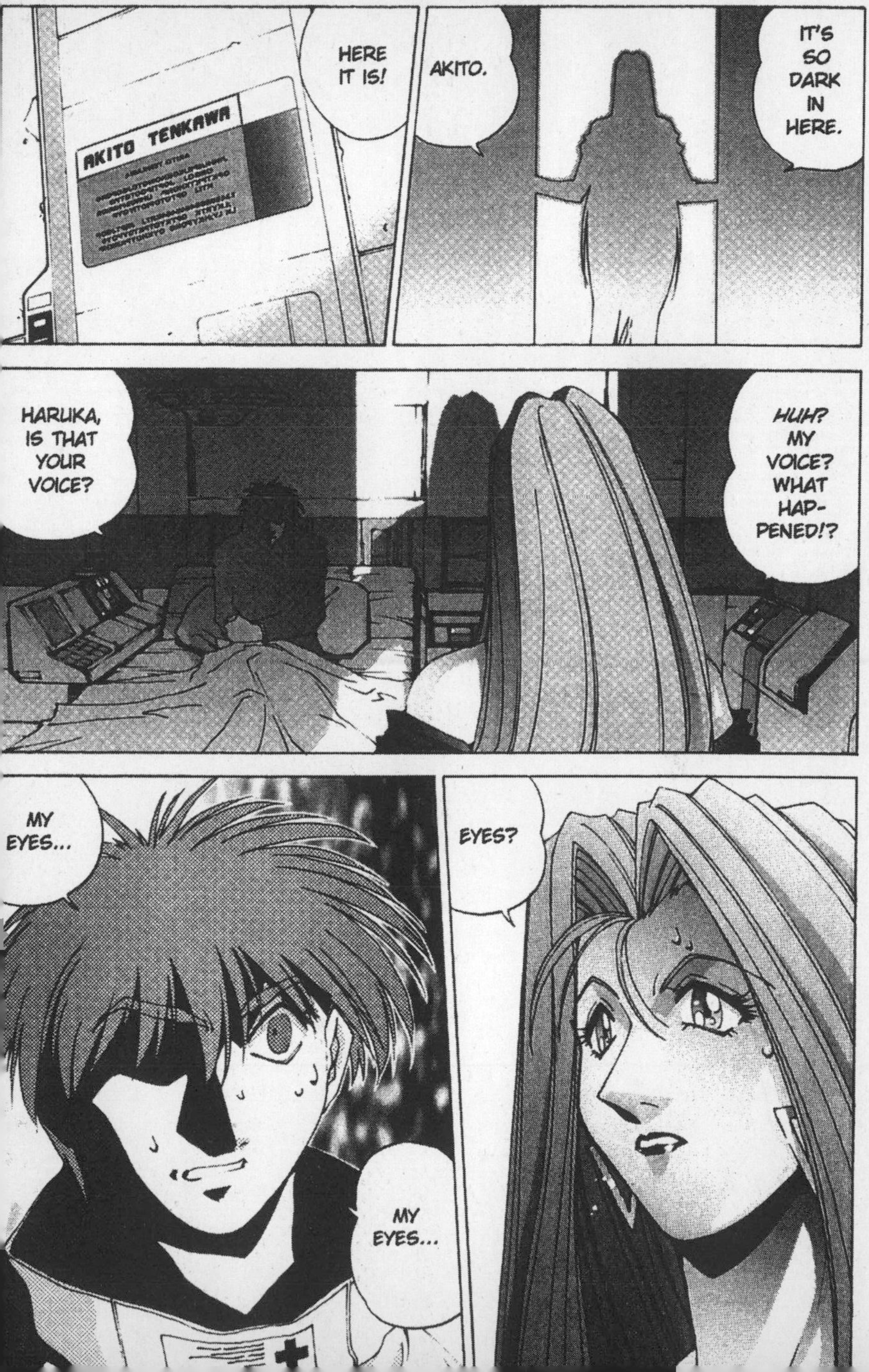
AKITO TENKAWA
HERE IT IS!
AKITO.
IT'S SO DARK IN HERE.
HARUKA, IS THAT YOUR VOICE?
HUH? MY VOICE? WHAT HAP-PENED!?
MY EYES...
MY EYES...
EYES?

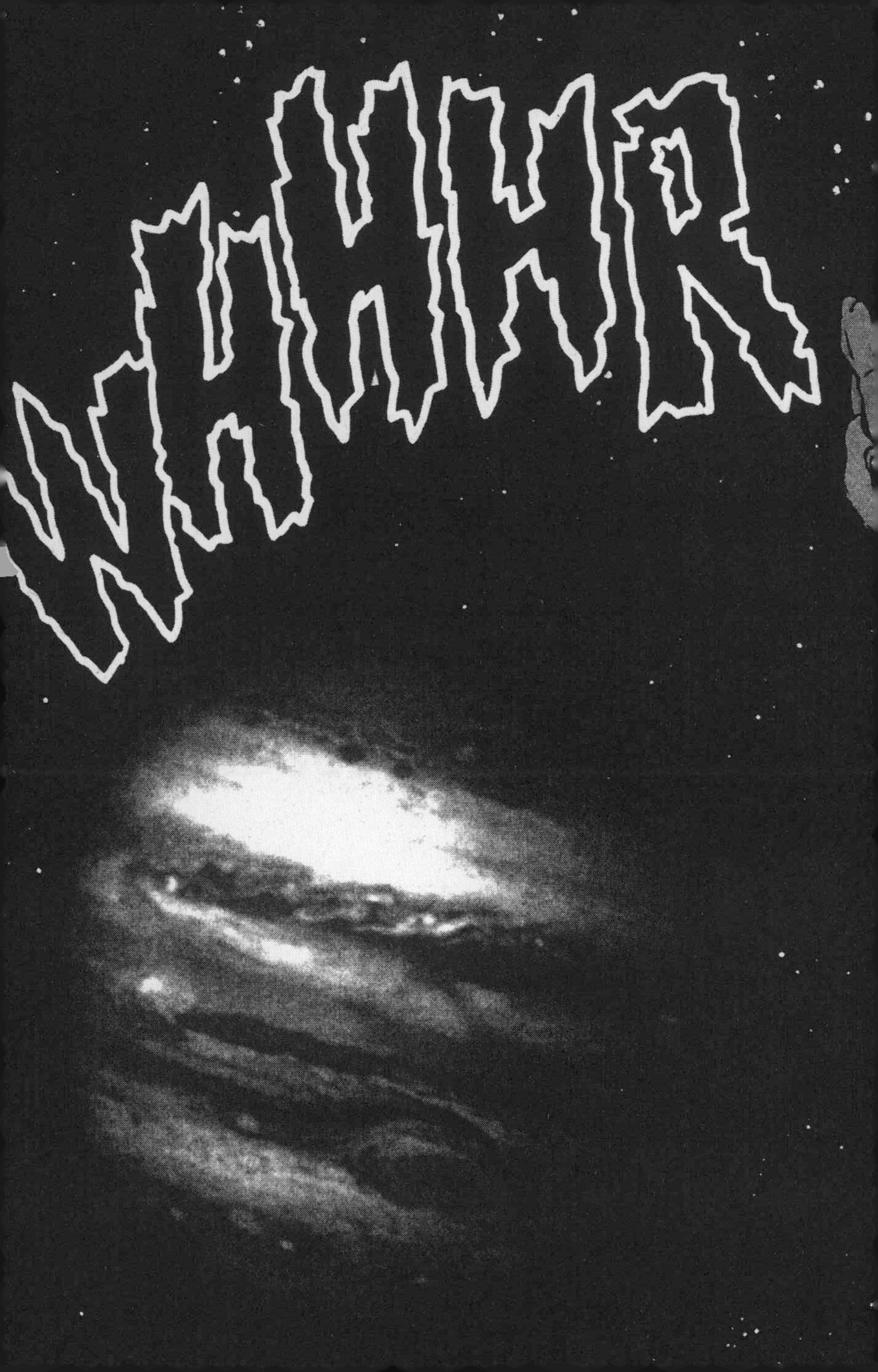
WHHHR

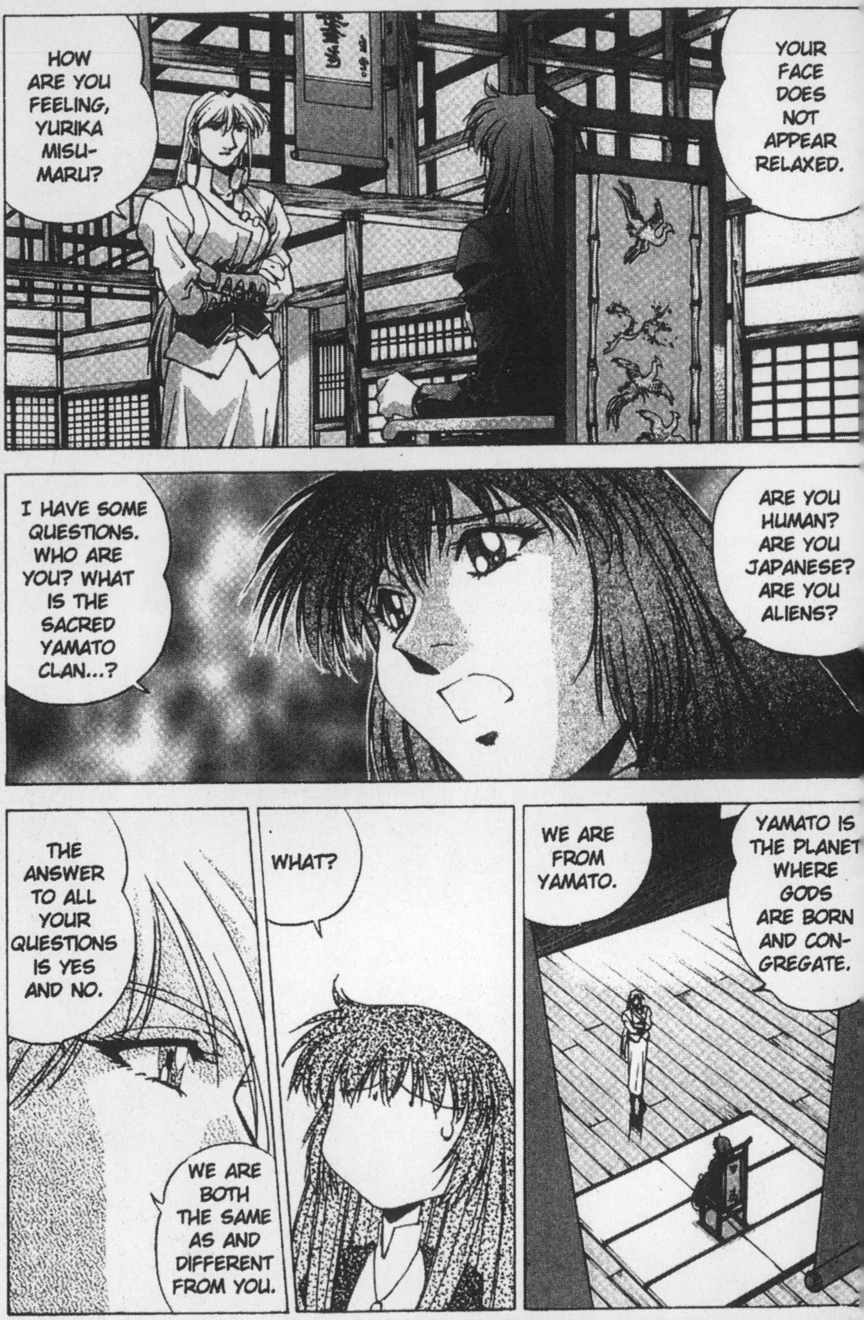
HOW ARE YOU FEELING, YURIKA MISU-MARU?
YOUR FACE DOES NOT APPEAR RELAXED.
I HAVE SOME QUESTIONS. WHO ARE YOU? WHAT IS THE SACRED YAMATO CLAN...?
ARE YOU HUMAN? ARE YOU JAPANESE? ARE YOU ALIENS?
THE ANSWER TO ALL YOUR QUESTIONS IS YES AND NO.
WE ARE BOTH THE SAME AS AND DIFFERENT FROM YOU.
WHAT?
WE ARE FROM YAMATO.
YAMATO IS THE PLANET WHERE GODS ARE BORN AND CON-GREGATE.

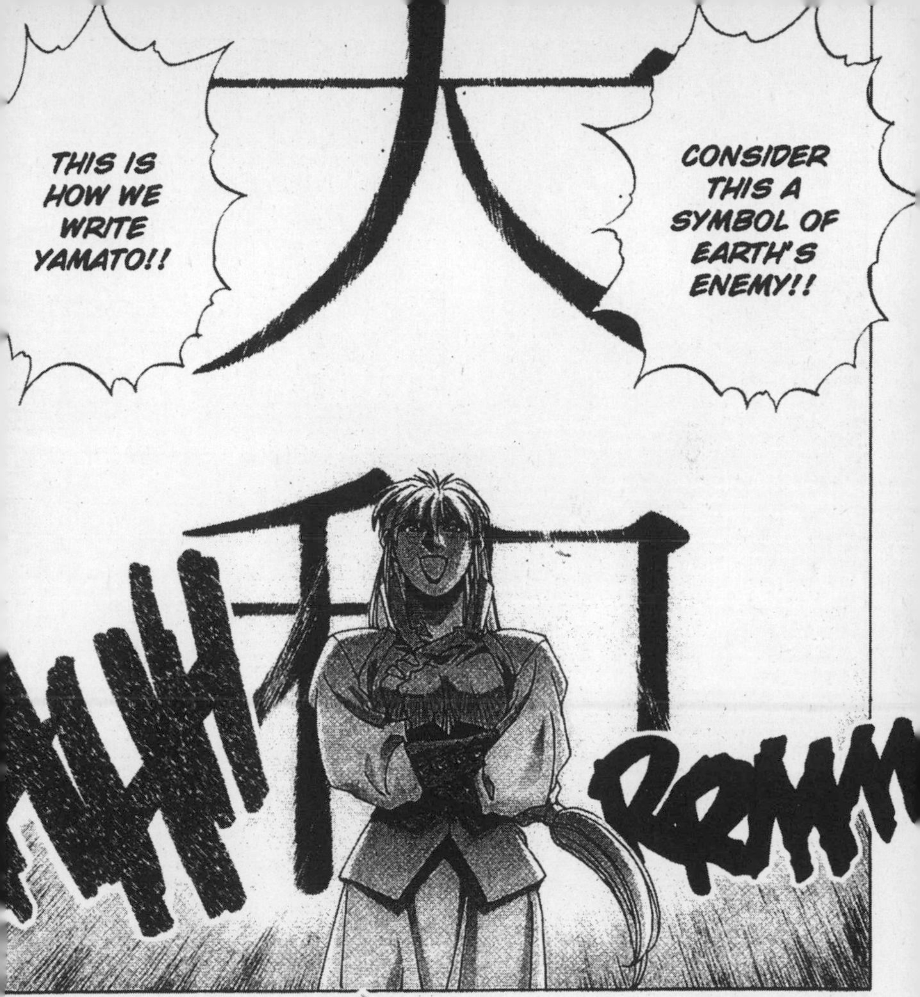
THIS IS HOW WE WRITE YAMATO!!
CONSIDER THIS A SYMBOL OF EARTH'S ENEMY!!
HURRMMM
HUH?

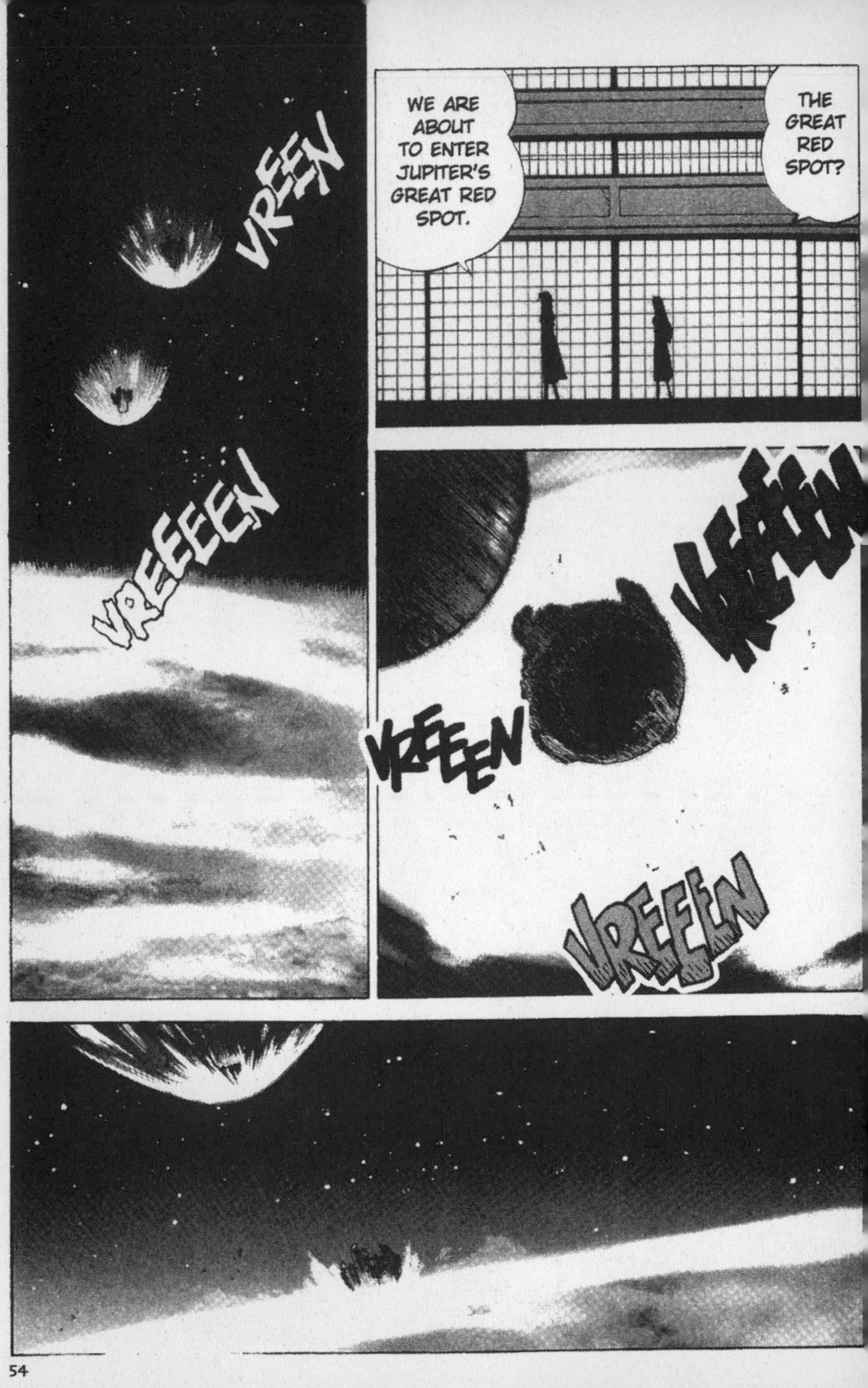
VREEN
VREEEEN
WE ARE ABOUT TO ENTER JUPITER'S GREAT RED SPOT.
THE GREAT RED SPOT?
VREEEN
VREEEN

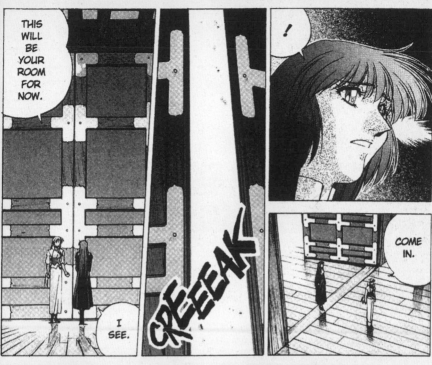

THIS WILL BE YOUR ROOM FOR NOW.

I SEE.

CREEEAK

!

COME IN.

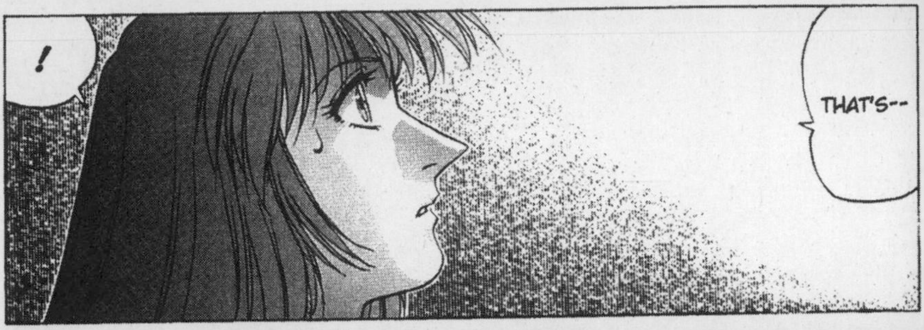
!
THAT'S--
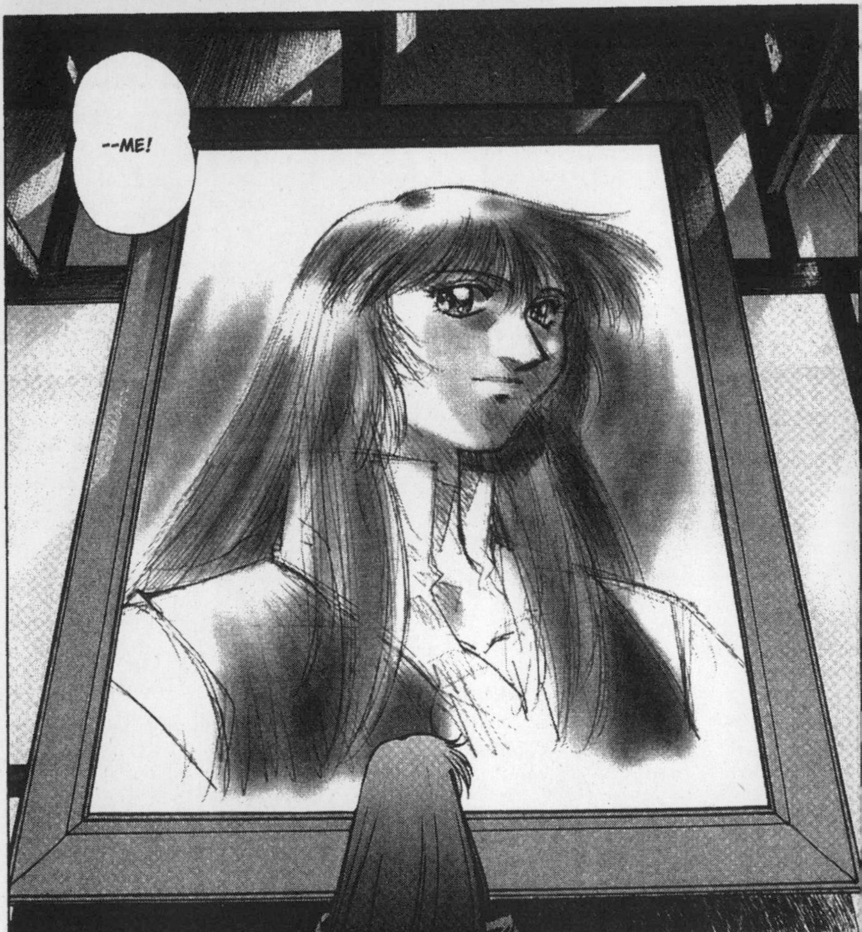
--ME!

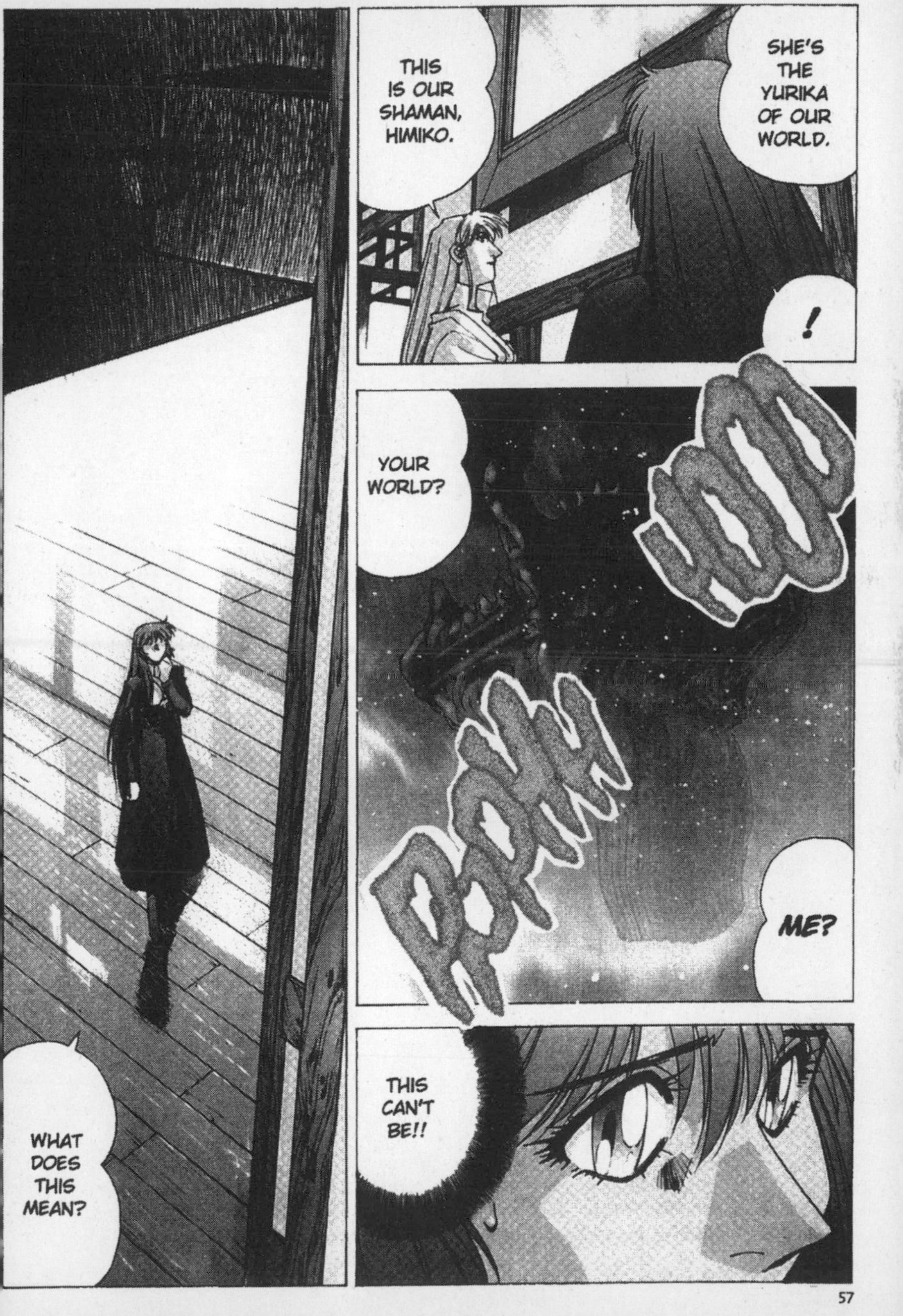
WHAT DOES THIS MEAN?
THIS IS OUR SHAMAN, HIMIKO.
SHE'S THE YURIKA OF OUR WORLD.
!
YOUR WORLD?
ME?
THIS CAN'T BE!!

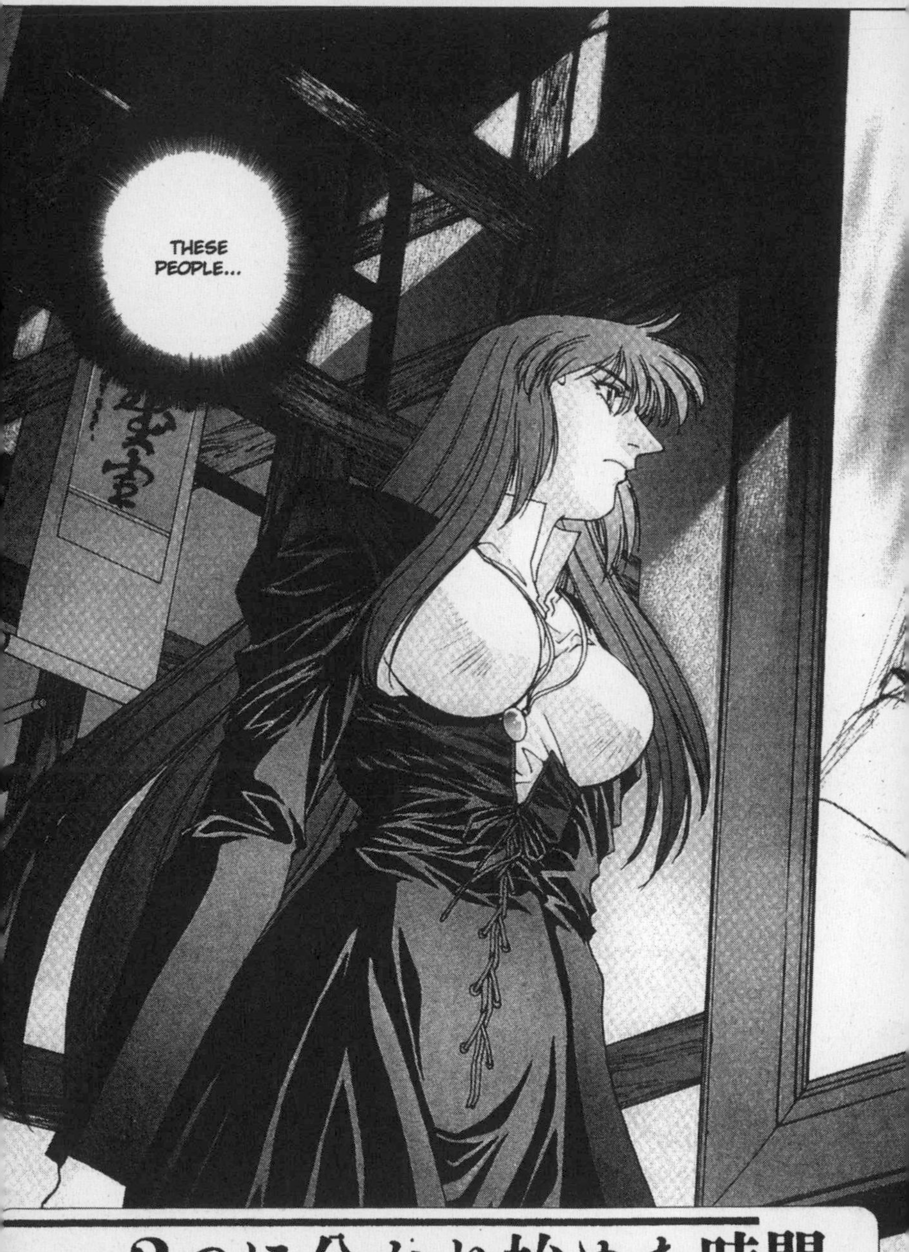
THESE PEOPLE...

第15話 2つに分かれ始めた時間

—DOUBLE-DEALING—

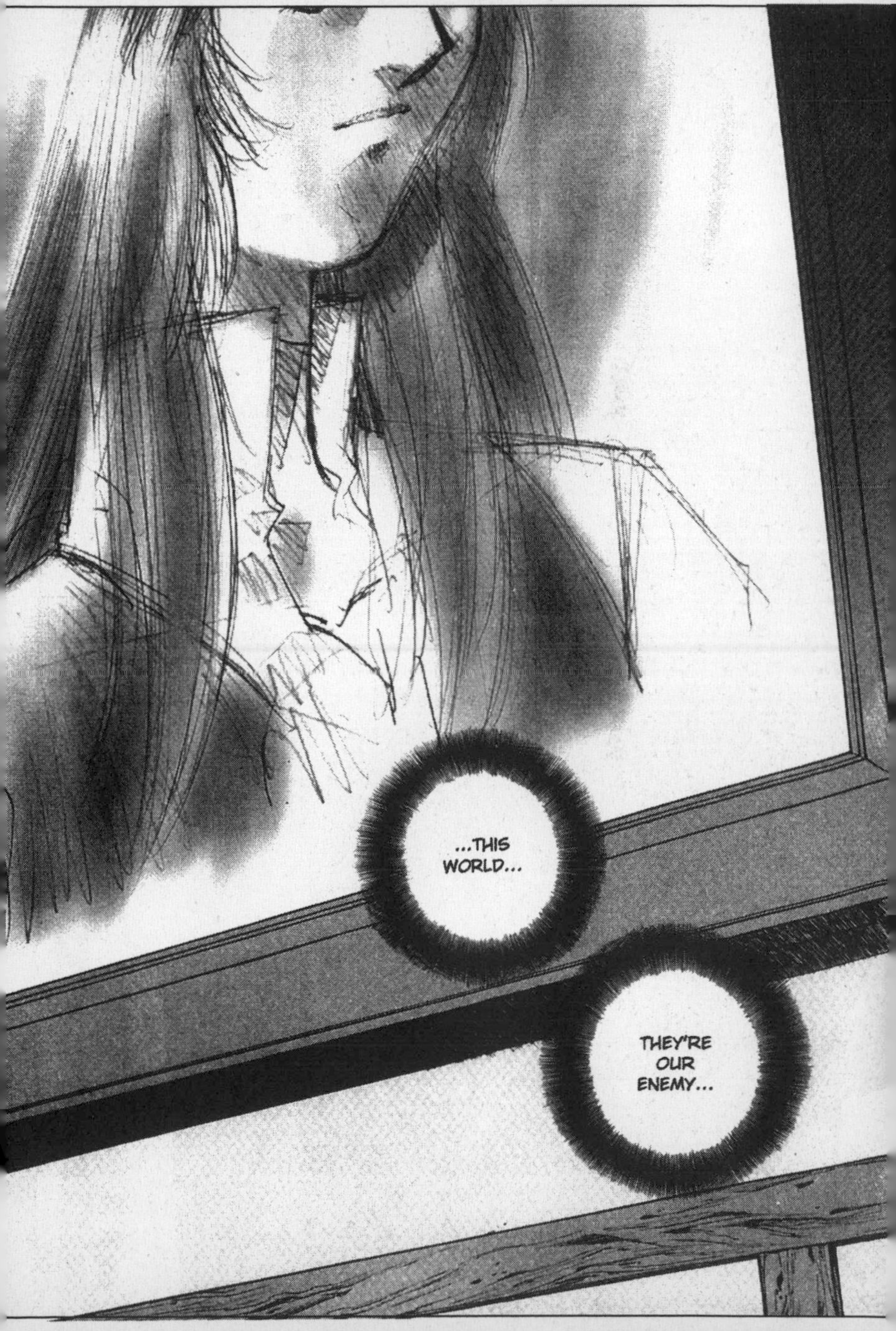
...THIS WORLD...
THEY'RE OUR ENEMY...

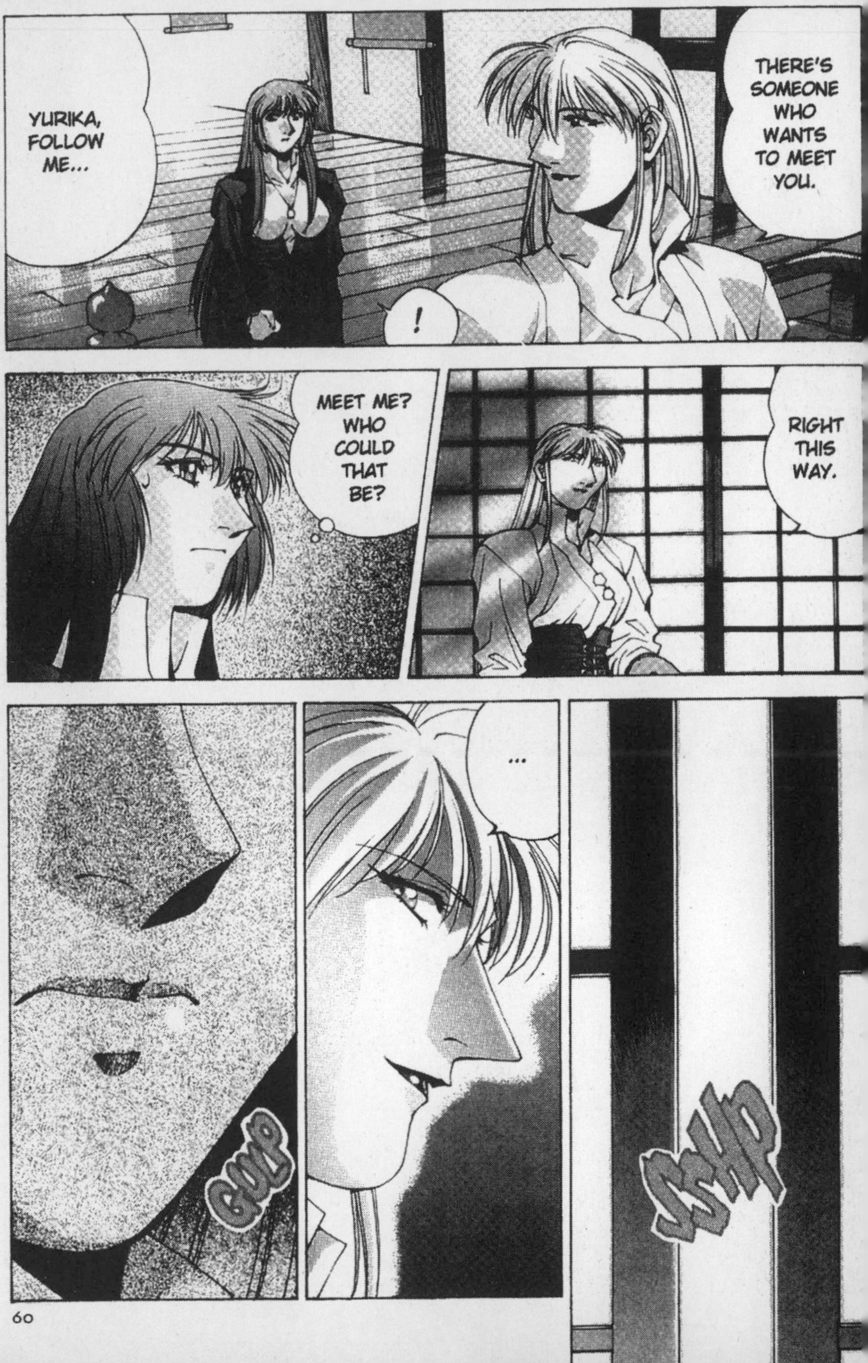
YURIKA, FOLLOW ME...
!
THERE'S SOMEONE WHO WANTS TO MEET YOU.
MEET ME? WHO COULD THAT BE?
RIGHT THIS WAY.
GULP
...
SSHP

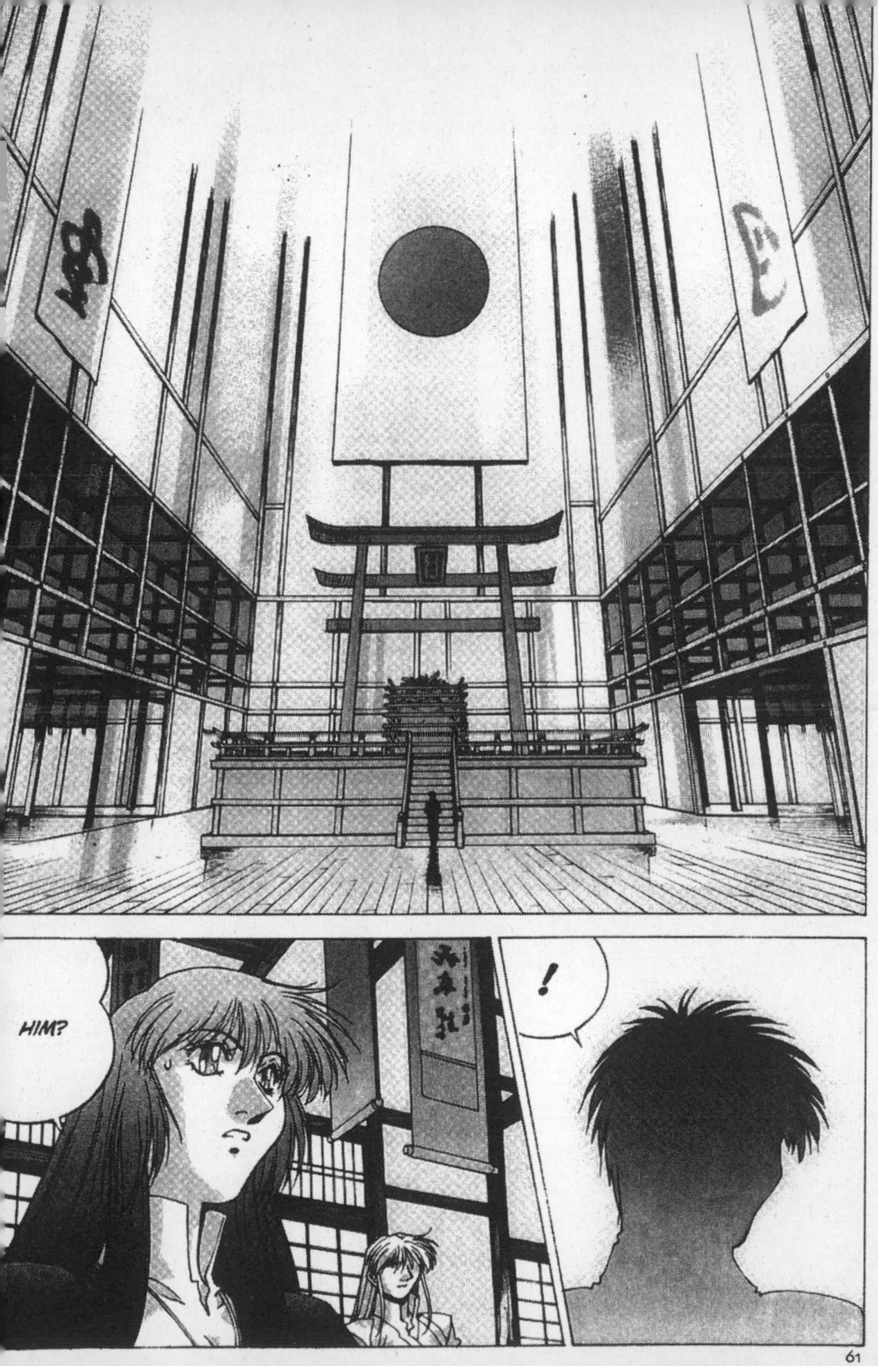
HIM?
!

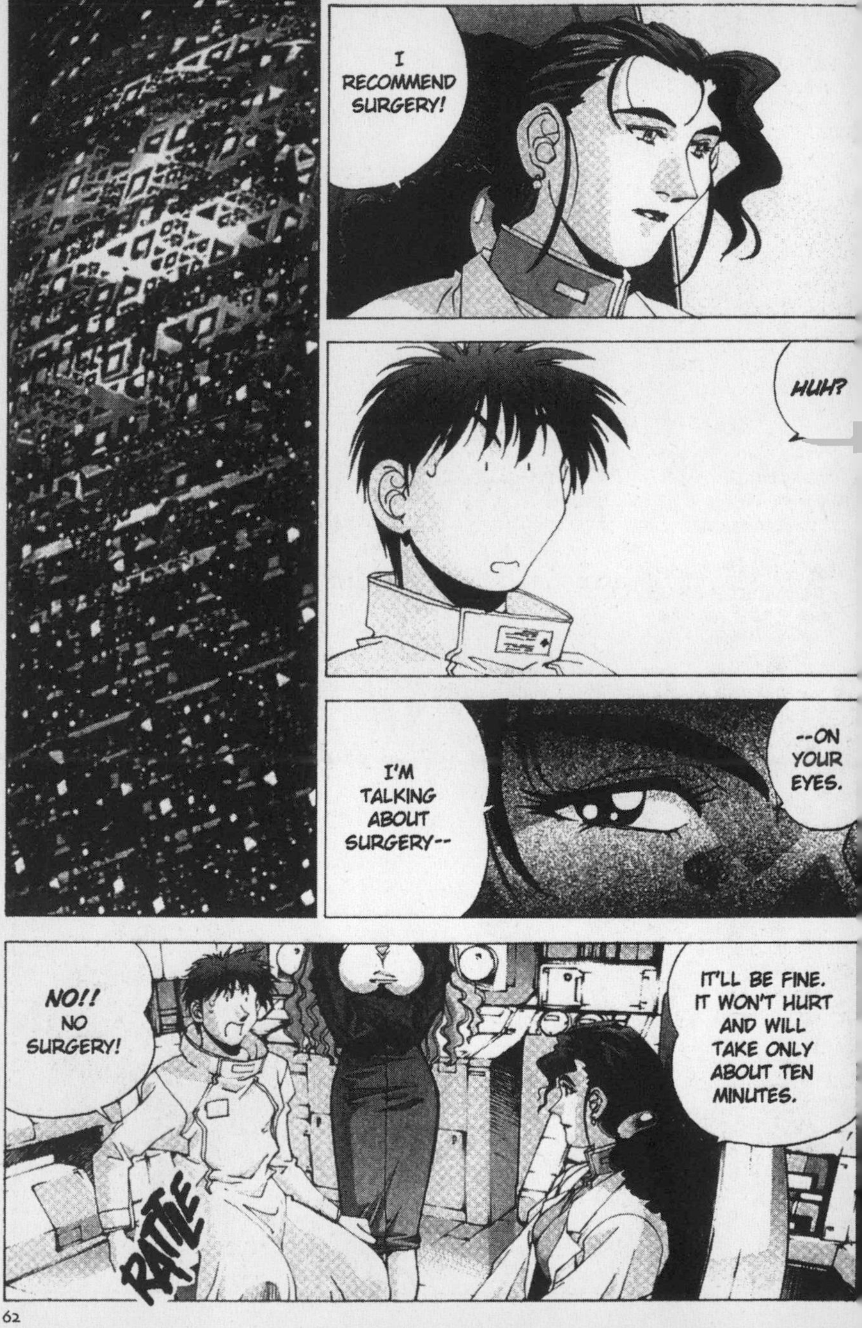
I RECOMMEND SURGERY!
HUH?
I'M TALKING ABOUT SURGERY--
--ON YOUR EYES.
NO!! NO SURGERY!
RATTLE
IT'LL BE FINE. IT WON'T HURT AND WILL TAKE ONLY ABOUT TEN MINUTES.

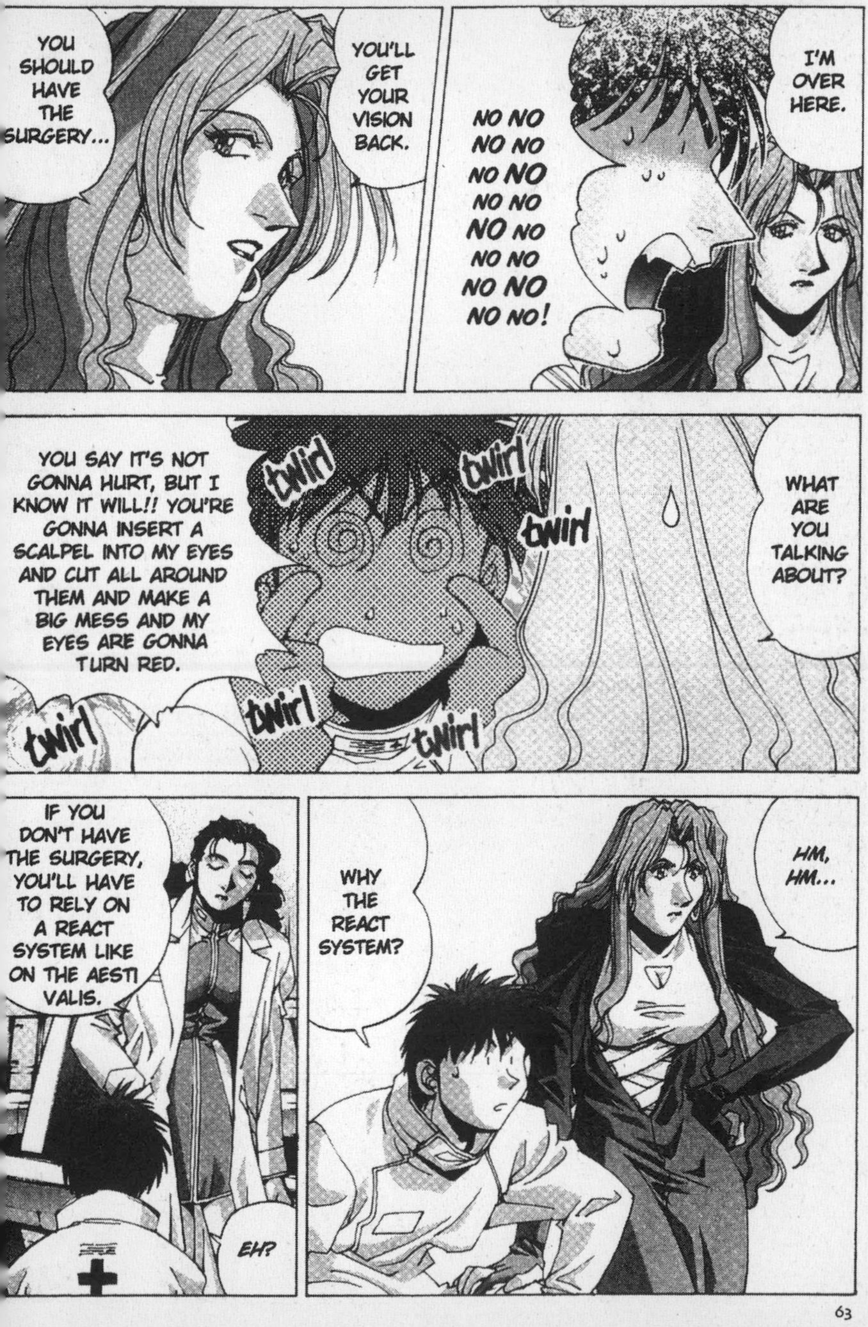

YOU SHOULD HAVE THE SURGERY...
YOU'LL GET YOUR VISION BACK.
NO NO NO NO NO NO NO NO NO NO NO NO NO NO NO NO!
I'M OVER HERE.
YOU SAY IT'S NOT GONNA HURT, BUT I KNOW IT WILL!! YOU'RE GONNA INSERT A SCALPEL INTO MY EYES AND CUT ALL AROUND THEM AND MAKE A BIG MESS AND MY EYES ARE GONNA TURN RED.
twirl
twirl
twirl
twirl
twirl
twirl
WHAT ARE YOU TALKING ABOUT?
IF YOU DON'T HAVE THE SURGERY, YOU'LL HAVE TO RELY ON A REACT SYSTEM LIKE ON THE AESTI VALIS.
EH?
WHY THE REACT SYSTEM?
HM, HM...

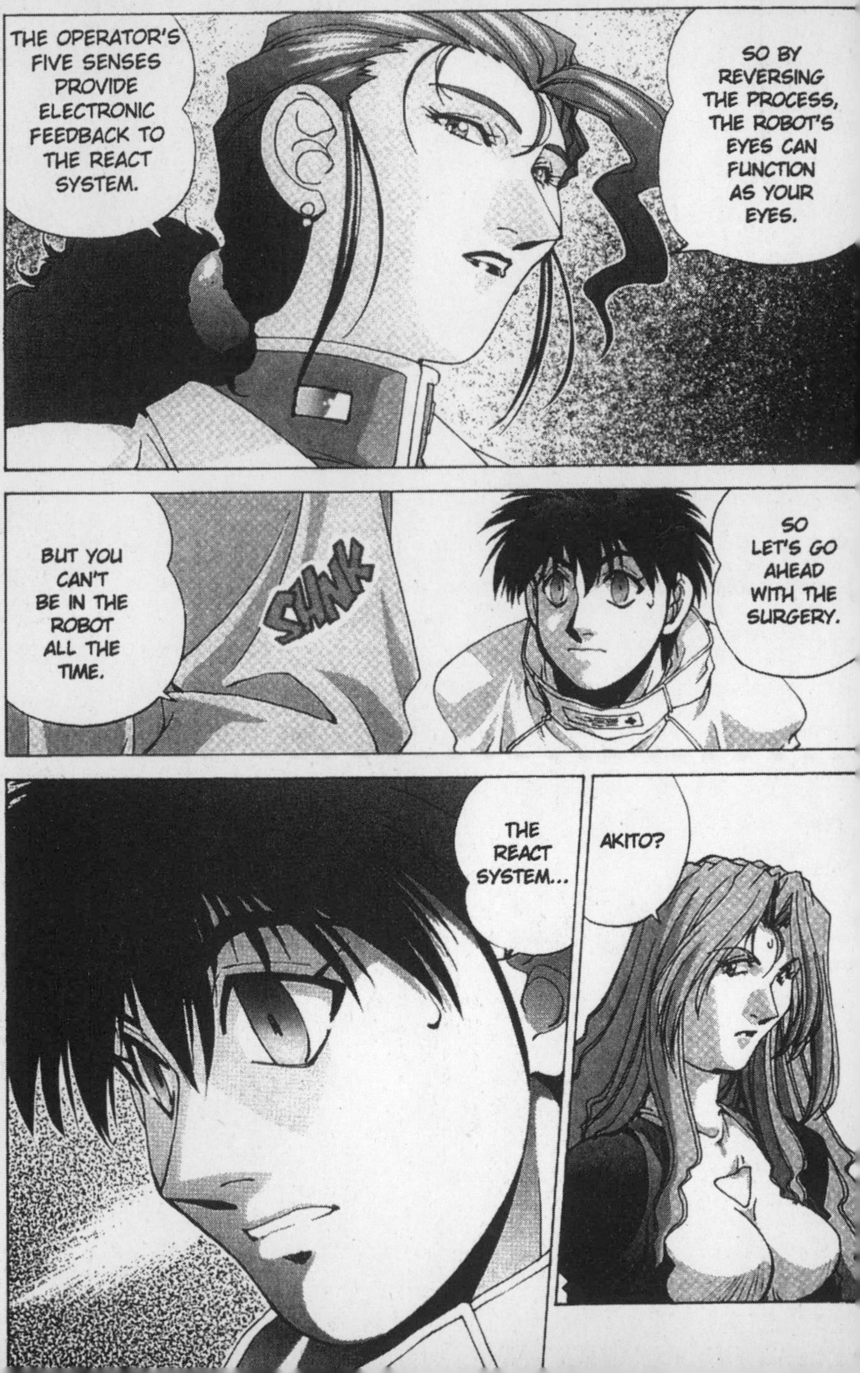
THE OPERATOR'S FIVE SENSES PROVIDE ELECTRONIC FEEDBACK TO THE REACT SYSTEM.
SO BY REVERSING THE PROCESS, THE ROBOT'S EYES CAN FUNCTION AS YOUR EYES.
BUT YOU CAN'T BE IN THE ROBOT ALL THE TIME.
SHINK
SO LET'S GO AHEAD WITH THE SURGERY.
THE REACT SYSTEM...
AKITO?

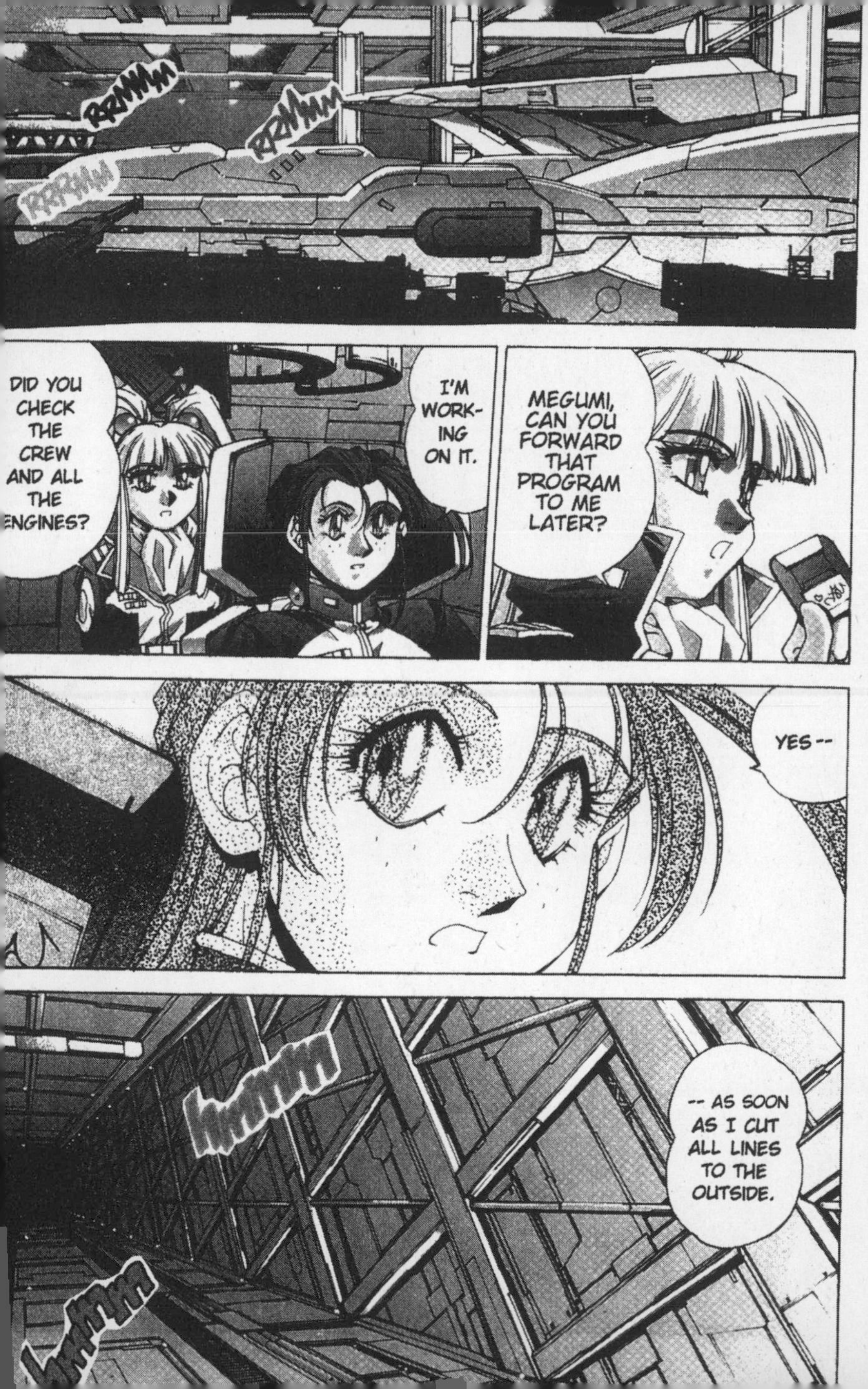
RRMMM!
RRMMM
RRRMMM
DID YOU CHECK THE CREW AND ALL THE ENGINES?
I'M WORK-ING ON IT.
MEGUMI, CAN YOU FORWARD THAT PROGRAM TO ME LATER?
YES --
-- AS SOON AS I CUT ALL LINES TO THE OUTSIDE.

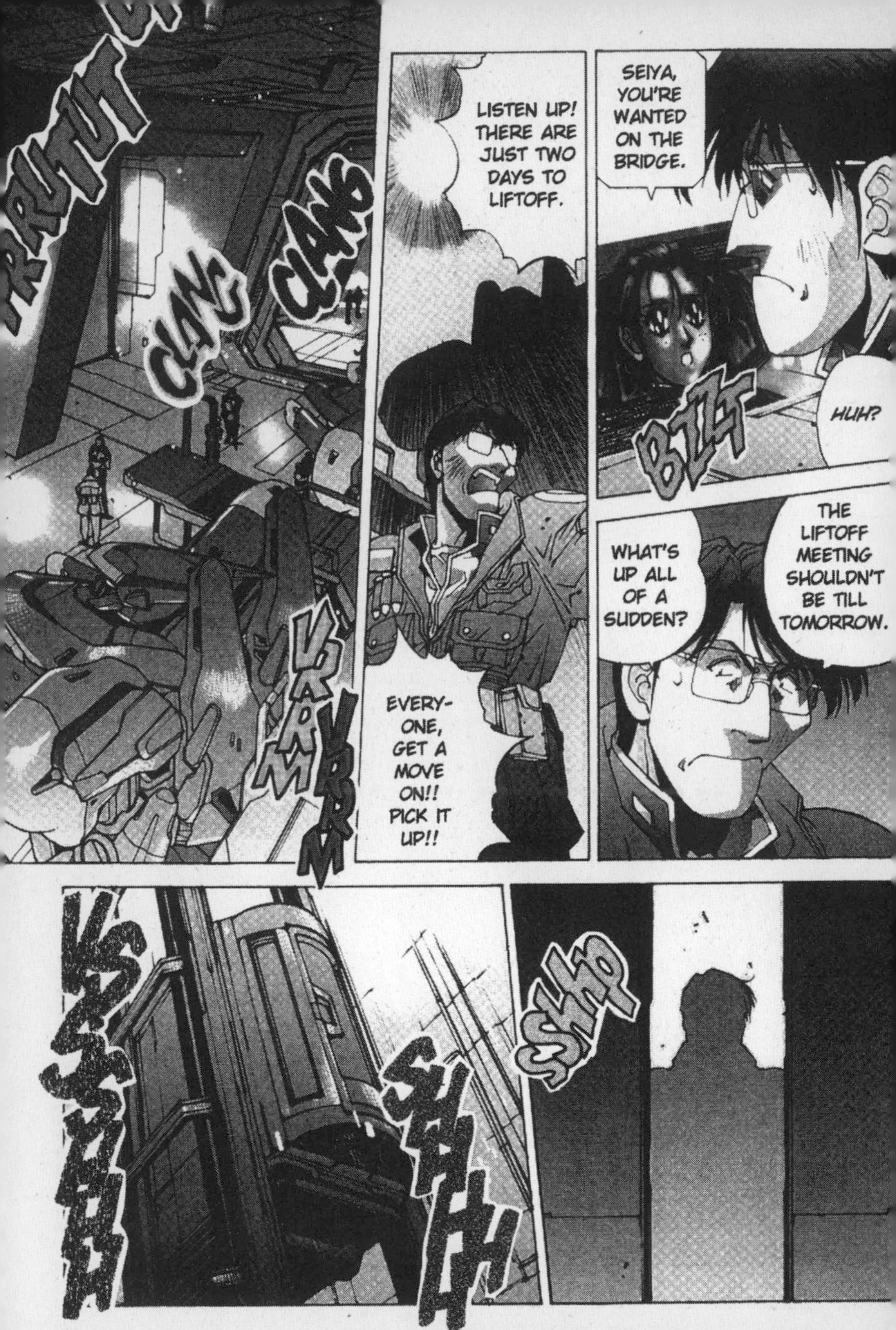
CLANG
CLANG
LISTEN UP! THERE ARE JUST TWO DAYS TO LIFTOFF.
EVERY-ONE, GET A MOVE ON!! PICK IT UP!!
SEIYA, YOU'RE WANTED ON THE BRIDGE.
BZZT
HUH?
WHAT'S UP ALL OF A SUDDEN?
THE LIFTOFF MEETING SHOULDN'T BE TILL TOMORROW.

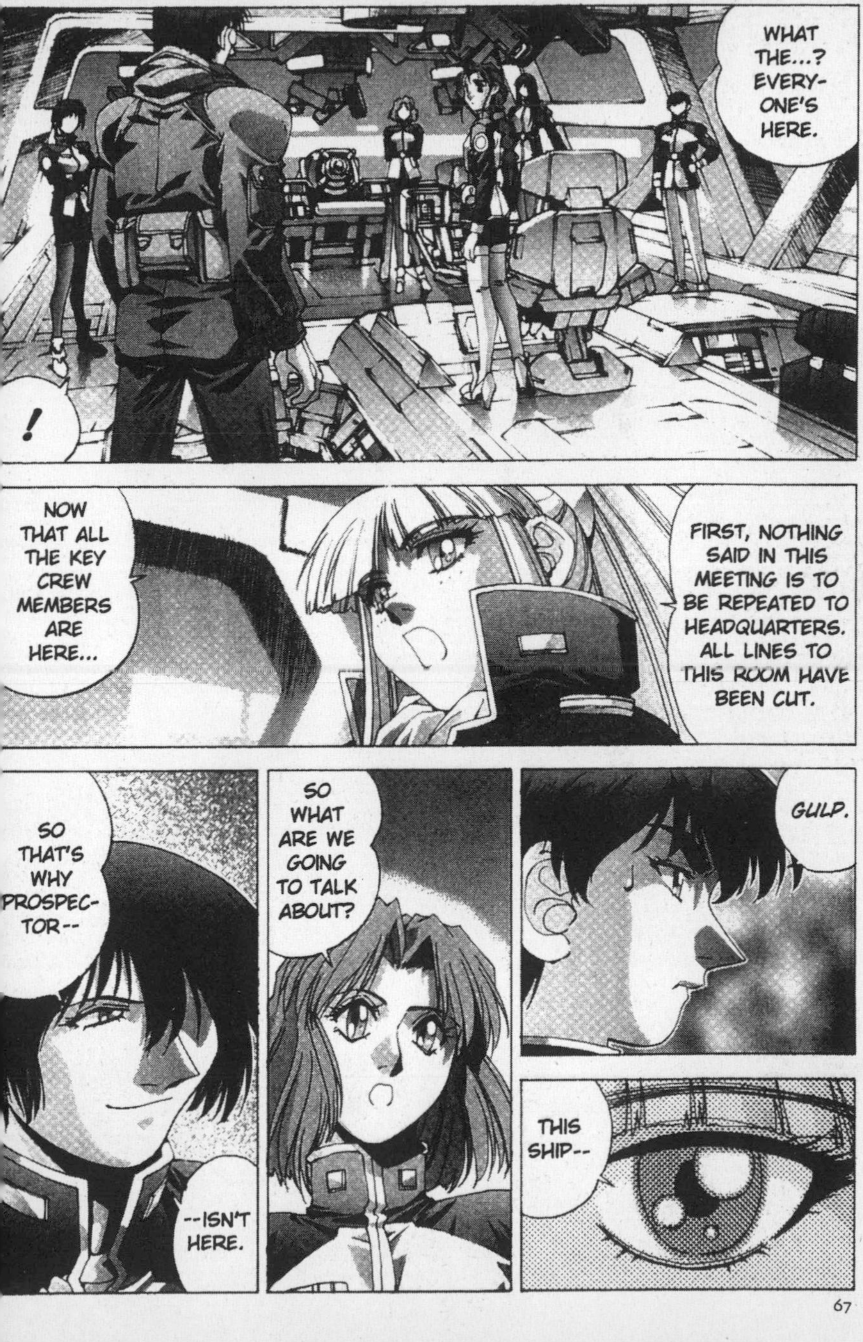
WHAT THE...? EVERYONE'S HERE.
!
NOW THAT ALL THE KEY CREW MEMBERS ARE HERE...
FIRST, NOTHING SAID IN THIS MEETING IS TO BE REPEATED TO HEADQUARTERS. ALL LINES TO THIS ROOM HAVE BEEN CUT.
SO THAT'S WHY PROSPECTOR--
--ISN'T HERE.
SO WHAT ARE WE GOING TO TALK ABOUT?
GULP.
THIS SHIP--

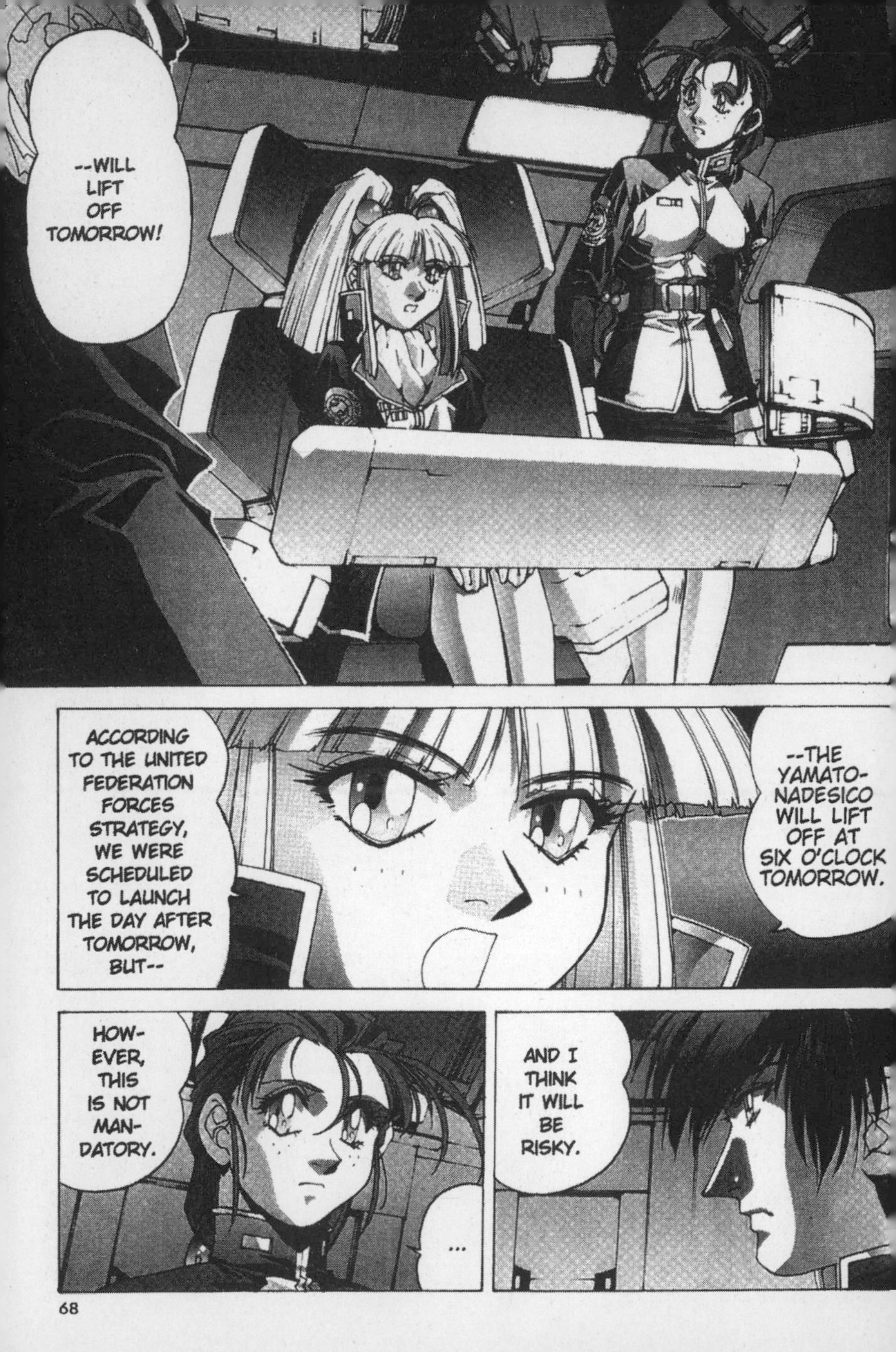
--WILL LIFT OFF TOMORROW!
ACCORDING TO THE UNITED FEDERATION FORCES STRATEGY, WE WERE SCHEDULED TO LAUNCH THE DAY AFTER TOMORROW, BUT--
--THE YAMATO-NADESICO WILL LIFT OFF AT SIX O'CLOCK TOMORROW.
HOW-EVER, THIS IS NOT MAN-DATORY.
...
AND I THINK IT WILL BE RISKY.

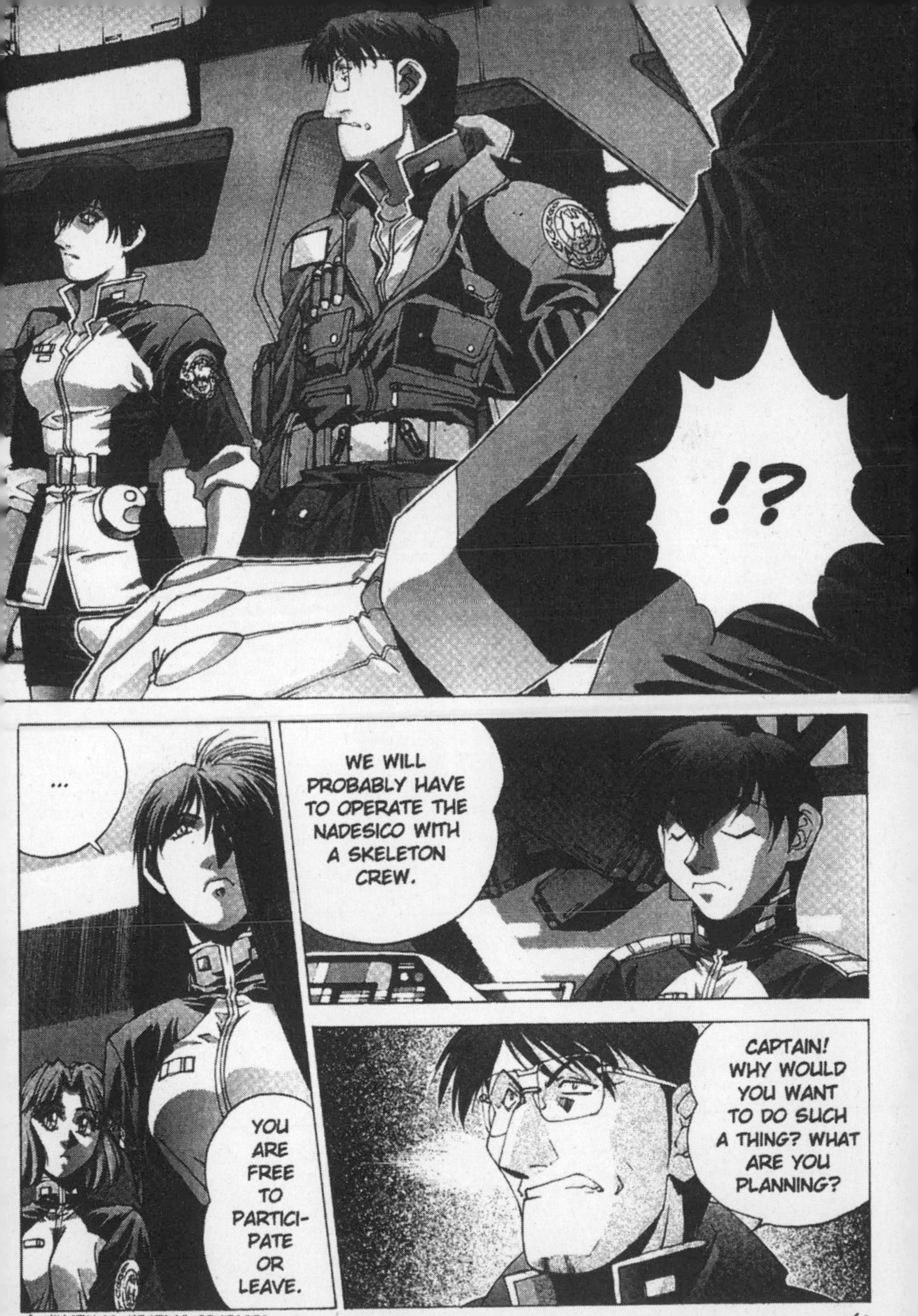
!?
...
YOU ARE FREE TO PARTICI-PATE OR LEAVE.
WE WILL PROBABLY HAVE TO OPERATE THE NADESICO WITH A SKELETON CREW.
CAPTAIN! WHY WOULD YOU WANT TO DO SUCH A THING? WHAT ARE YOU PLANNING?

▲ HIKARU IS WEARING CONTACTS.

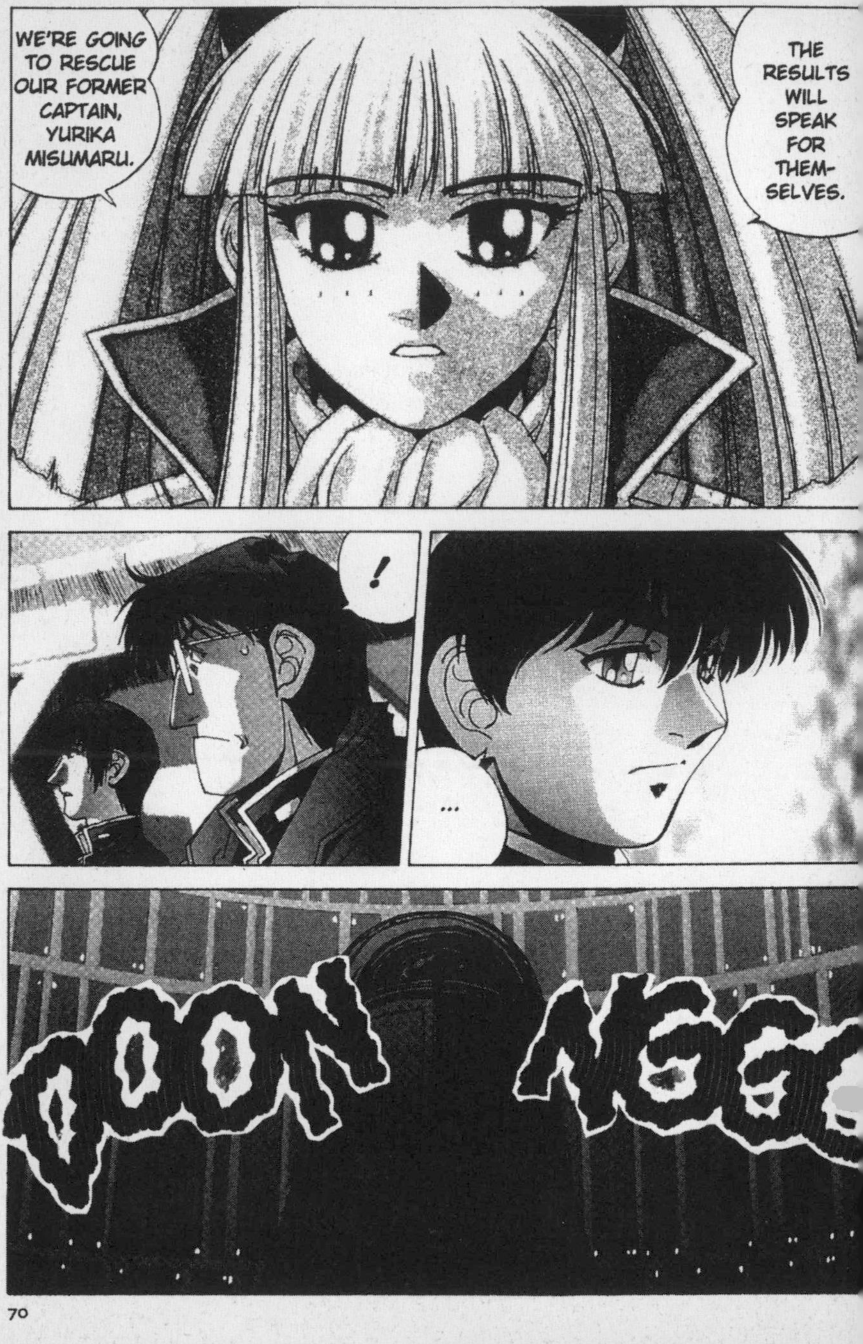
WE'RE GOING TO RESCUE OUR FORMER CAPTAIN, YURIKA MISUMARU.
THE RESULTS WILL SPEAK FOR THEM-SELVES.
!
...
DOON NGG

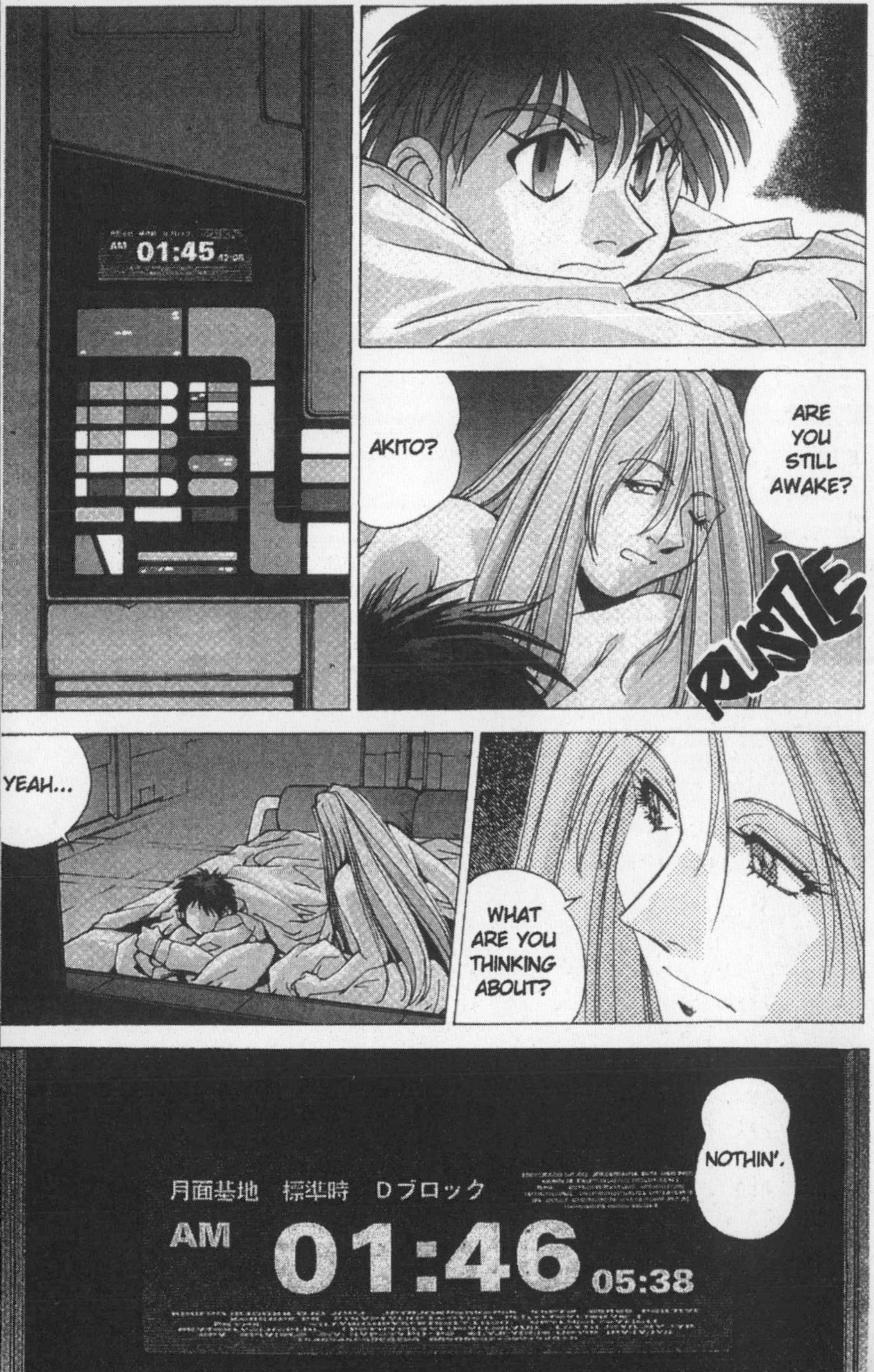
AM
01:45
AKITO?
ARE YOU STILL AWAKE?
RUSTLE
YEAH...
WHAT ARE YOU THINKING ABOUT?
月面基地　標準時　Dブロック
AM
01:46
05:38
NOTHIN'.

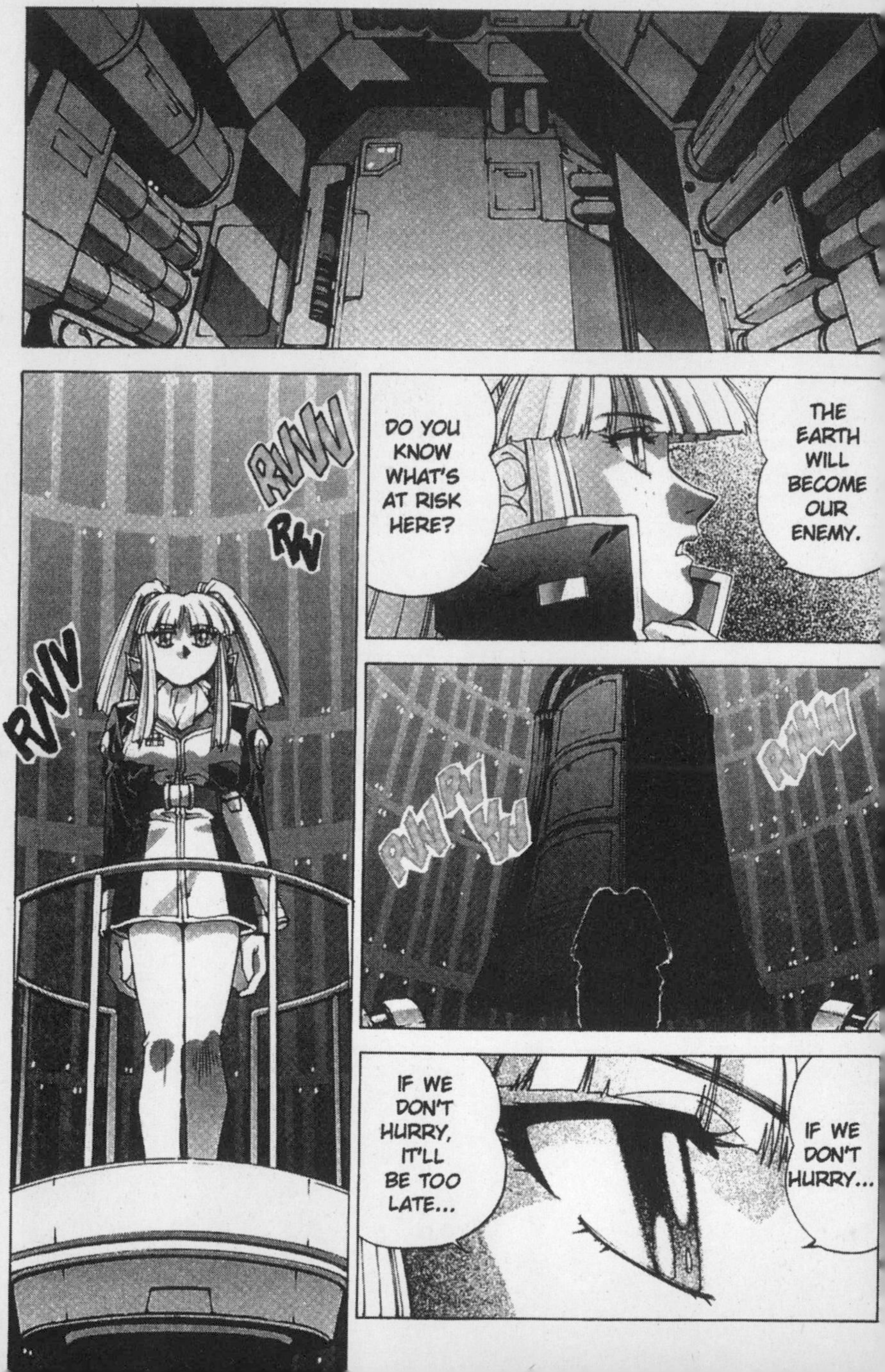
RW
DO YOU KNOW WHAT'S AT RISK HERE?
THE EARTH WILL BECOME OUR ENEMY.
IF WE DON'T HURRY, IT'LL BE TOO LATE...
IF WE DON'T HURRY...

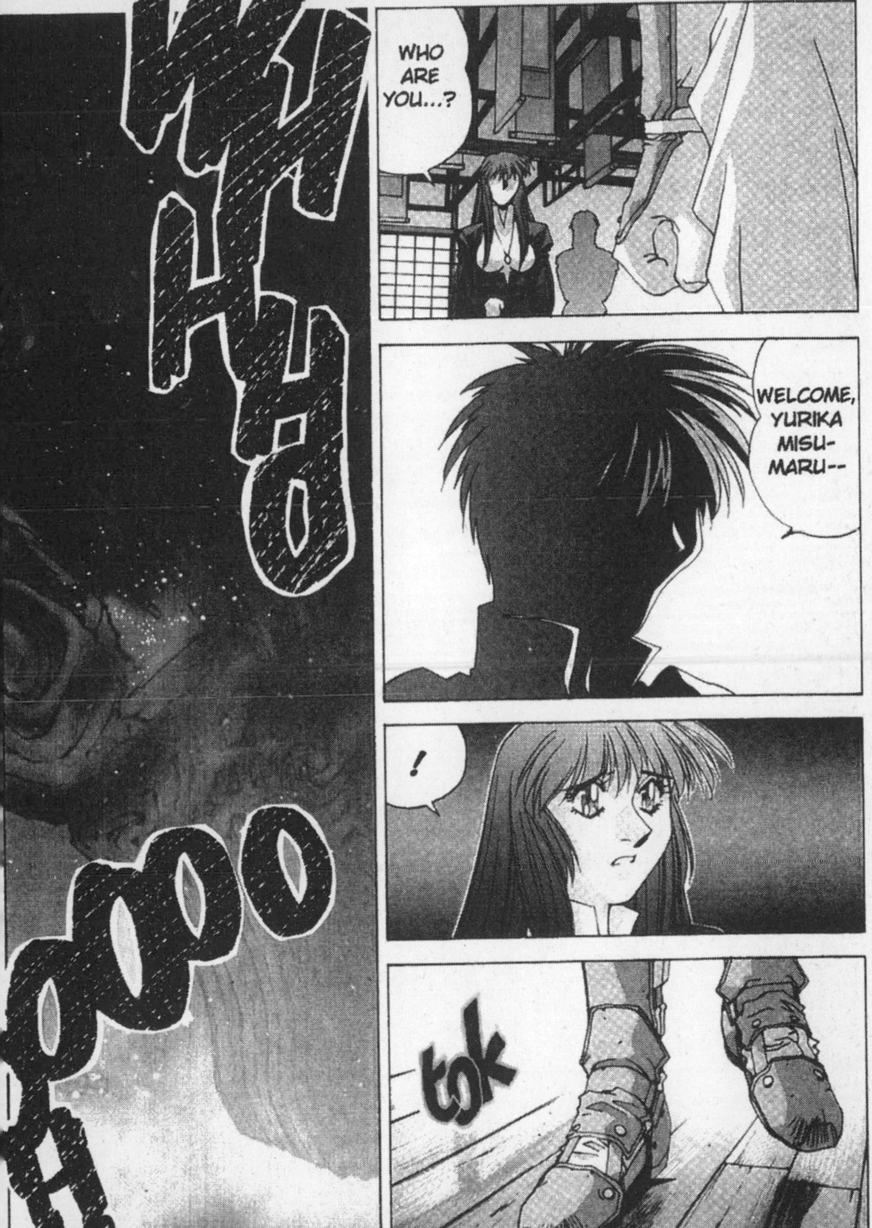
WHO ARE YOU...?
WELCOME, YURIKA MISU-MARU--
!
tok

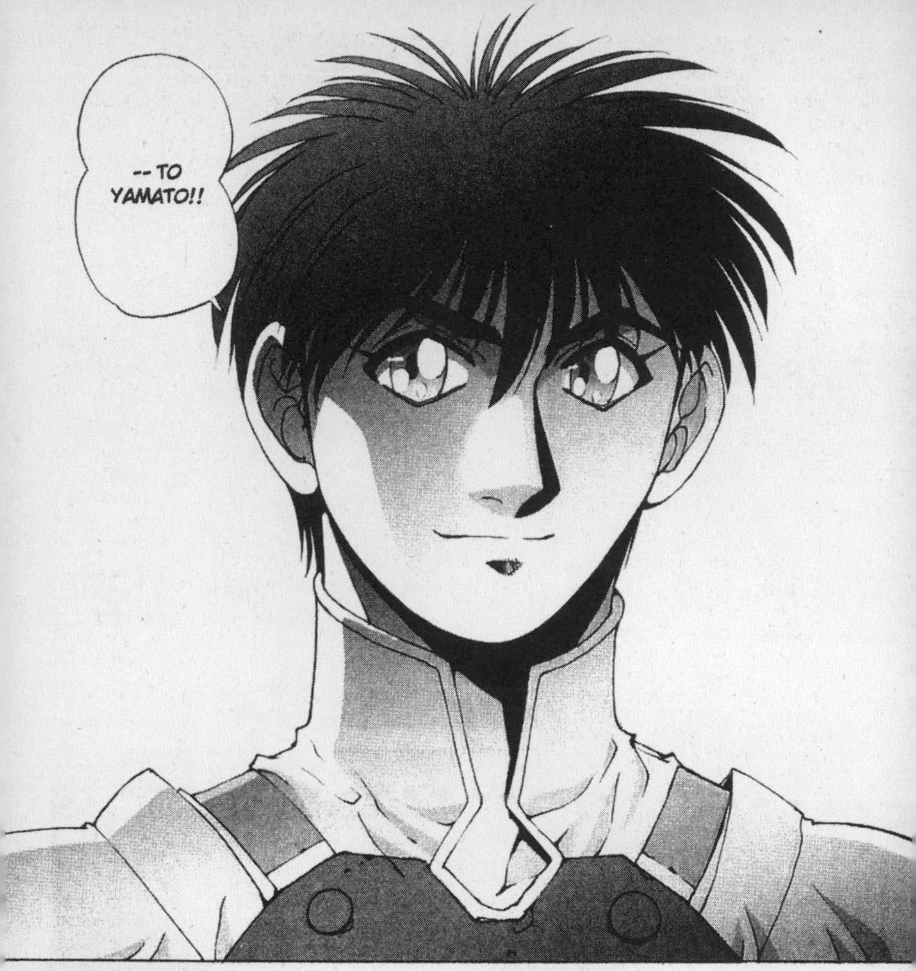
-- TO YAMATO!!

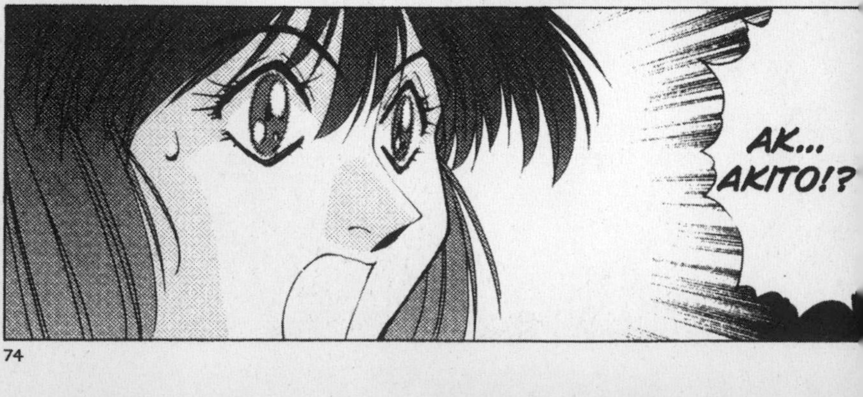
AK... AKITO!?

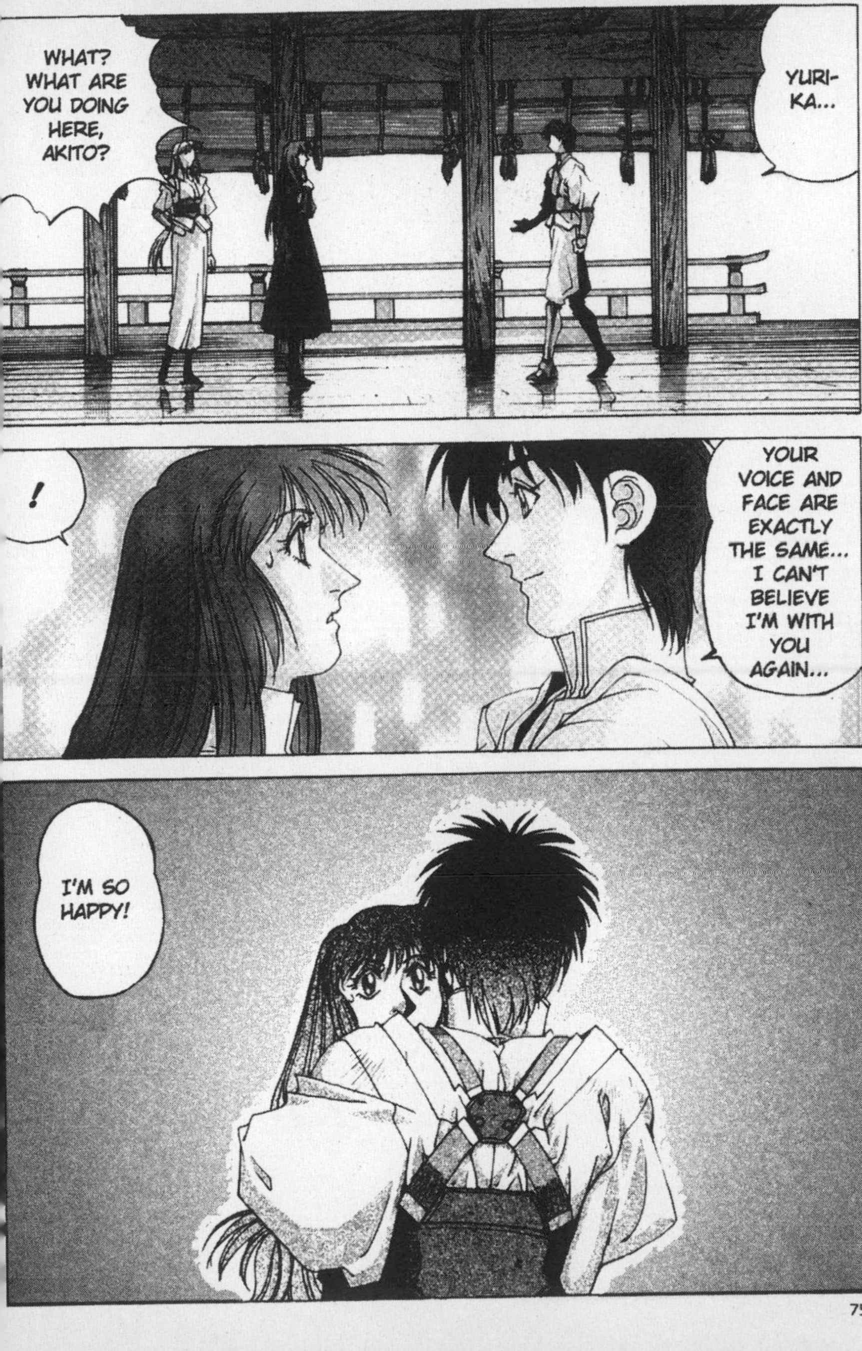
WHAT? WHAT ARE YOU DOING HERE, AKITO?
YURI-KA...
!
YOUR VOICE AND FACE ARE EXACTLY THE SAME... I CAN'T BELIEVE I'M WITH YOU AGAIN...
I'M SO HAPPY!

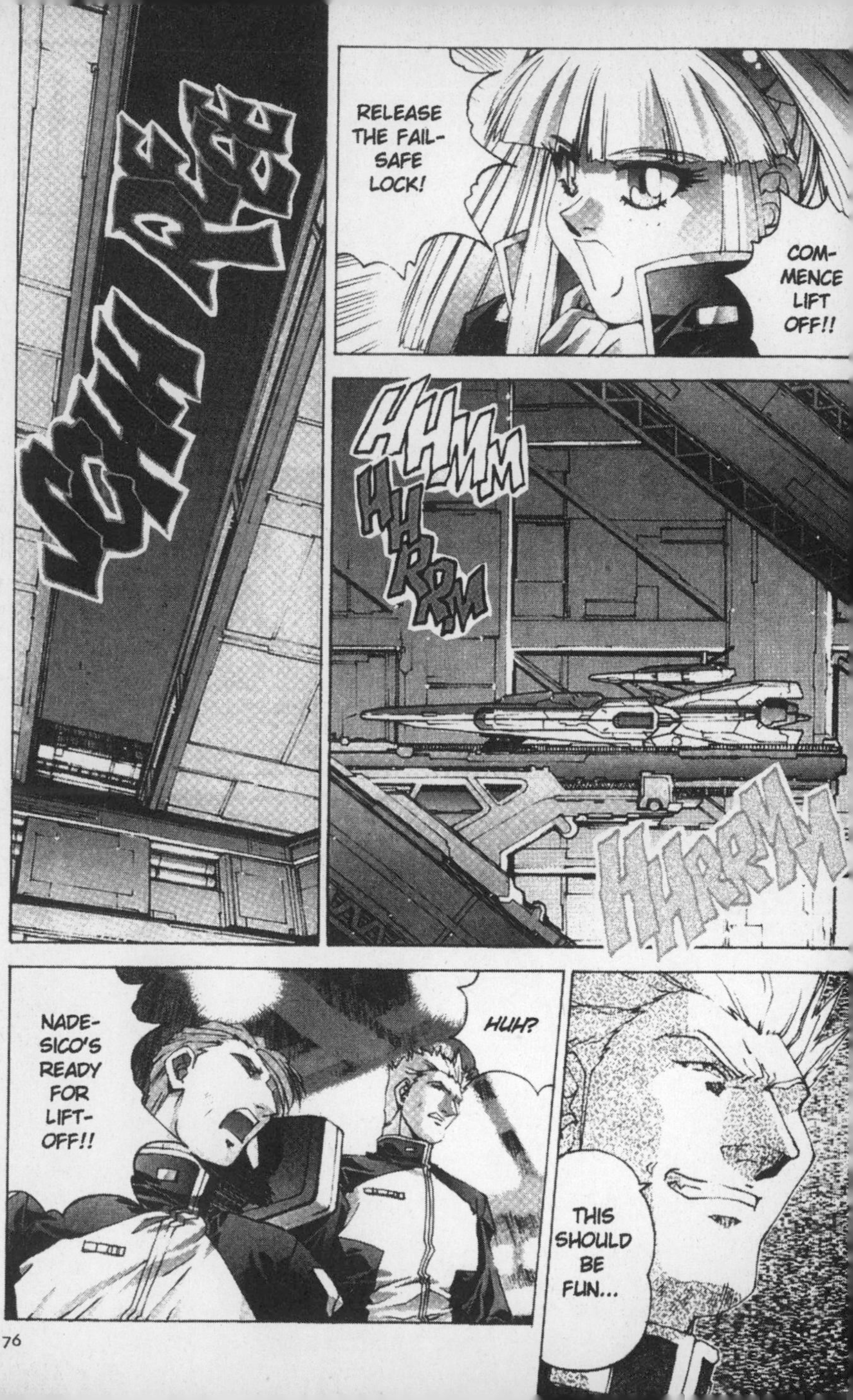
RELEASE THE FAIL-SAFE LOCK!
COMMENCE LIFT OFF!!
HUMMM
HURRM
HURRM
NADESICO'S READY FOR LIFT-OFF!!
HUH?
THIS SHOULD BE FUN...

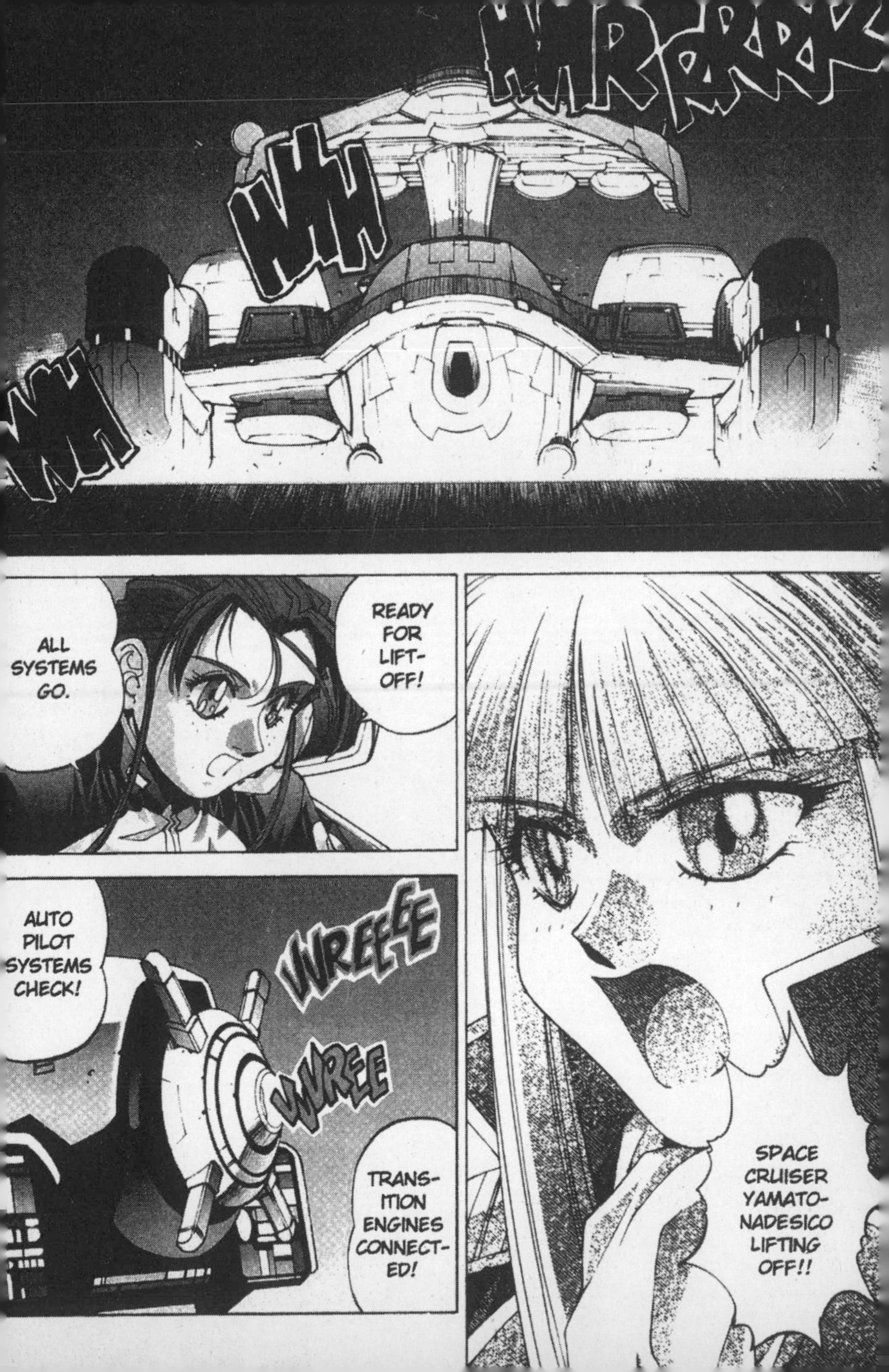
WHH
WHH
WHRRRRRK
ALL SYSTEMS GO.
READY FOR LIFT-OFF!
AUTO PILOT SYSTEMS CHECK!
VVREEEE
VVREE
TRANS-ITION ENGINES CONNECT-ED!
SPACE CRUISER YAMATO-NADESICO LIFTING OFF!!

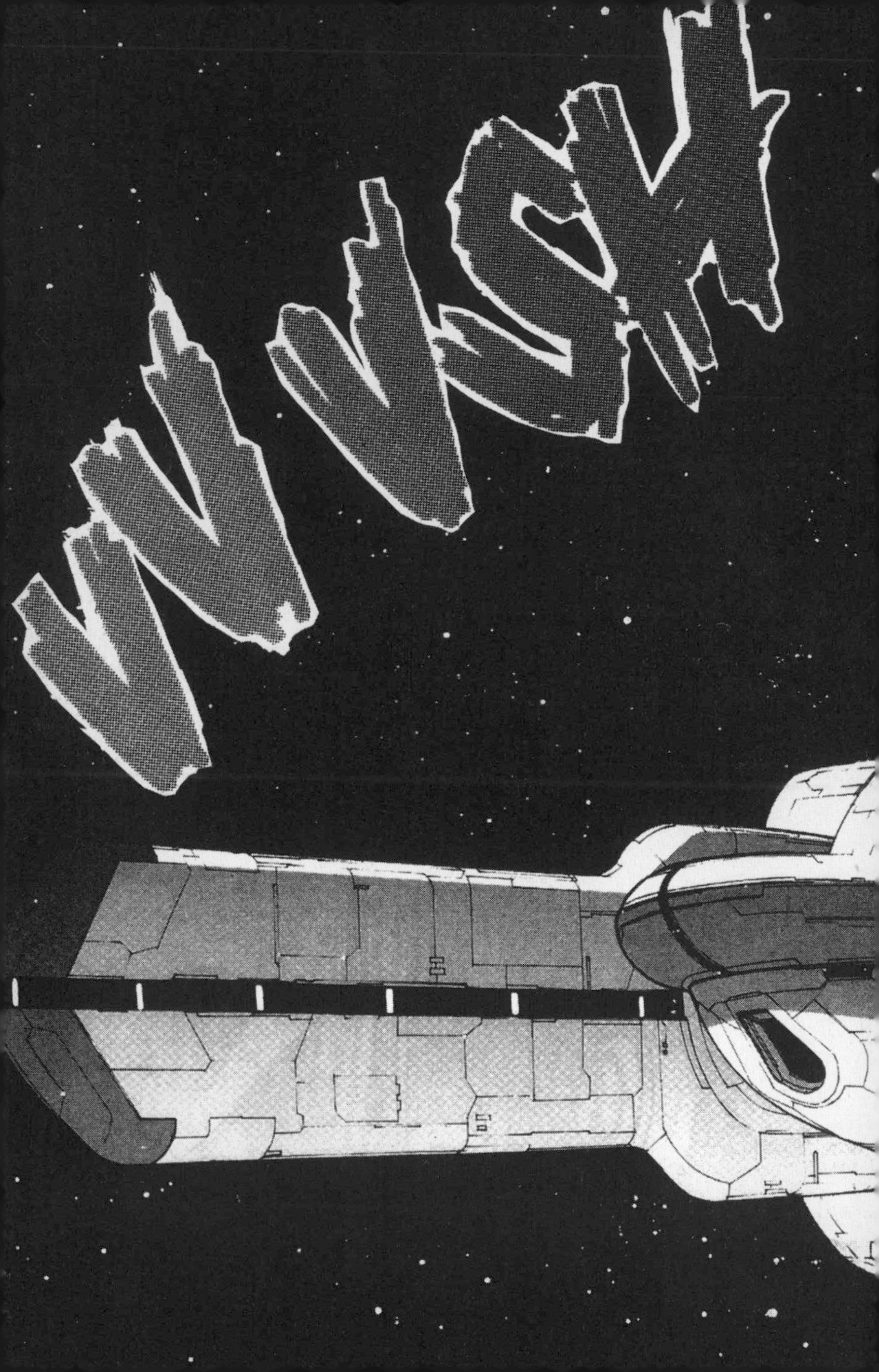

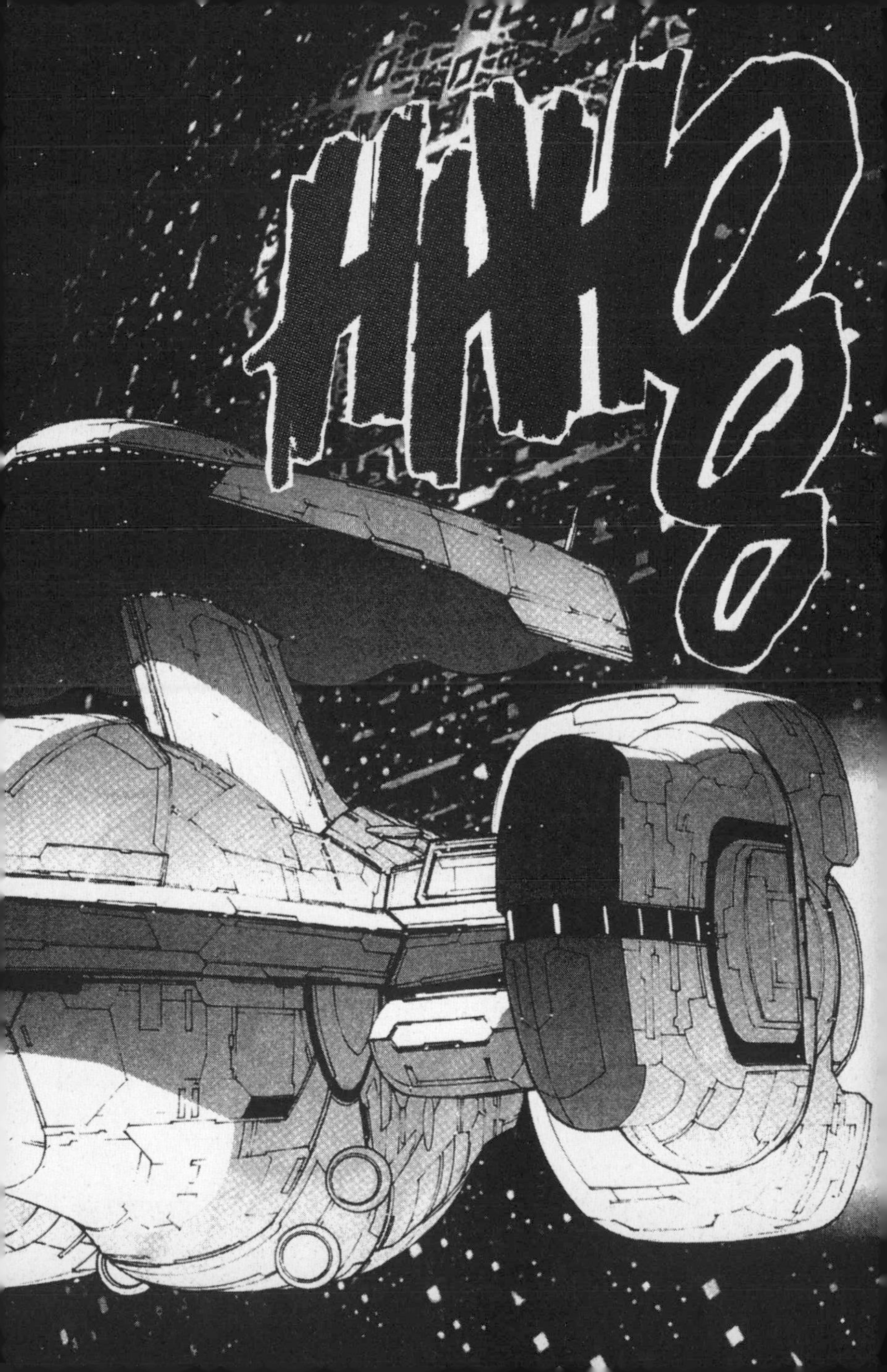

VRREEN

VRREEN

THE NADESICO IS VEERING OFF LUNAR ORBIT.

I NEED A QUICK COURSE CALCULATION!!

BEEP BEEP

JABBER JABBER

ARE YOU PLANNING A REVOLT?

NADESICO!!

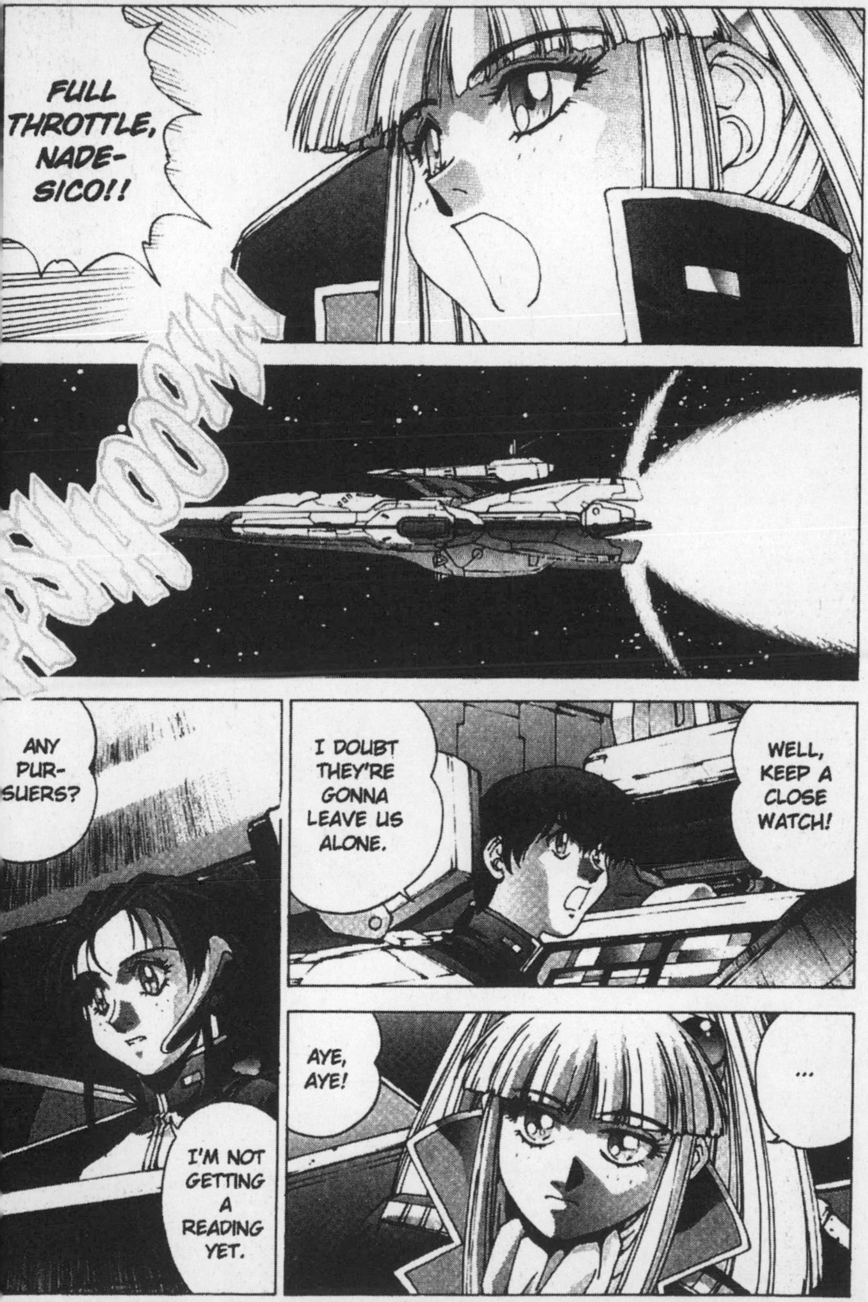
FULL THROTTLE, NADE-SICO!!
ANY PUR-SUERS?
I'M NOT GETTING A READING YET.
I DOUBT THEY'RE GONNA LEAVE US ALONE.
WELL, KEEP A CLOSE WATCH!
AYE, AYE!
...

第16話 とりあえずの真実

A TEMPORARY STEP OF TRUTH

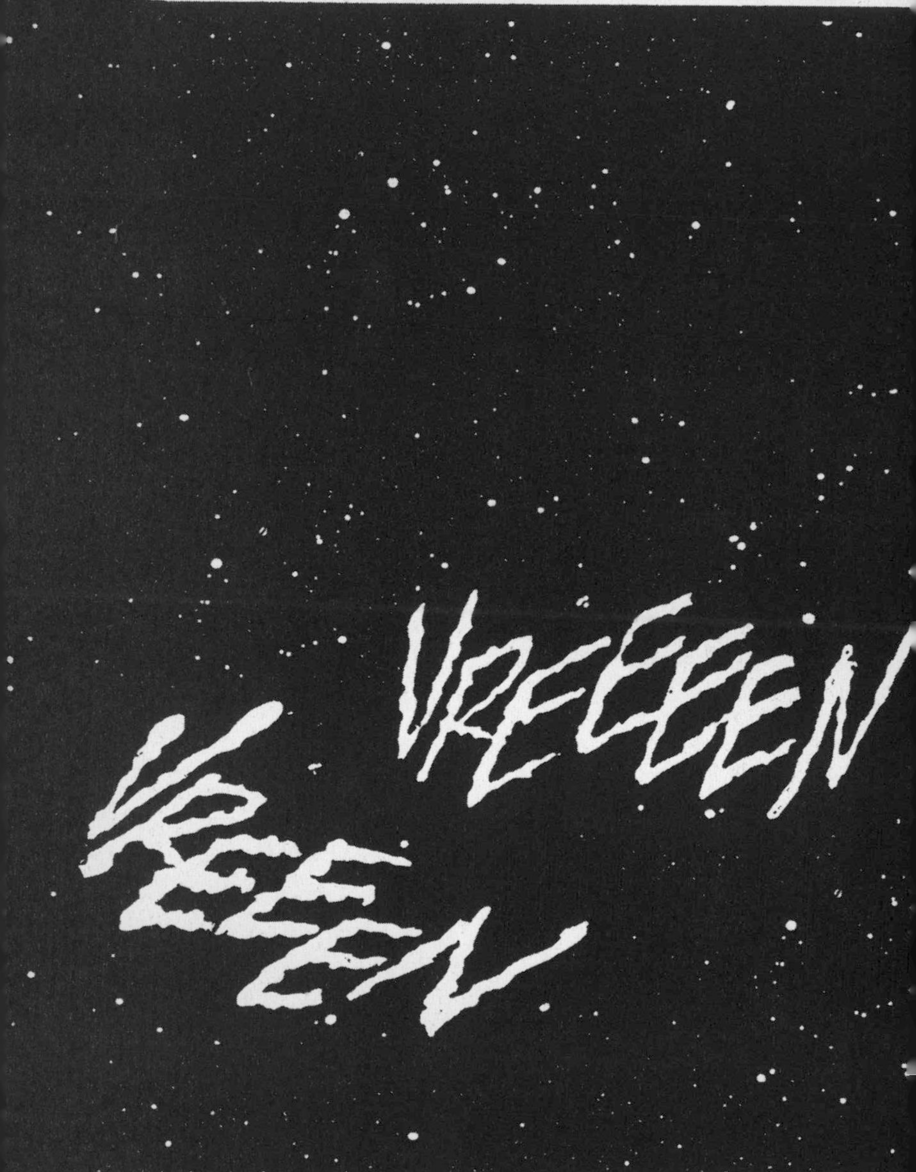
VREEEEN
VREEEN

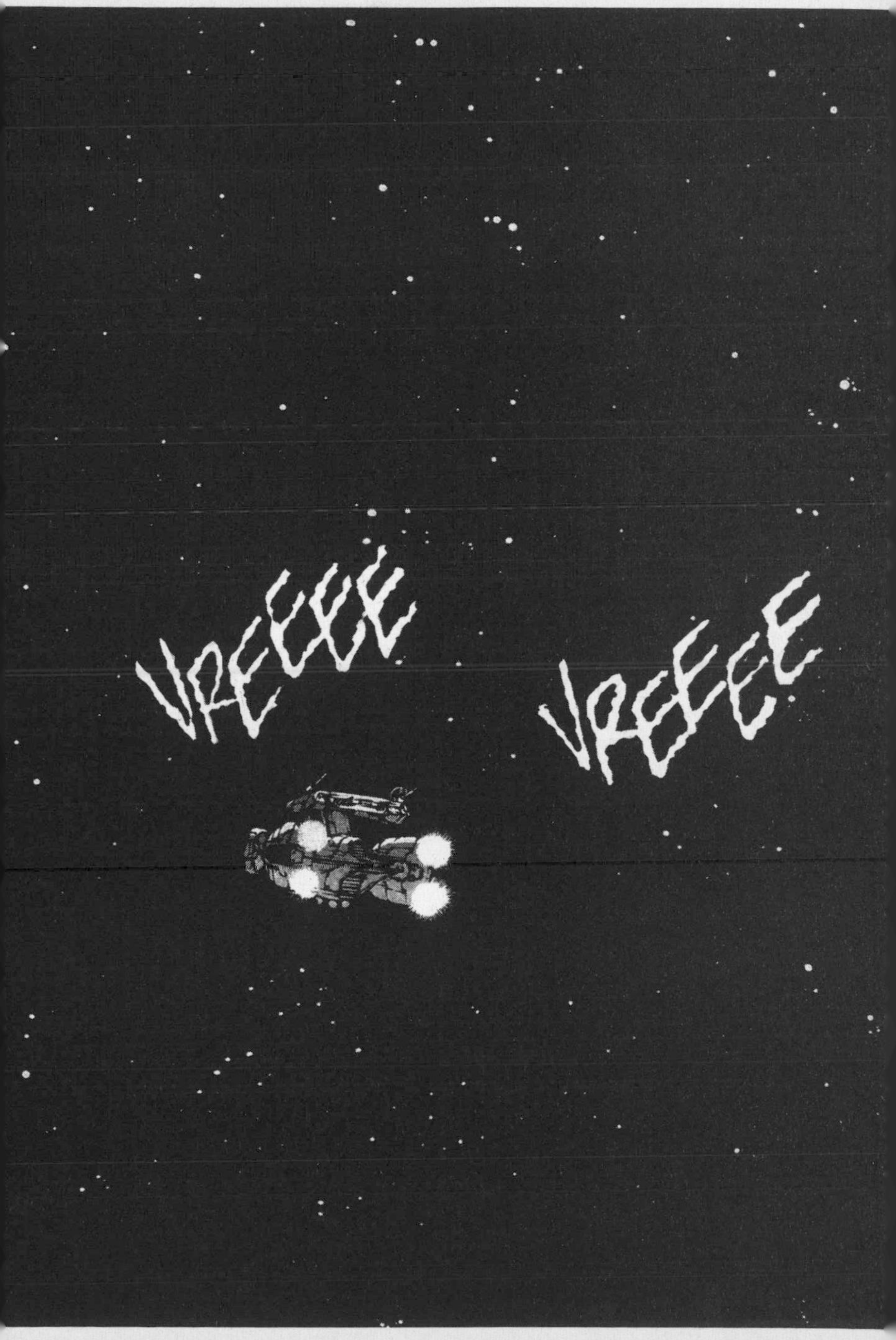
VREEEE
VREEEE

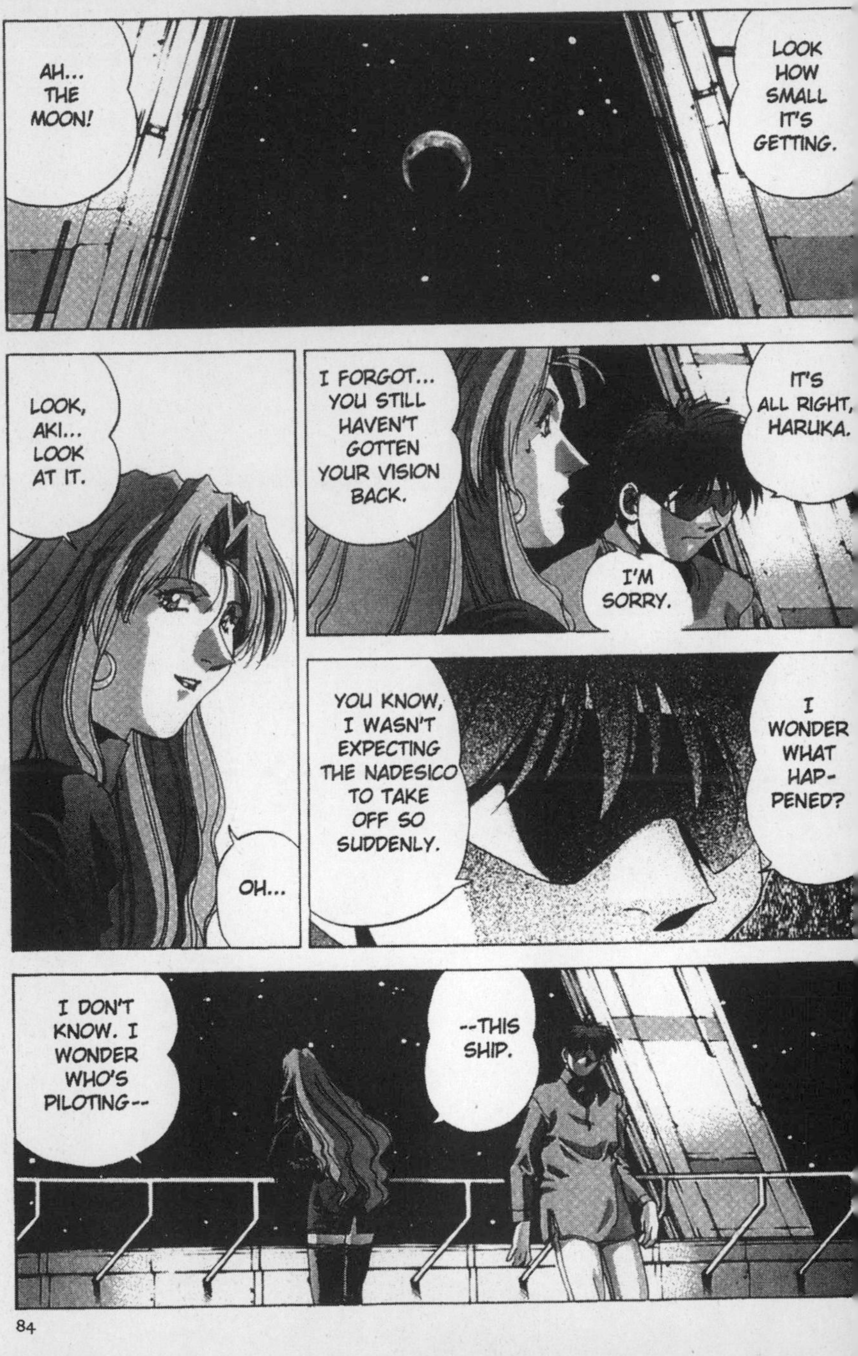
AH... THE MOON!
LOOK HOW SMALL IT'S GETTING.
LOOK, AKI... LOOK AT IT.
OH...
I FORGOT... YOU STILL HAVEN'T GOTTEN YOUR VISION BACK.
I'M SORRY.
IT'S ALL RIGHT, HARUKA.
YOU KNOW, I WASN'T EXPECTING THE NADESICO TO TAKE OFF SO SUDDENLY.
I WONDER WHAT HAP-PENED?
I DON'T KNOW. I WONDER WHO'S PILOTING--
--THIS SHIP.

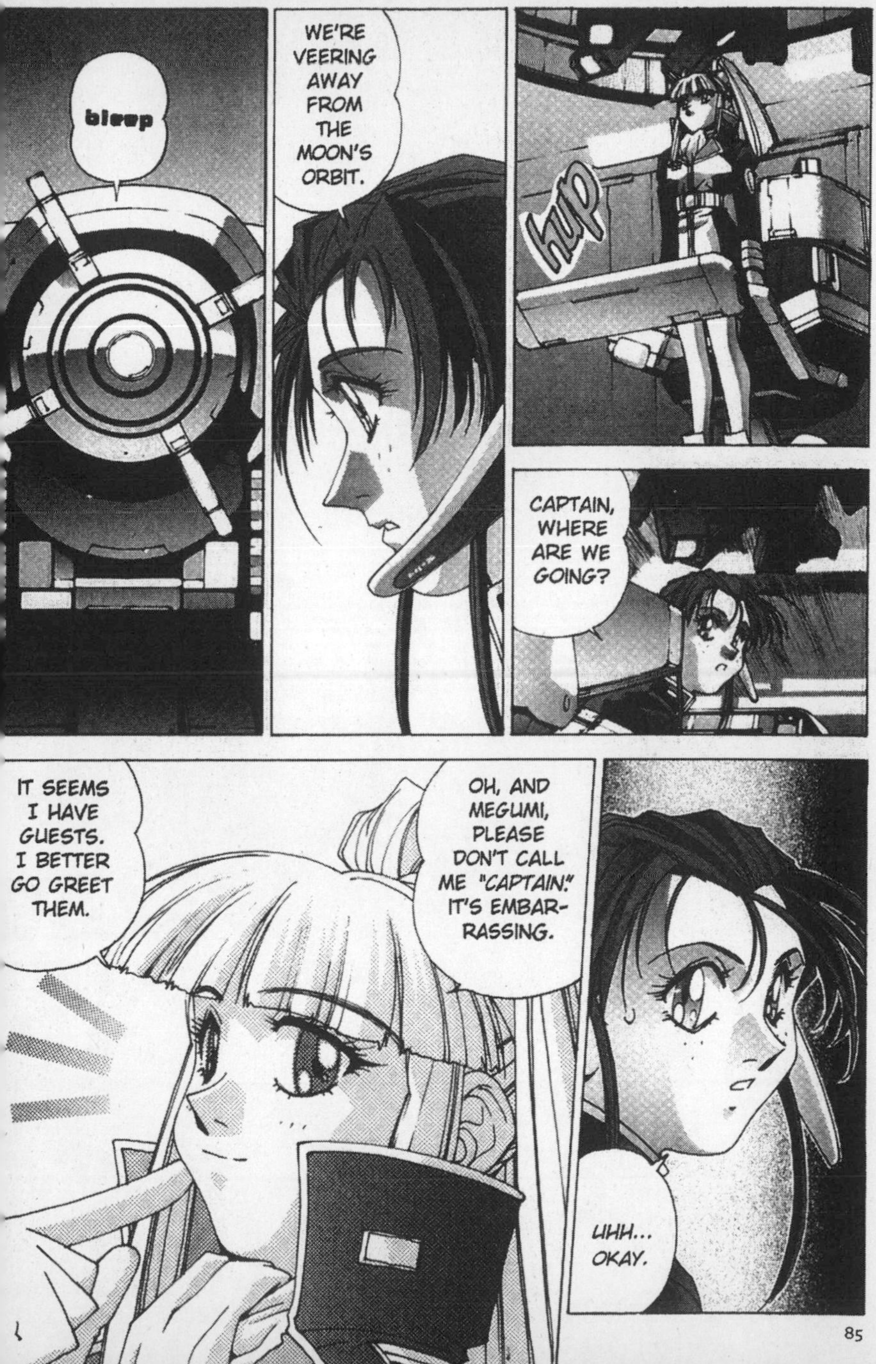

bleep
WE'RE VEERING AWAY FROM THE MOON'S ORBIT.
hup
CAPTAIN, WHERE ARE WE GOING?
IT SEEMS I HAVE GUESTS. I BETTER GO GREET THEM.
OH, AND MEGUMI, PLEASE DON'T CALL ME "CAPTAIN." IT'S EMBARRASSING.
UHH... OKAY.

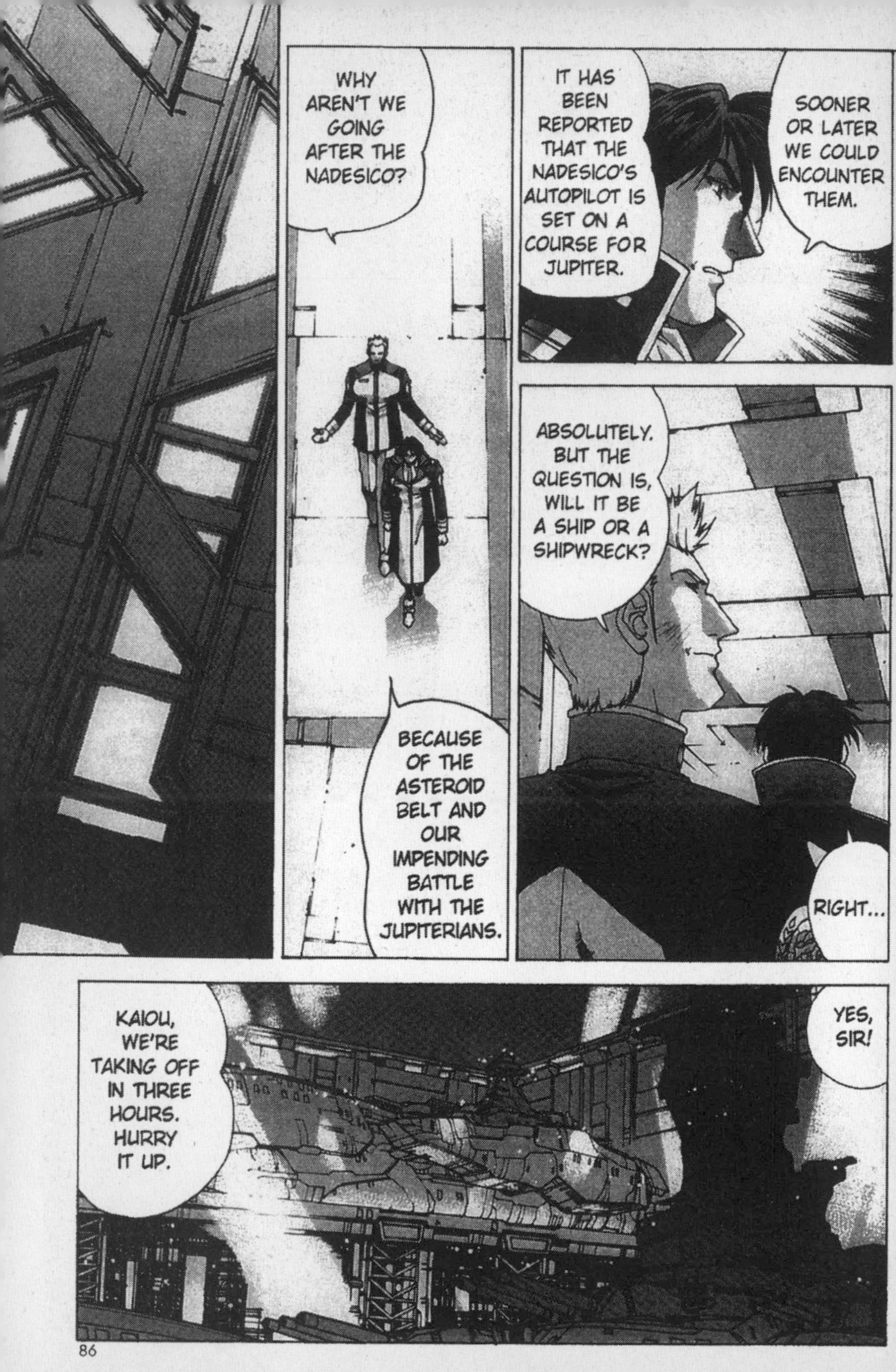
WHY AREN'T WE GOING AFTER THE NADESICO?
BECAUSE OF THE ASTEROID BELT AND OUR IMPENDING BATTLE WITH THE JUPITERIANS.
IT HAS BEEN REPORTED THAT THE NADESICO'S AUTOPILOT IS SET ON A COURSE FOR JUPITER.
SOONER OR LATER WE COULD ENCOUNTER THEM.
ABSOLUTELY. BUT THE QUESTION IS, WILL IT BE A SHIP OR A SHIPWRECK?
RIGHT...
KAIOU, WE'RE TAKING OFF IN THREE HOURS. HURRY IT UP.
YES, SIR!

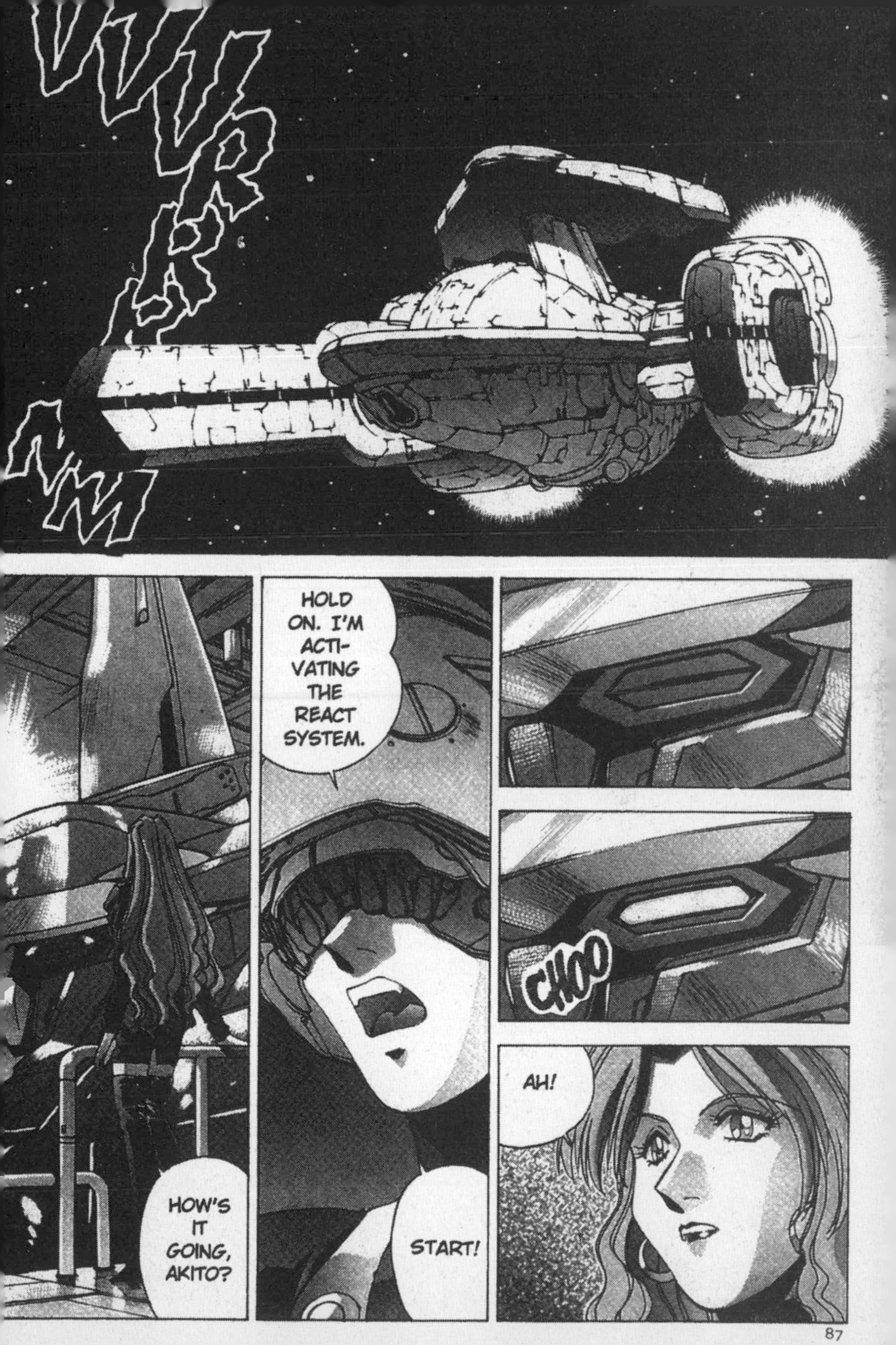
HOW'S IT GOING, AKITO?
HOLD ON. I'M ACTI-VATING THE REACT SYSTEM.
START!
CHOO
AH!

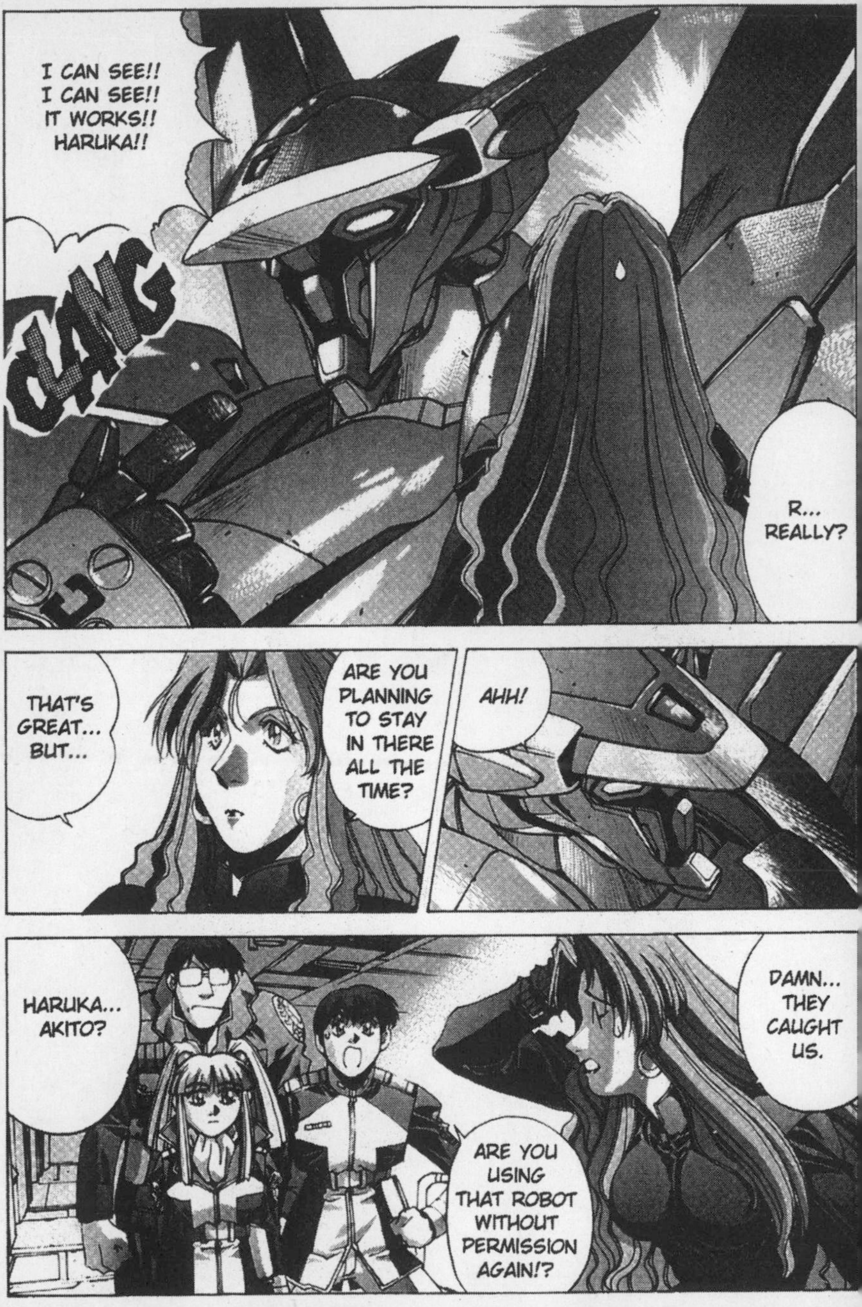
I CAN SEE!! I CAN SEE!! IT WORKS!! HARUKA!!
CLANG
R... REALLY?
THAT'S GREAT... BUT...
ARE YOU PLANNING TO STAY IN THERE ALL THE TIME?
AHH!
HARUKA... AKITO?
DAMN... THEY CAUGHT US.
ARE YOU USING THAT ROBOT WITHOUT PERMISSION AGAIN!?

AND? YOU THINK YOU CAN REGAIN YOUR VISION BY USING THE REACT SYSTEM AGAIN?

作戦艦橋
TACTICAL ROOM

I TRIED IT AND IT WORKED.

OF COURSE I'D NEED TO USE THE EXABYTE CAMERA.

WHAT SHOULD WE DO WITH THESE TWO?

WHAT... WHAT DO YOU MEAN?

...

WE'RE NOT REALLY AN ARMY AND WE'RE NOT A COMPANY.

AND WE CAN'T SEND HARUKA AND AKITO BACK TO EARTH.

SO WHY DID THE NADESICO TAKE OFF?

THAT'S THE REAL QUES-TION.

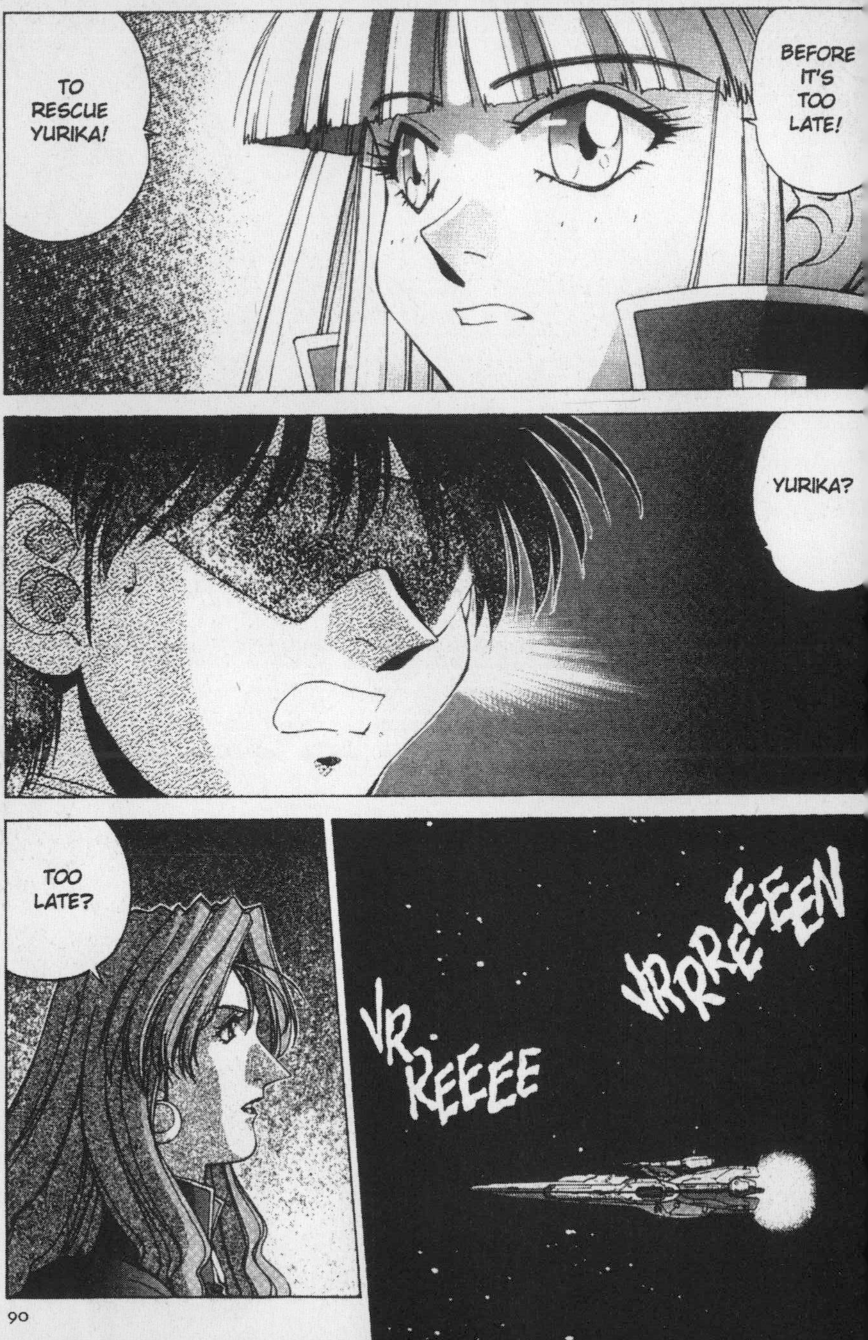
TO RESCUE YURIKA!
BEFORE IT'S TOO LATE!
YURIKA?
TOO LATE?
VR- REEEE
VRREEEN
REEN

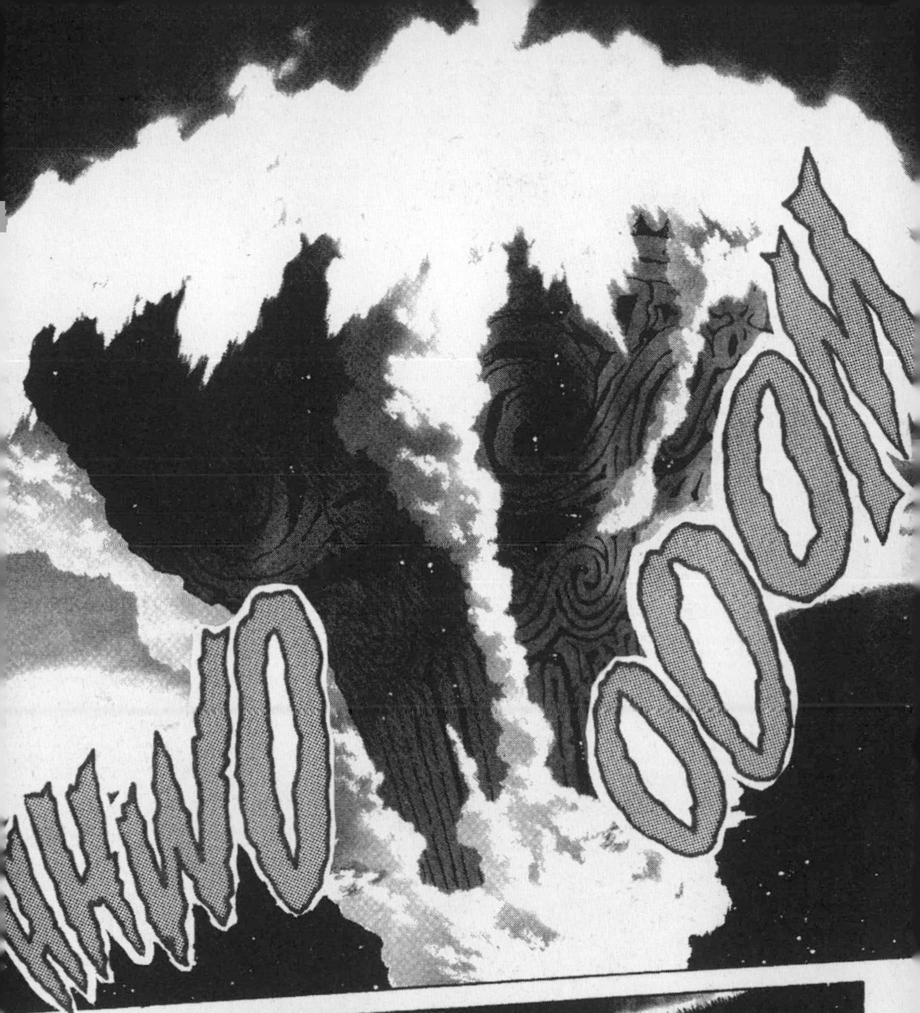
HWOOOOOM
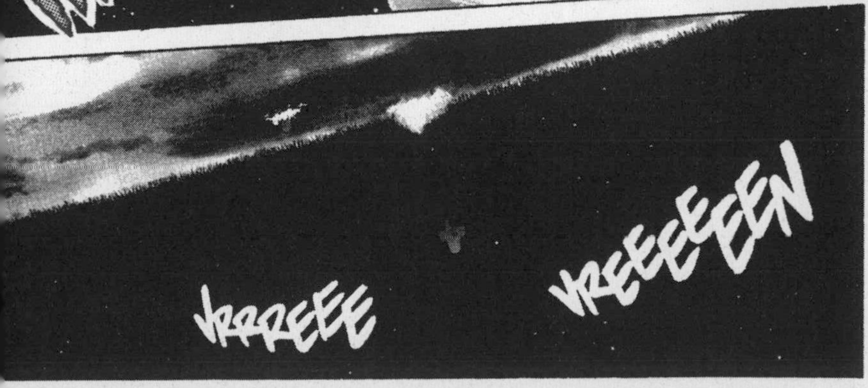
VRRREEE
VREEEEEEN

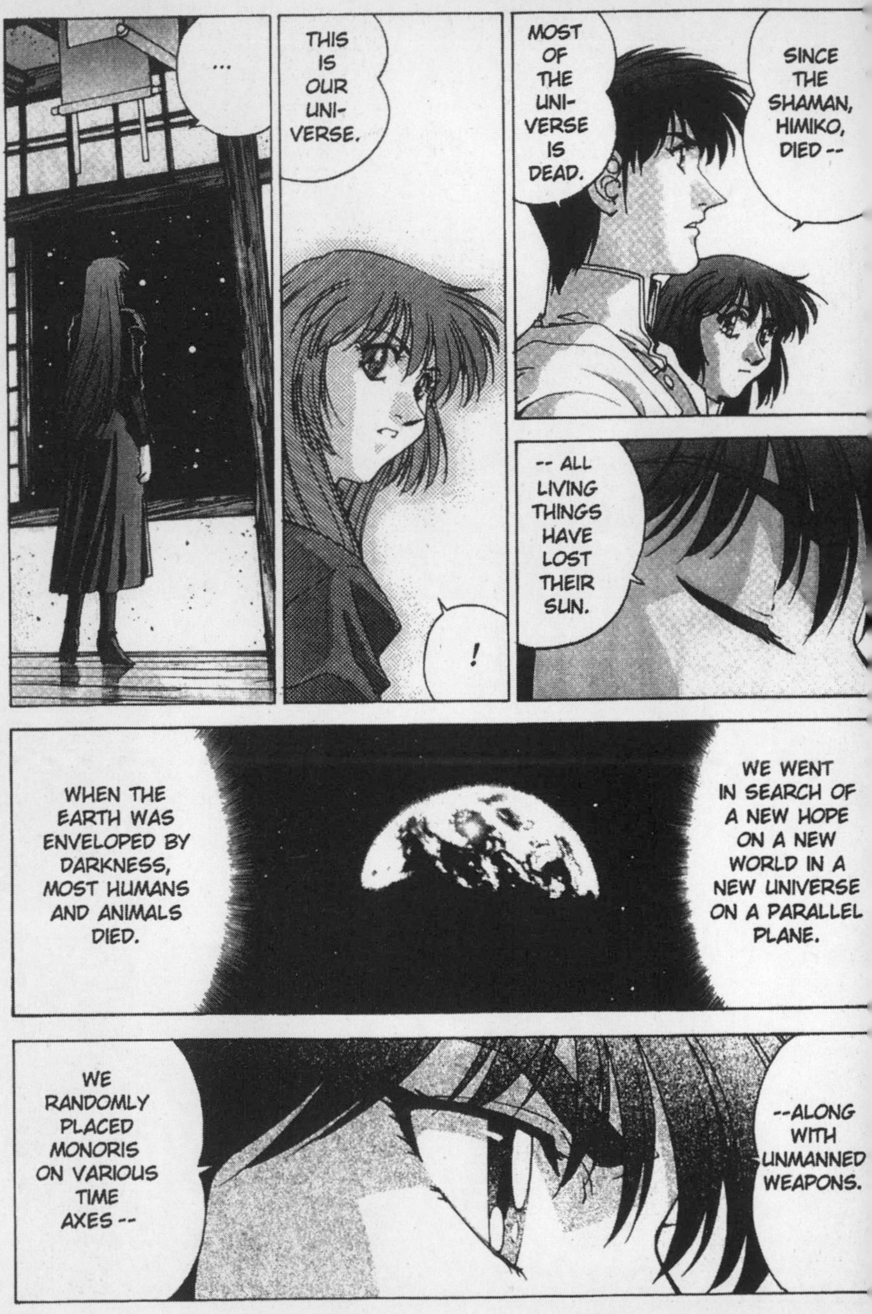
...
THIS IS OUR UNIVERSE.
!
MOST OF THE UNIVERSE IS DEAD.
SINCE THE SHAMAN, HIMIKO, DIED --
-- ALL LIVING THINGS HAVE LOST THEIR SUN.
WHEN THE EARTH WAS ENVELOPED BY DARKNESS, MOST HUMANS AND ANIMALS DIED.
WE WENT IN SEARCH OF A NEW HOPE ON A NEW WORLD IN A NEW UNIVERSE ON A PARALLEL PLANE.
WE RANDOMLY PLACED MONORIS ON VARIOUS TIME AXES --
--ALONG WITH UNMANNED WEAPONS.

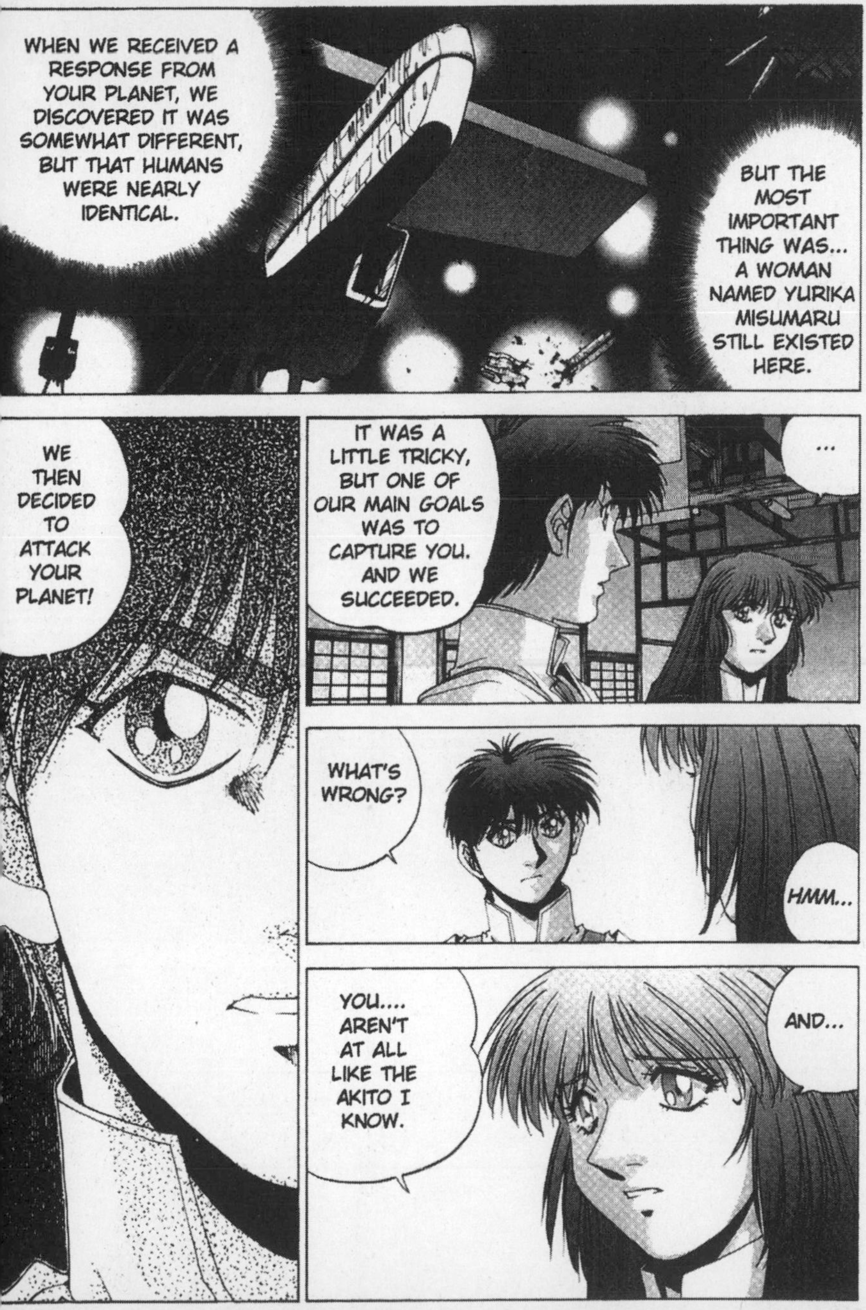
WHEN WE RECEIVED A RESPONSE FROM YOUR PLANET, WE DISCOVERED IT WAS SOMEWHAT DIFFERENT, BUT THAT HUMANS WERE NEARLY IDENTICAL.
BUT THE MOST IMPORTANT THING WAS... A WOMAN NAMED YURIKA MISUMARU STILL EXISTED HERE.
WE THEN DECIDED TO ATTACK YOUR PLANET!
IT WAS A LITTLE TRICKY, BUT ONE OF OUR MAIN GOALS WAS TO CAPTURE YOU. AND WE SUCCEEDED.
...
WHAT'S WRONG?
HMM...
YOU.... AREN'T AT ALL LIKE THE AKITO I KNOW.
AND...

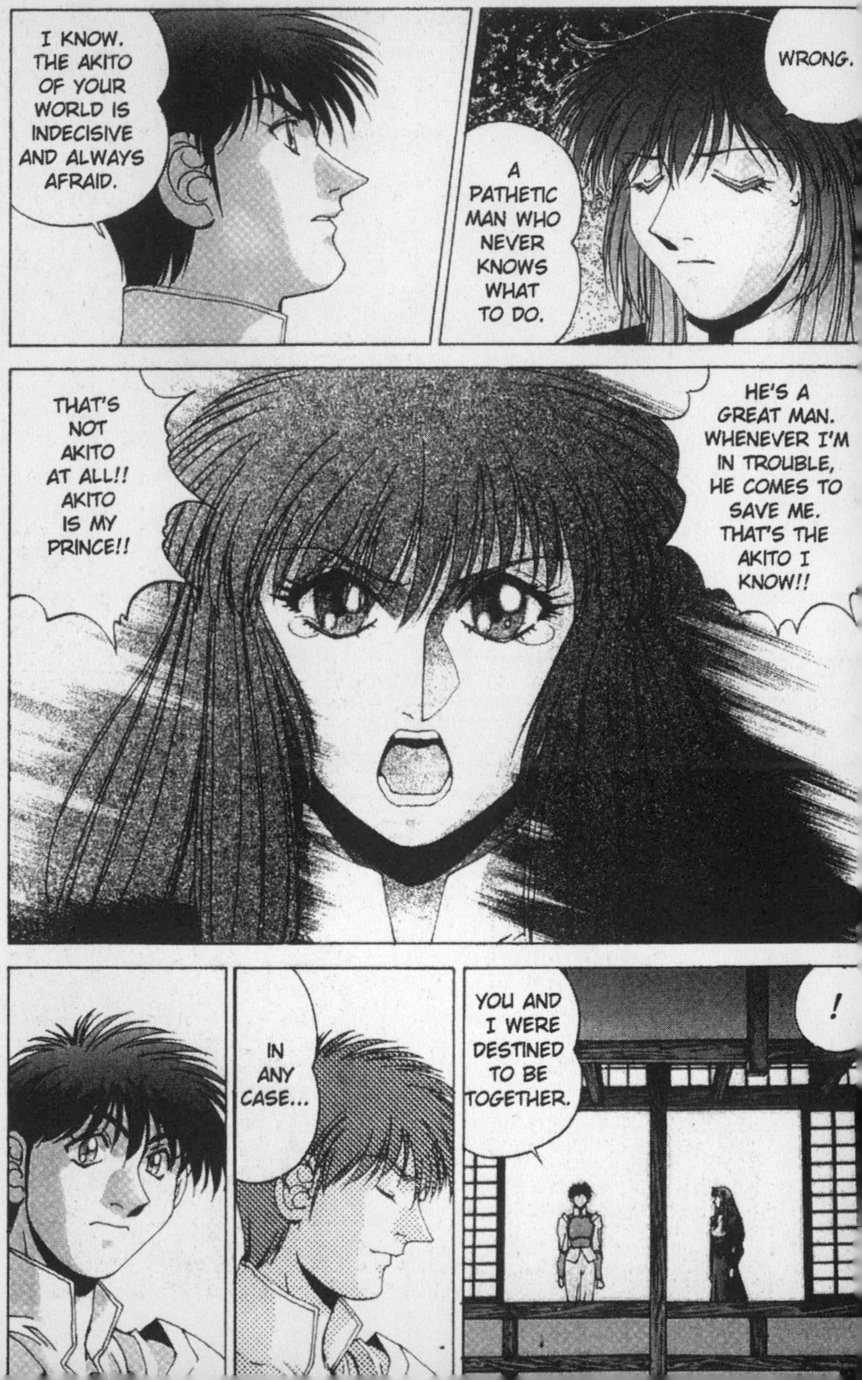
I KNOW. THE AKITO OF YOUR WORLD IS INDECISIVE AND ALWAYS AFRAID.
WRONG.
A PATHETIC MAN WHO NEVER KNOWS WHAT TO DO.
THAT'S NOT AKITO AT ALL!! AKITO IS MY PRINCE!!
HE'S A GREAT MAN. WHENEVER I'M IN TROUBLE, HE COMES TO SAVE ME. THAT'S THE AKITO I KNOW!!
IN ANY CASE...
YOU AND I WERE DESTINED TO BE TOGETHER.
!

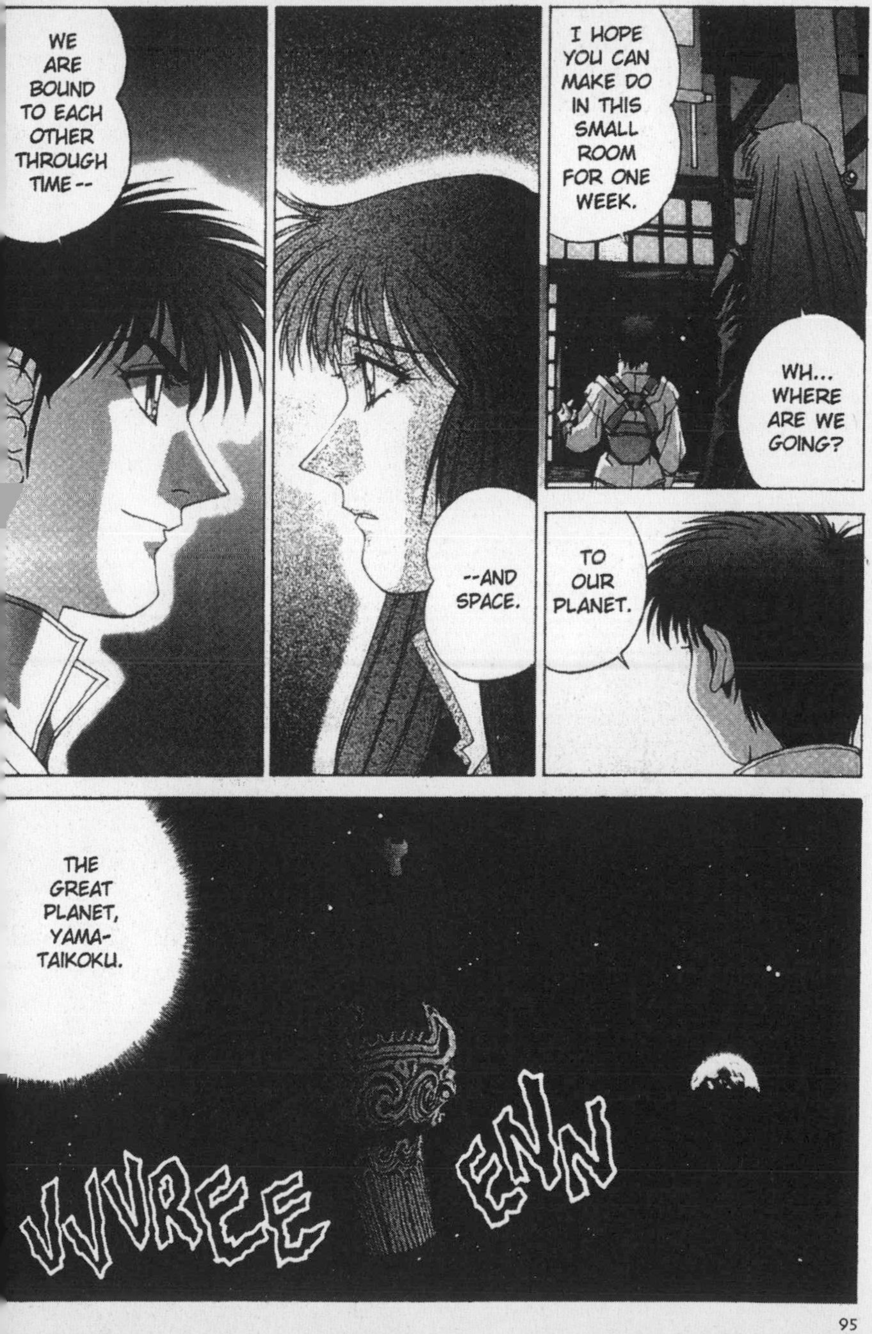
WE ARE BOUND TO EACH OTHER THROUGH TIME --
--AND SPACE.
I HOPE YOU CAN MAKE DO IN THIS SMALL ROOM FOR ONE WEEK.
WH... WHERE ARE WE GOING?
TO OUR PLANET.
THE GREAT PLANET, YAMA-TAIKOKU.
VVREE ENN

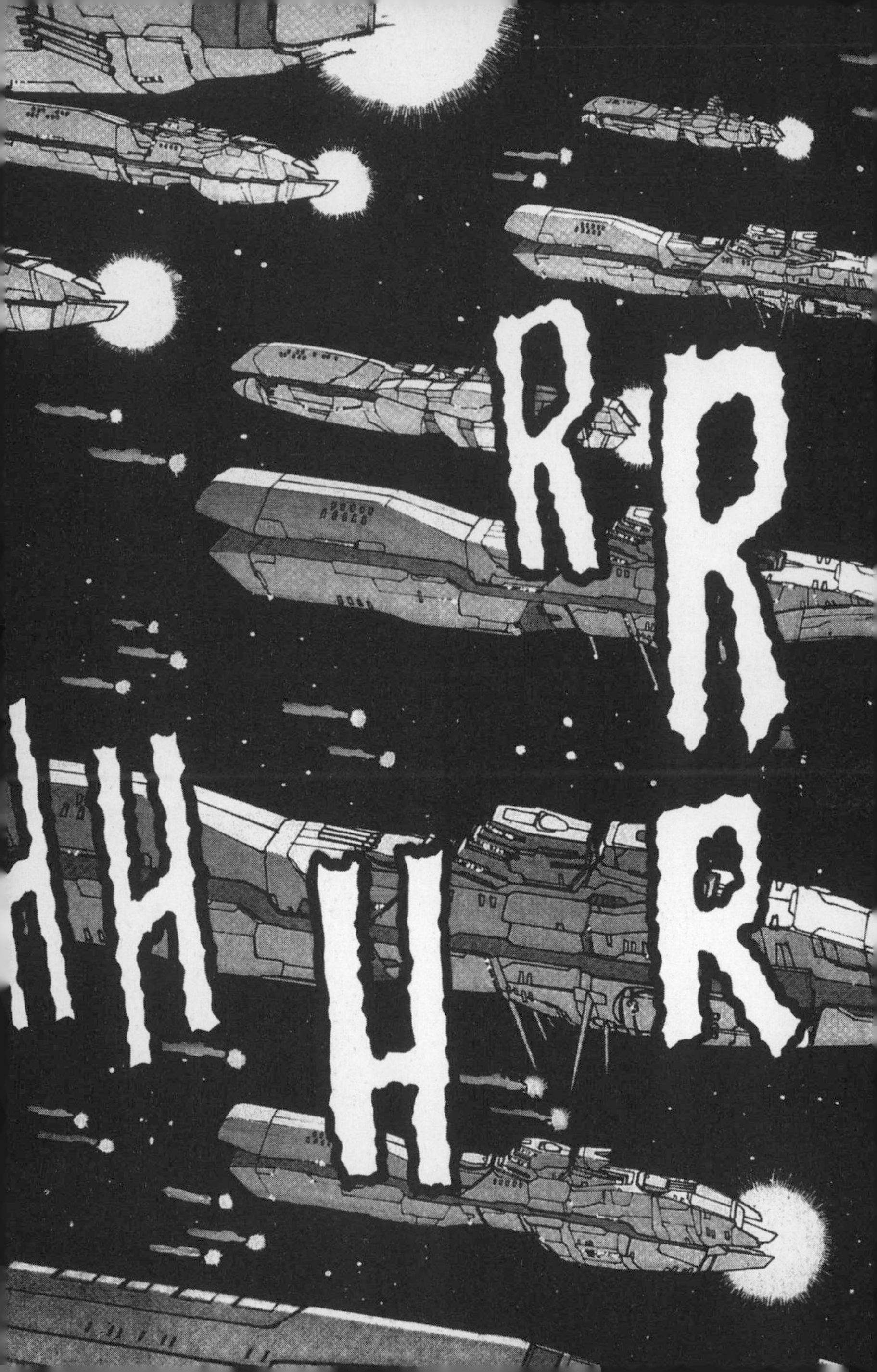
RR
HR

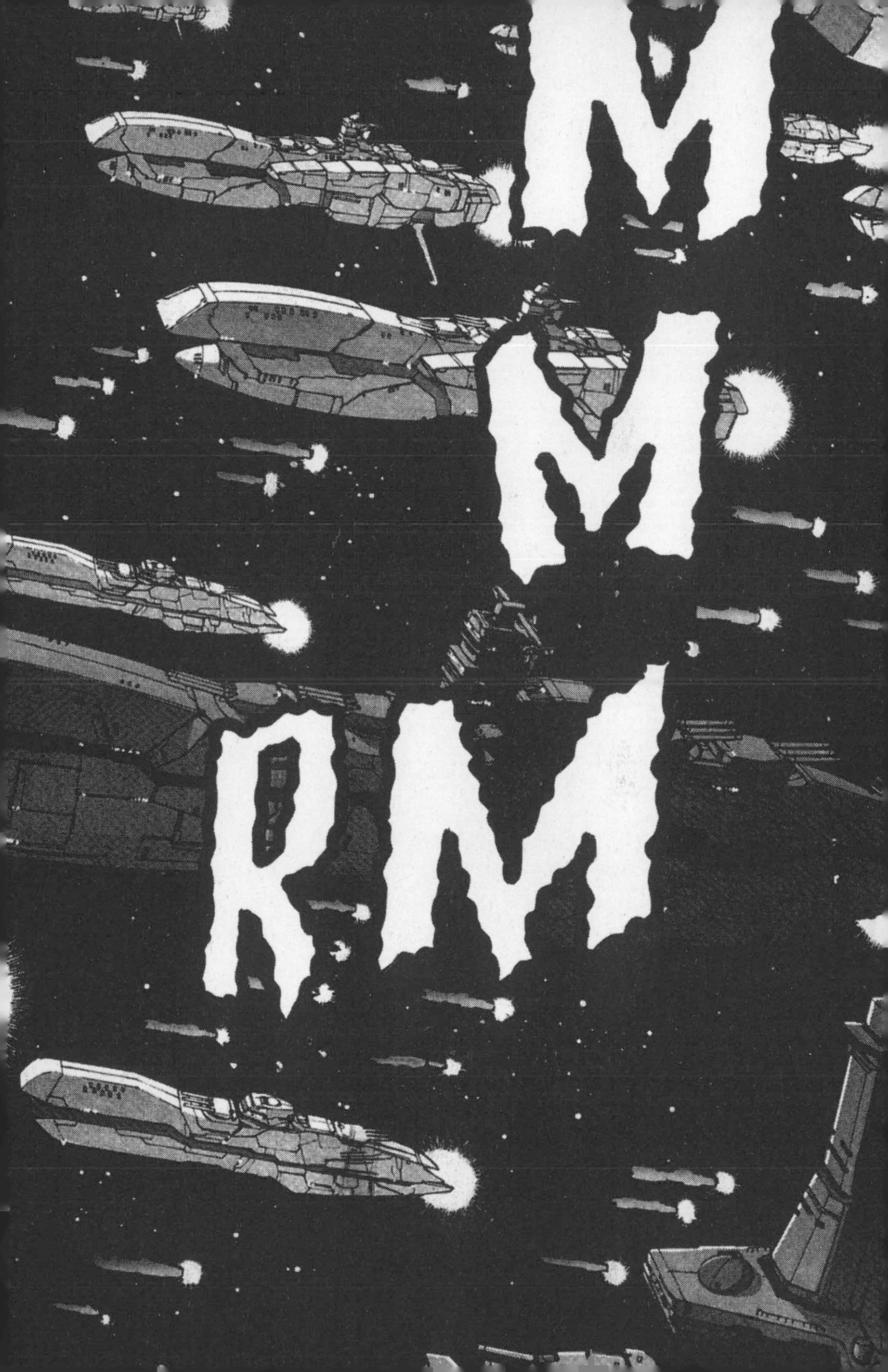

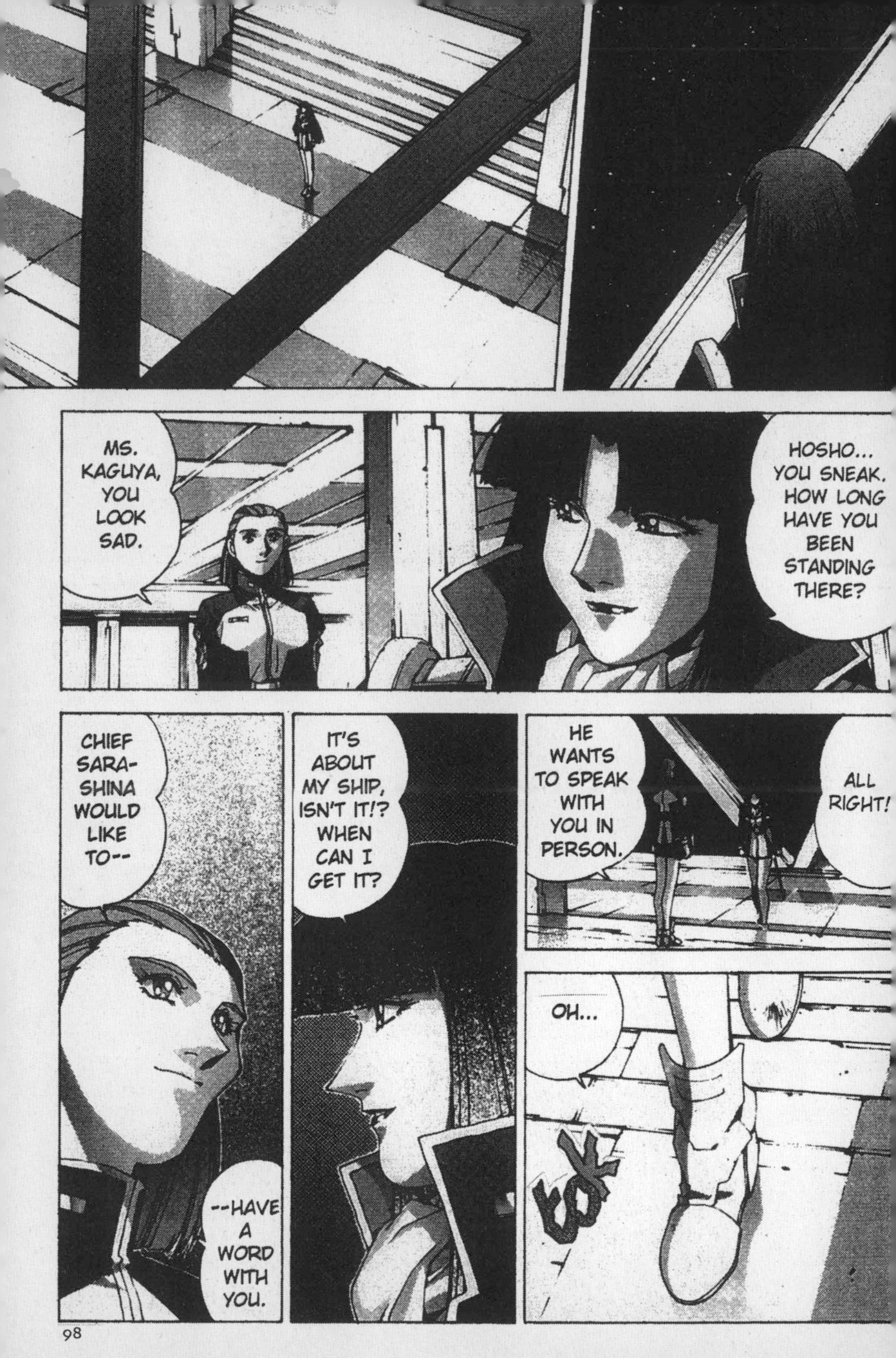
MS. KAGUYA, YOU LOOK SAD.
HOSHO... YOU SNEAK. HOW LONG HAVE YOU BEEN STANDING THERE?
CHIEF SARA-SHINA WOULD LIKE TO--
--HAVE A WORD WITH YOU.
IT'S ABOUT MY SHIP, ISN'T IT!? WHEN CAN I GET IT?
HE WANTS TO SPEAK WITH YOU IN PERSON.
ALL RIGHT!
OH...

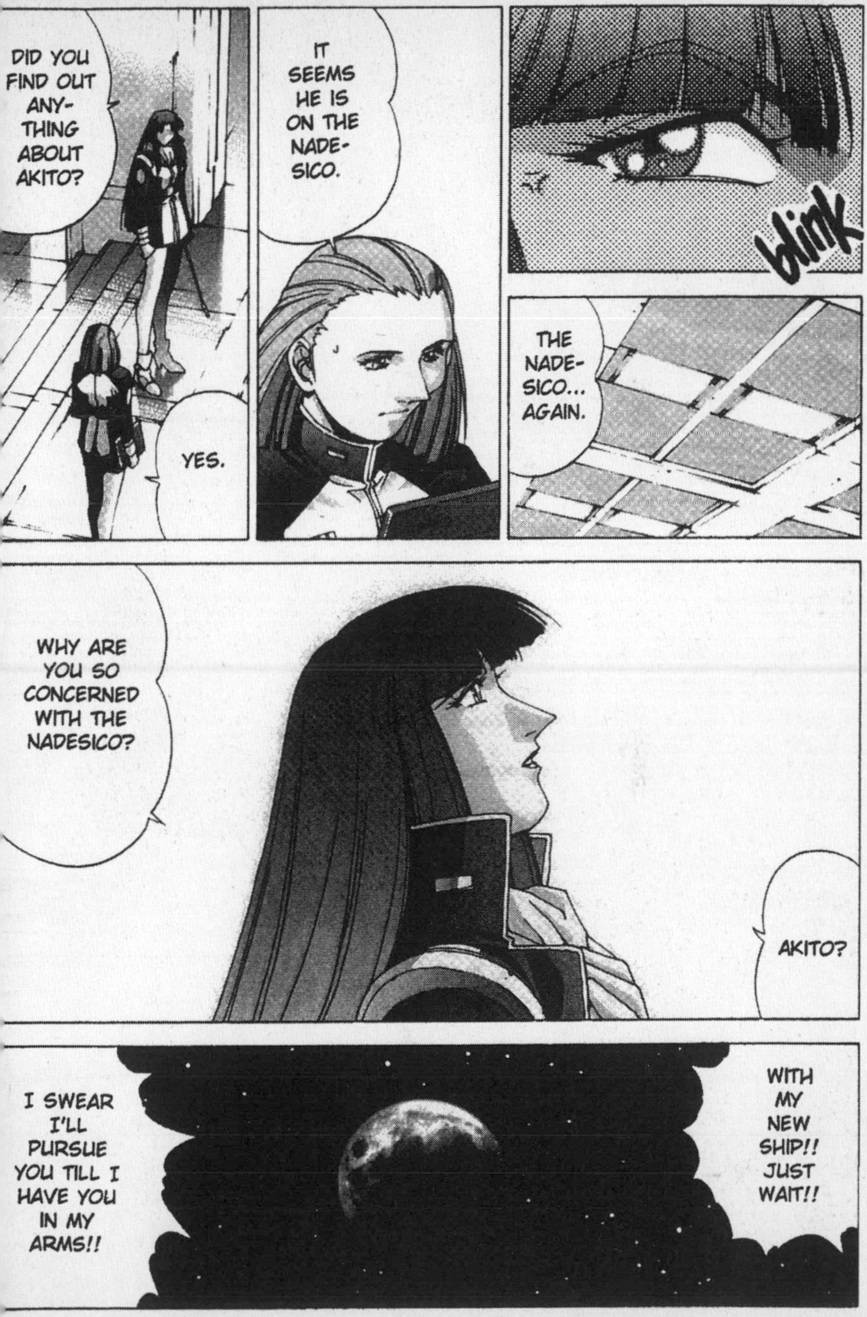
DID YOU FIND OUT ANY-THING ABOUT AKITO?
YES.
IT SEEMS HE IS ON THE NADE-SICO.
blink
THE NADE-SICO... AGAIN.
WHY ARE YOU SO CONCERNED WITH THE NADESICO?
AKITO?
I SWEAR I'LL PURSUE YOU TILL I HAVE YOU IN MY ARMS!!
WITH MY NEW SHIP!! JUST WAIT!!

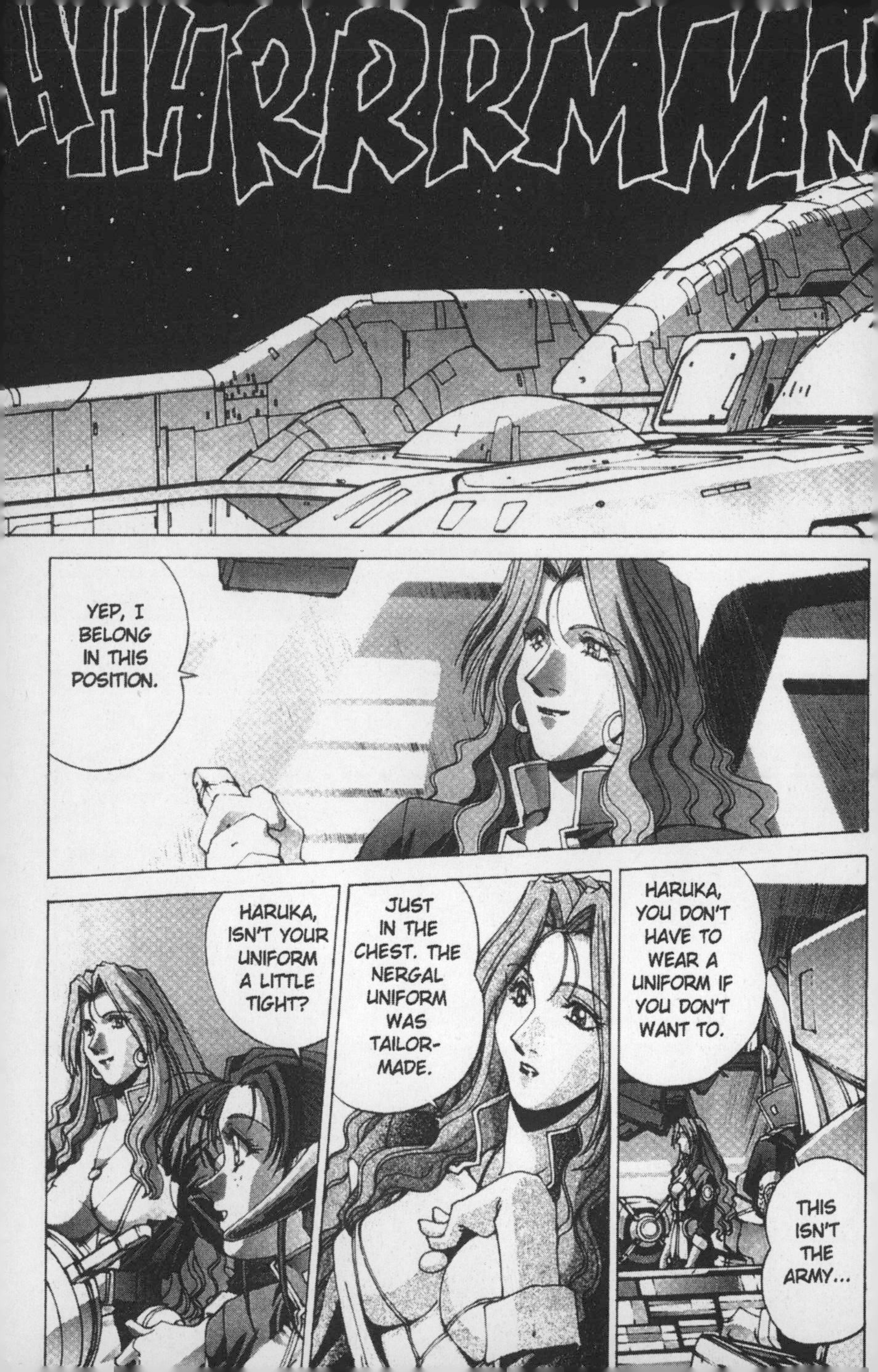
WHRRRMMMM
YEP, I BELONG IN THIS POSITION.
HARUKA, ISN'T YOUR UNIFORM A LITTLE TIGHT?
JUST IN THE CHEST. THE NERGAL UNIFORM WAS TAILOR-MADE.
HARUKA, YOU DON'T HAVE TO WEAR A UNIFORM IF YOU DON'T WANT TO.
THIS ISN'T THE ARMY...

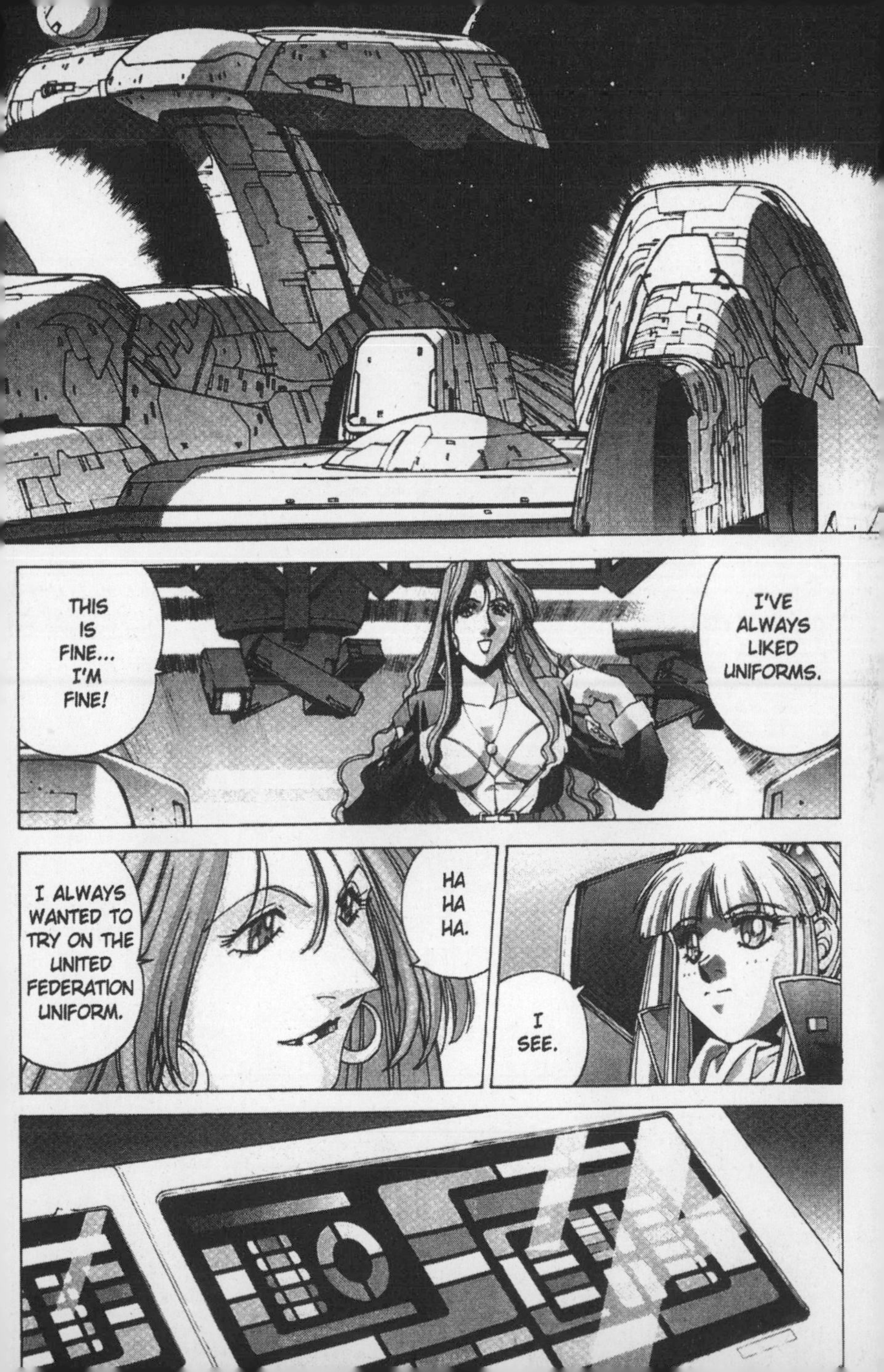
THIS IS FINE... I'M FINE!
I'VE ALWAYS LIKED UNIFORMS.
I ALWAYS WANTED TO TRY ON THE UNITED FEDERATION UNIFORM.
HA HA HA.
I SEE.

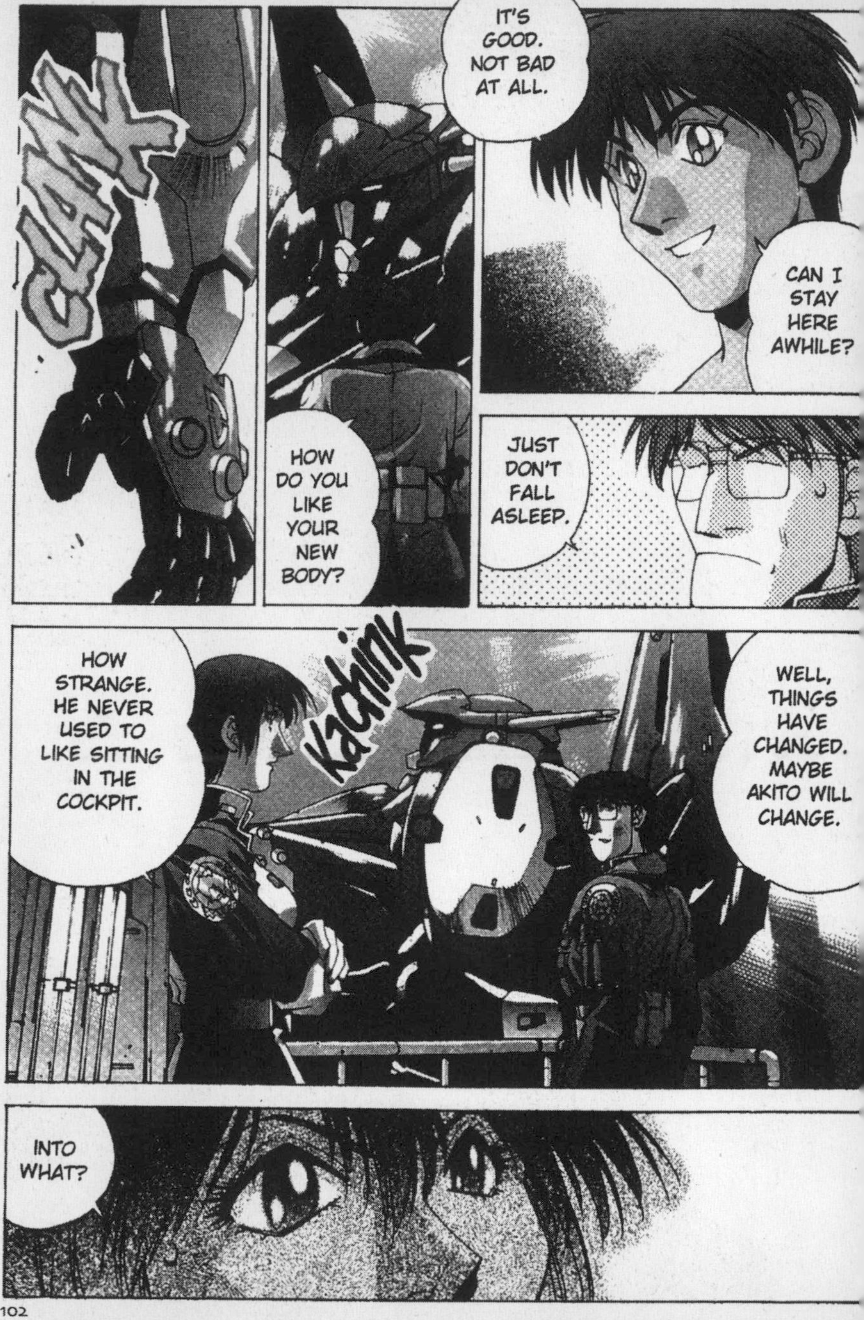
CLANK
HOW DO YOU LIKE YOUR NEW BODY?
IT'S GOOD. NOT BAD AT ALL.
CAN I STAY HERE AWHILE?
JUST DON'T FALL ASLEEP.
HOW STRANGE. HE NEVER USED TO LIKE SITTING IN THE COCKPIT.
KACHINK
WELL, THINGS HAVE CHANGED. MAYBE AKITO WILL CHANGE.
INTO WHAT?

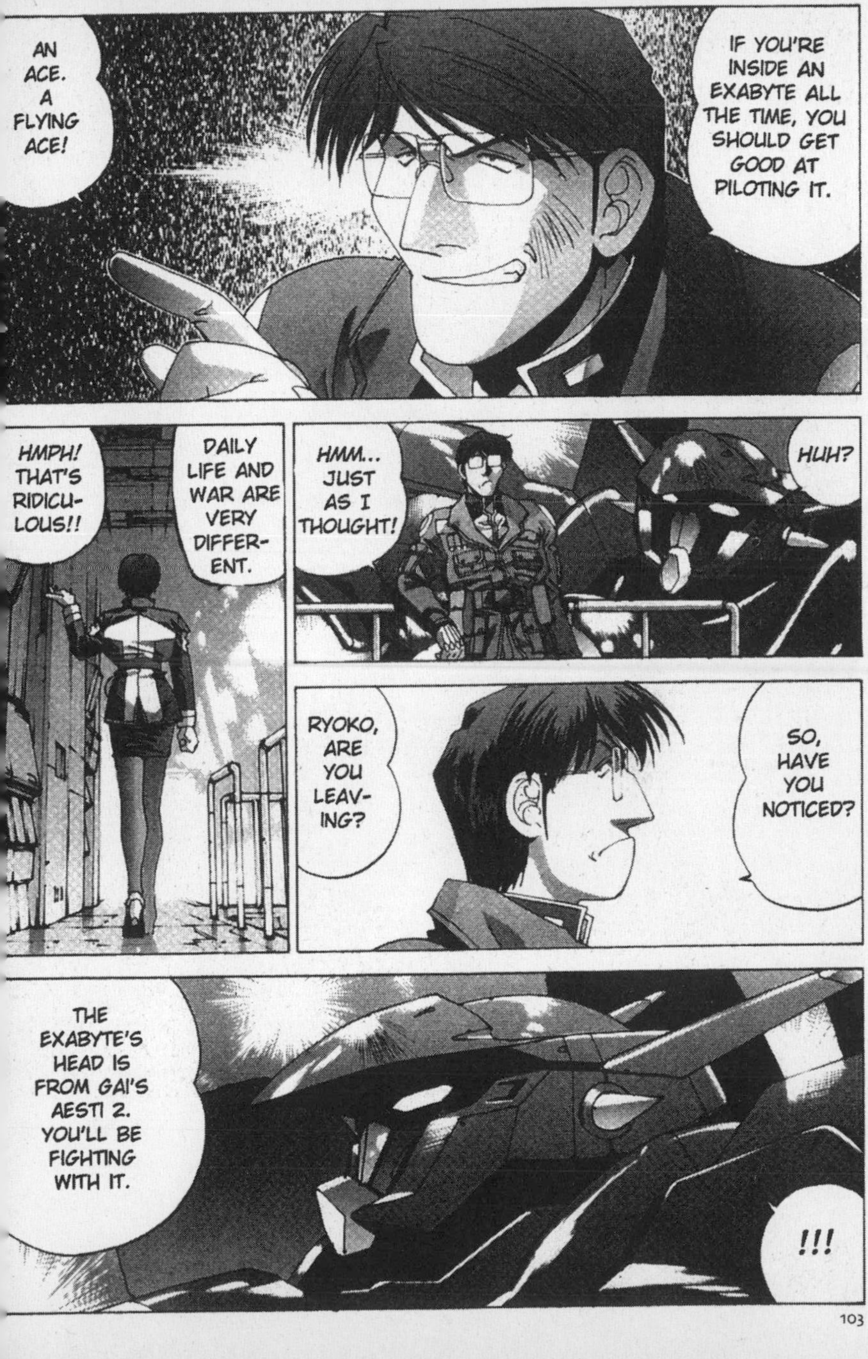
AN ACE. A FLYING ACE!
IF YOU'RE INSIDE AN EXABYTE ALL THE TIME, YOU SHOULD GET GOOD AT PILOTING IT.
HMPH! THAT'S RIDICU-LOUS!!
DAILY LIFE AND WAR ARE VERY DIFFER-ENT.
HMM... JUST AS I THOUGHT!
HUH?
RYOKO, ARE YOU LEAV-ING?
SO, HAVE YOU NOTICED?
THE EXABYTE'S HEAD IS FROM GAI'S AESTI 2. YOU'LL BE FIGHTING WITH IT.
!!!

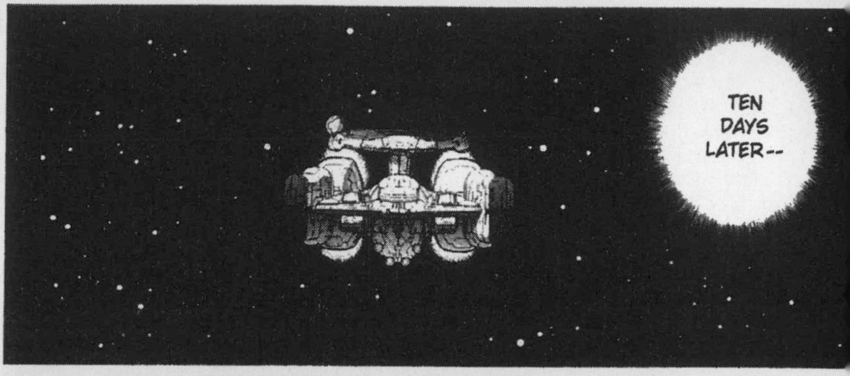
TEN DAYS LATER--

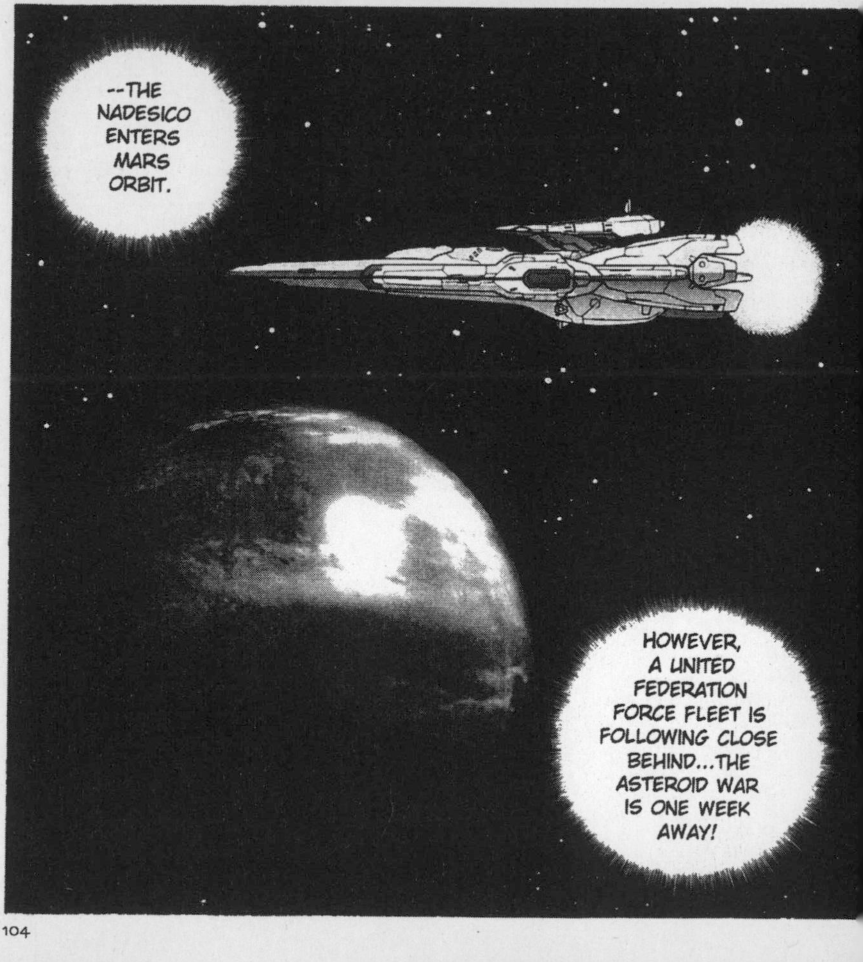
--THE NADESICO ENTERS MARS ORBIT.
HOWEVER, A UNITED FEDERATION FORCE FLEET IS FOLLOWING CLOSE BEHIND...THE ASTEROID WAR IS ONE WEEK AWAY!

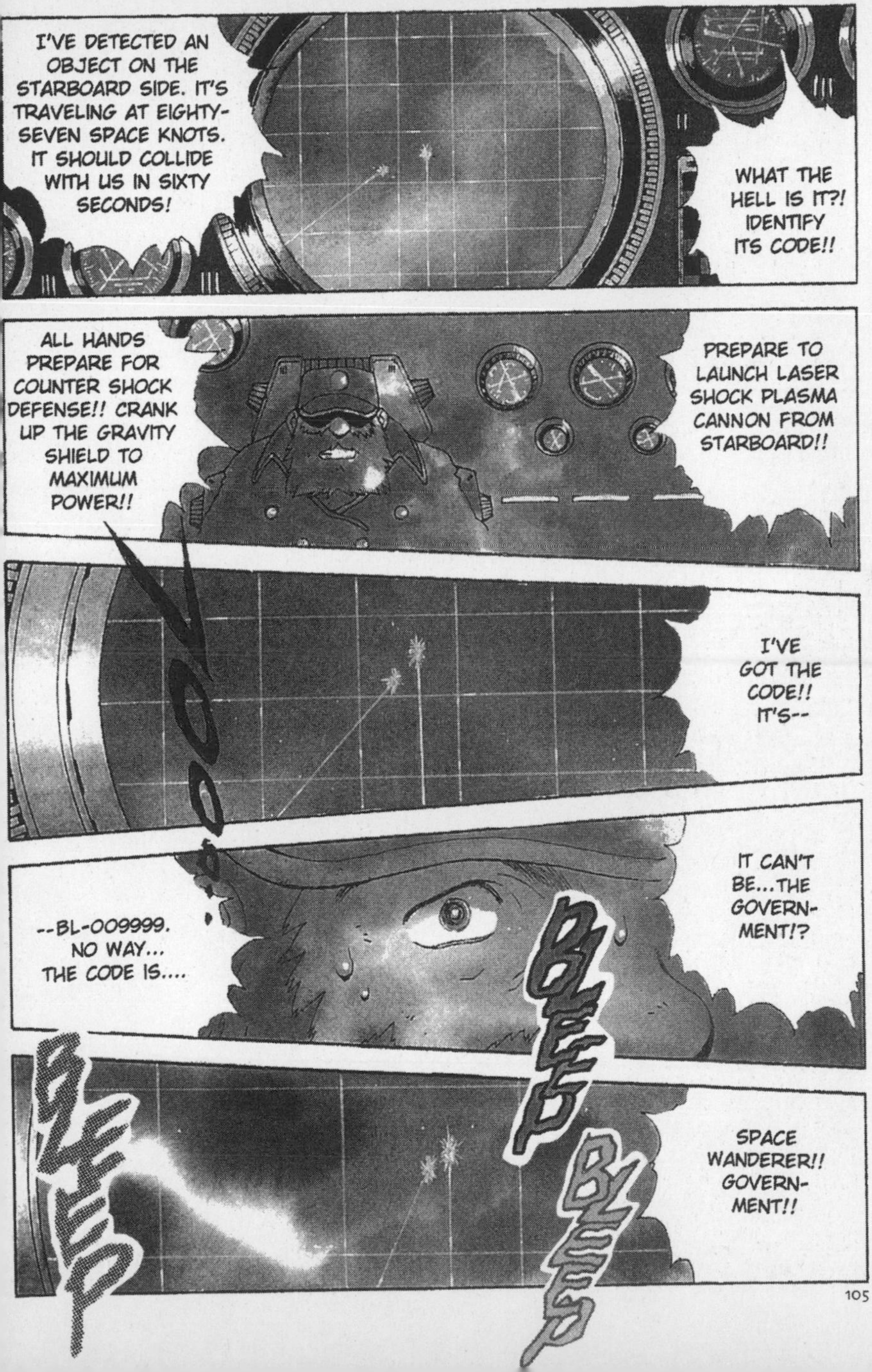
I'VE DETECTED AN OBJECT ON THE STARBOARD SIDE. IT'S TRAVELING AT EIGHTY-SEVEN SPACE KNOTS. IT SHOULD COLLIDE WITH US IN SIXTY SECONDS!
WHAT THE HELL IS IT?! IDENTIFY ITS CODE!!
ALL HANDS PREPARE FOR COUNTER SHOCK DEFENSE!! CRANK UP THE GRAVITY SHIELD TO MAXIMUM POWER!!
PREPARE TO LAUNCH LASER SHOCK PLASMA CANNON FROM STARBOARD!!
I'VE GOT THE CODE!! IT'S--
--BL-009999. NO WAY... THE CODE IS....
IT CAN'T BE...THE GOVERN-MENT!?
BLEEP
SPACE WANDERER!! GOVERN-MENT!!
BLEEP
BLEEP

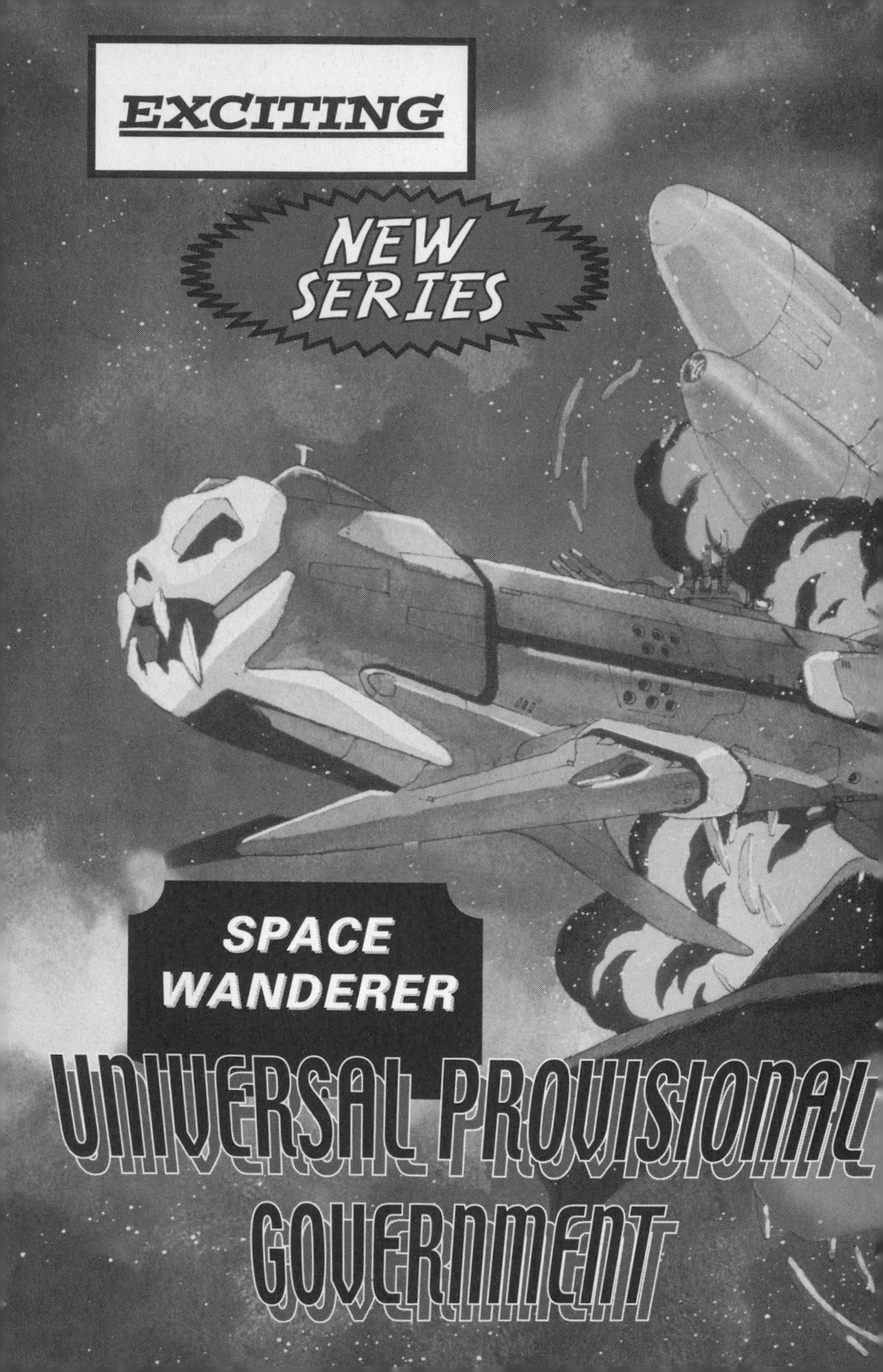
EXCITING
NEW SERIES
SPACE WANDERER
UNIVERSAL PROVISIONAL GOVERNMENT

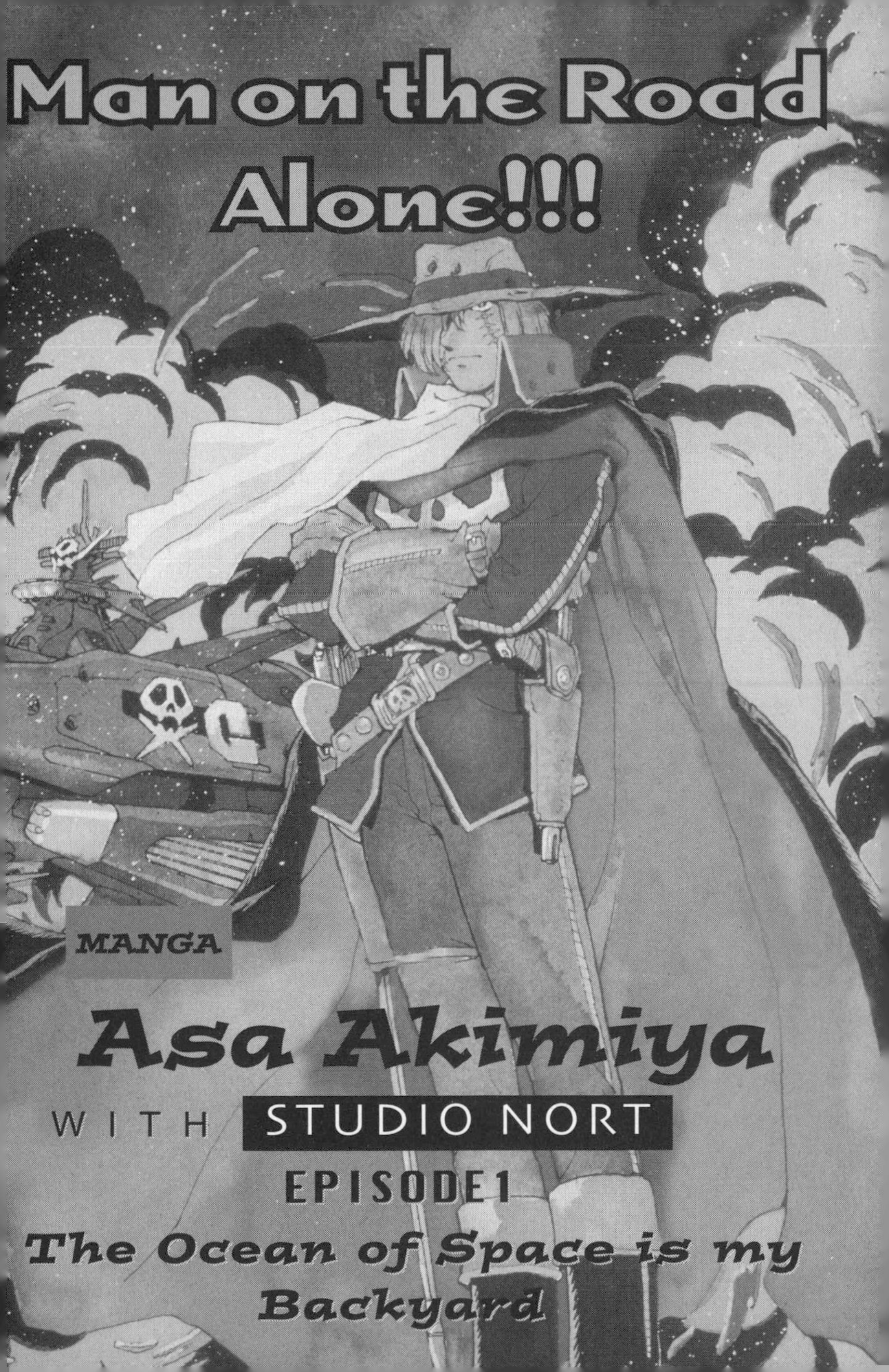

Man on the Road Alone!!!

MANGA

Asa Akimiya

WITH STUDIO NORT

EPISODE 1

The Ocean of Space is my Backyard

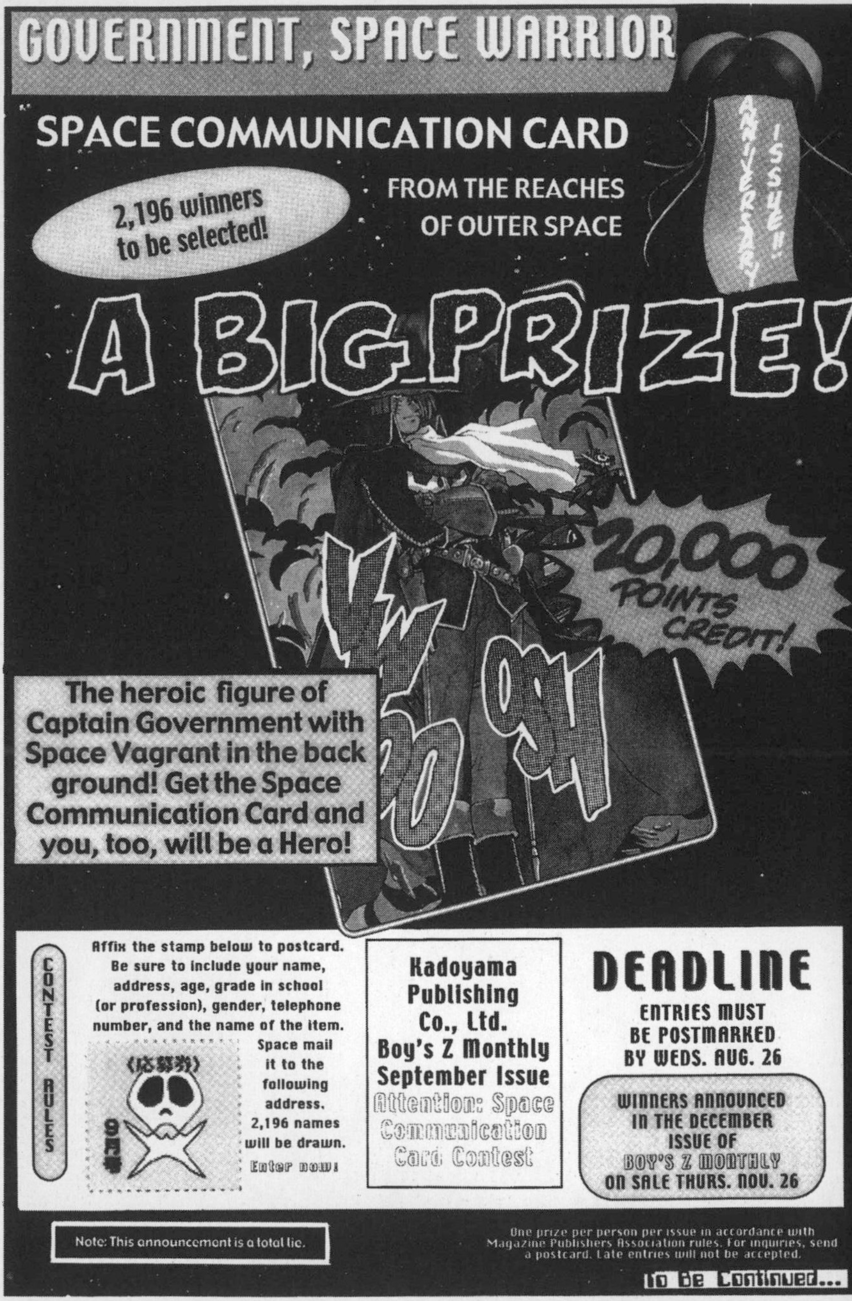

GOVERNMENT, SPACE WARRIOR
ANNIVERSARY ISSUE!!
SPACE COMMUNICATION CARD
2,196 winners to be selected!
FROM THE REACHES OF OUTER SPACE
A BIG PRIZE!
20,000 POINTS CREDIT!
The heroic figure of Captain Government with Space Vagrant in the back ground! Get the Space Communication Card and you, too, will be a Hero!
CONTEST RULES
Affix the stamp below to postcard. Be sure to include your name, address, age, grade in school (or profession), gender, telephone number, and the name of the item.
《応募券》
9月号
Space mail it to the following address. 2,196 names will be drawn.
Enter now!
Kadoyama Publishing Co., Ltd. Boy's Z Monthly September Issue
Attention: Space Communication Card Contest
DEADLINE
ENTRIES MUST BE POSTMARKED BY WEDS. AUG. 26
WINNERS ANNOUNCED IN THE DECEMBER ISSUE OF BOY'S Z MONTHLY ON SALE THURS. NOV. 26
Note: This announcement is a total lie.
One prize per person per issue in accordance with Magazine Publishers Association rules. For inquiries, send a postcard. Late entries will not be accepted.
To Be Continued...

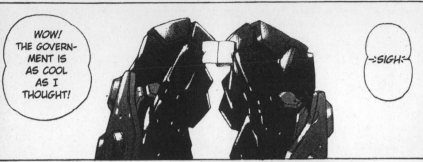

WOW! THE GOVERNMENT IS AS COOL AS I THOUGHT!

⸝SIGH⸝

A ROBOT READING A MANGA AND ENJOYING IT...

WHOA!

AKITO'S BEEN IN THERE ALL THE TIME LATELY.

DOESN'T REACT SYNCHRONICITY RATE VARY WITH THE INDIVIDUAL?

I GUESS SO.

AS FAR AS THE SYNC RATE GOES, AKITO'S A PRETTY PERFECT MATCH.

THEN I HOPE HE PRACTICES THE BATTLE SIMULATION.

I WONDER IF HE PLANS TO COOK IN THE EXABYTE ARMOR.

WHOA!

WHAT AN IDIOT.

109

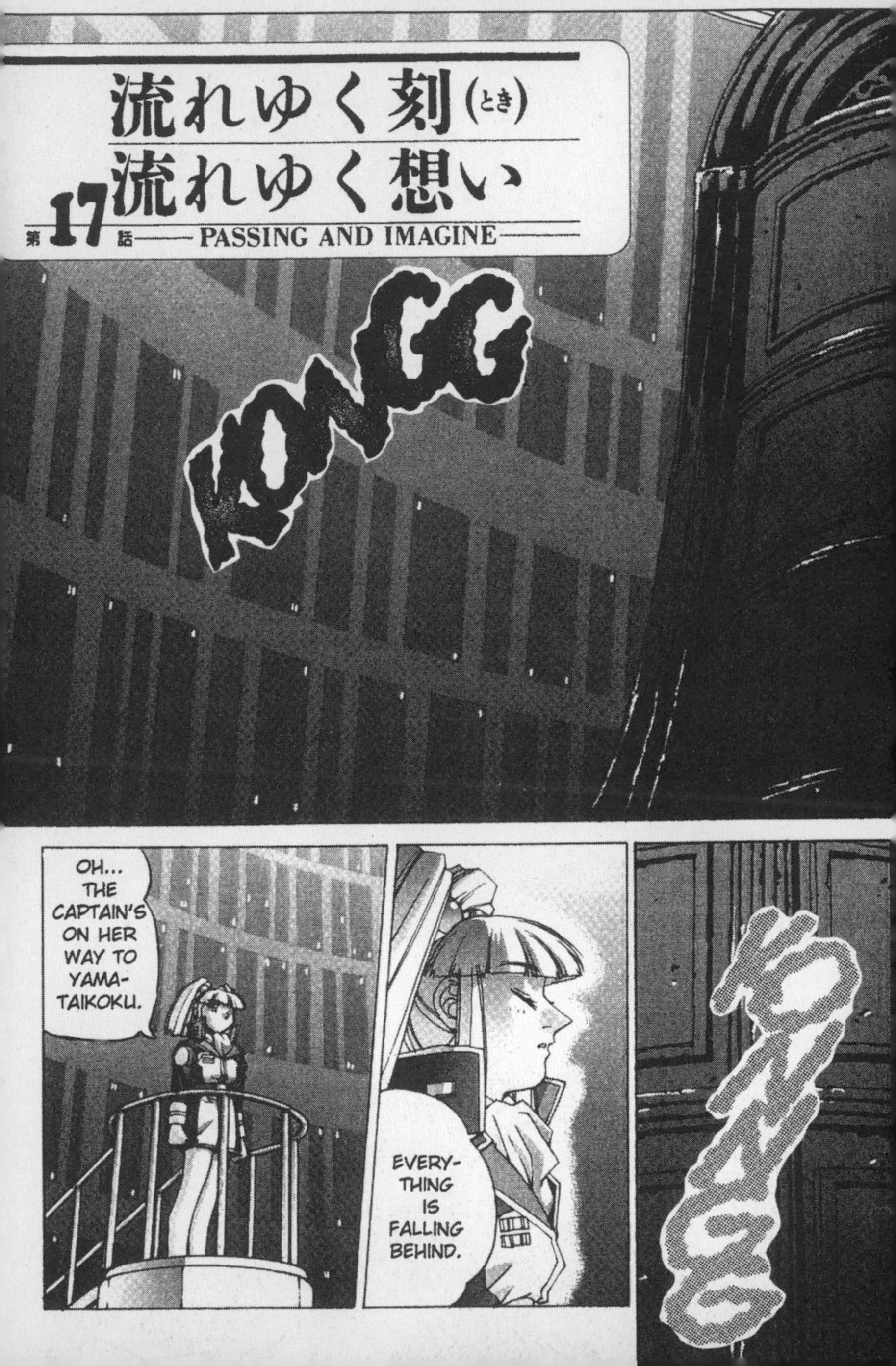
流れゆく刻(とき)
流れゆく想い
第17話—PASSING AND IMAGINE—
KONGG
OH... THE CAPTAIN'S ON HER WAY TO YAMA-TAIKOKU.
EVERY-THING IS FALLING BEHIND.

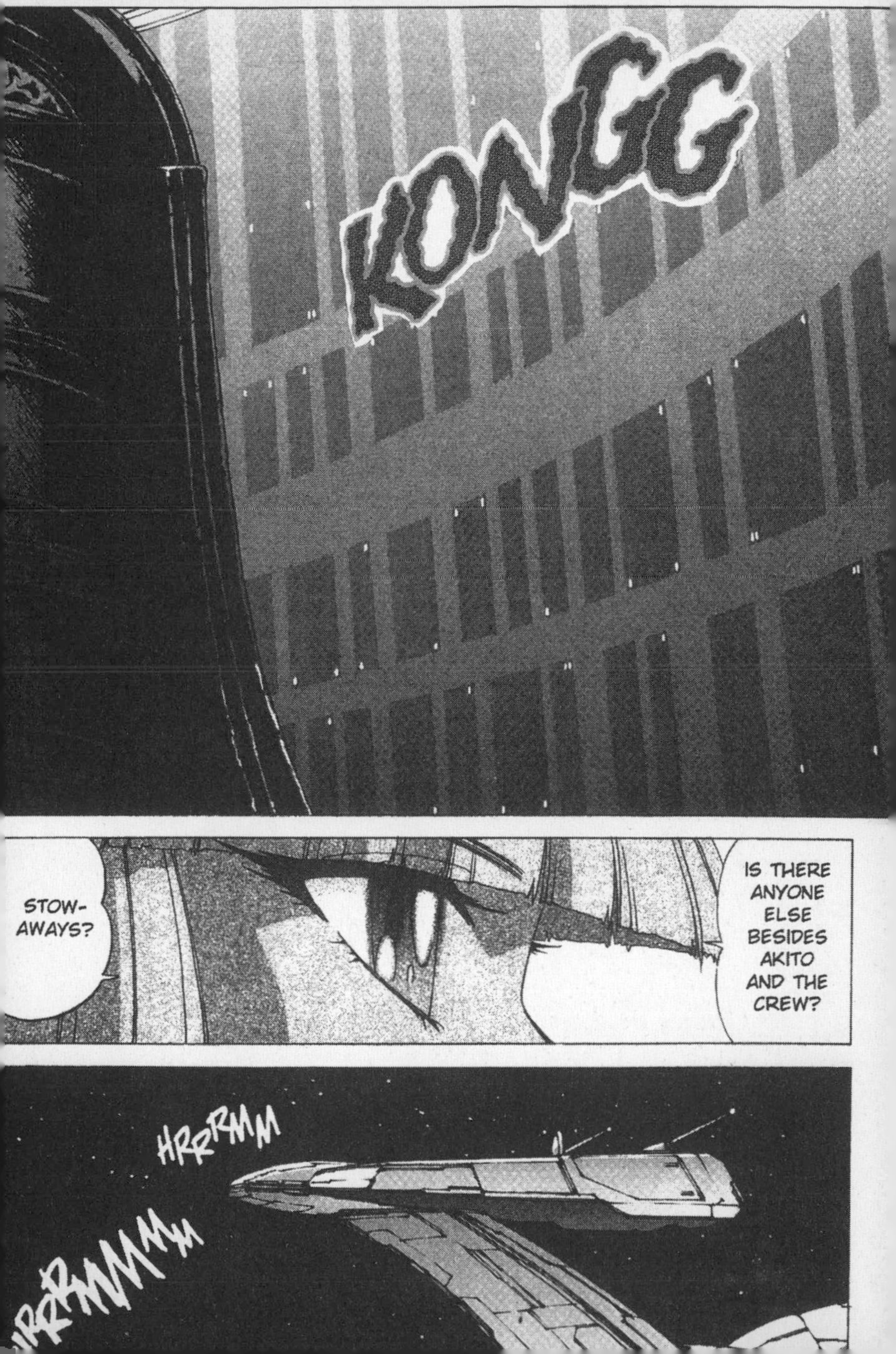
KONGG
STOW-AWAYS?
IS THERE ANYONE ELSE BESIDES AKITO AND THE CREW?
HRRRMM
HRRRMMMM

...AND THAT'S ALL I'VE GOT TO SAY.

MUNE-TAKE!?

LIKE I SAID... GET THE NADESICO TO THE NERGAL DOCK ON MARS!

MOVE IT!!

WE CAN'T DO THAT WITHOUT AUTHORIZATION!

FIRST OF ALL, THE CAPTAIN...

YOU CAN'T DO IT ON YOUR OWN... THAT'S WHY WE'RE STUCK HERE.

YOU'RE A LITTLE SLOW, AREN'T YA?

BUT WHY MARS? THERE'S NOTHING THERE.

THAT'S BECAUSE WE HUMANS MADE IT THAT WAY. MARS MEANS EVERYTHING TO ME.

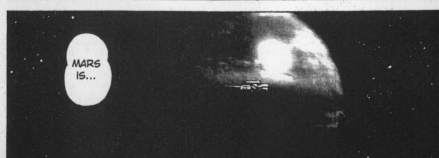

MARS IS...

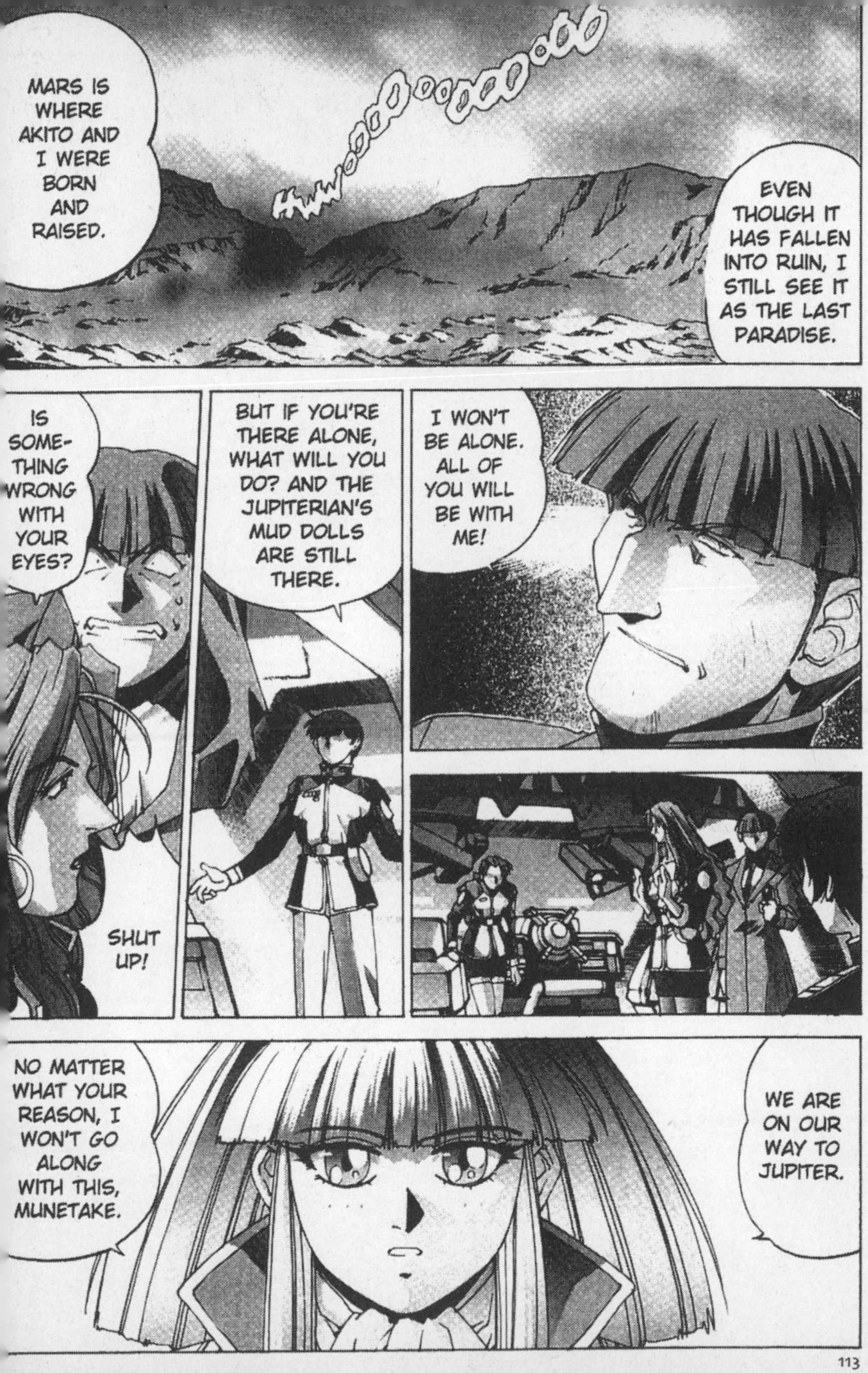
MARS IS WHERE AKITO AND I WERE BORN AND RAISED.
EVEN THOUGH IT HAS FALLEN INTO RUIN, I STILL SEE IT AS THE LAST PARADISE.
IS SOMETHING WRONG WITH YOUR EYES?
SHUT UP!
BUT IF YOU'RE THERE ALONE, WHAT WILL YOU DO? AND THE JUPITERIAN'S MUD DOLLS ARE STILL THERE.
I WON'T BE ALONE. ALL OF YOU WILL BE WITH ME!
NO MATTER WHAT YOUR REASON, I WON'T GO ALONG WITH THIS, MUNETAKE.
WE ARE ON OUR WAY TO JUPITER.

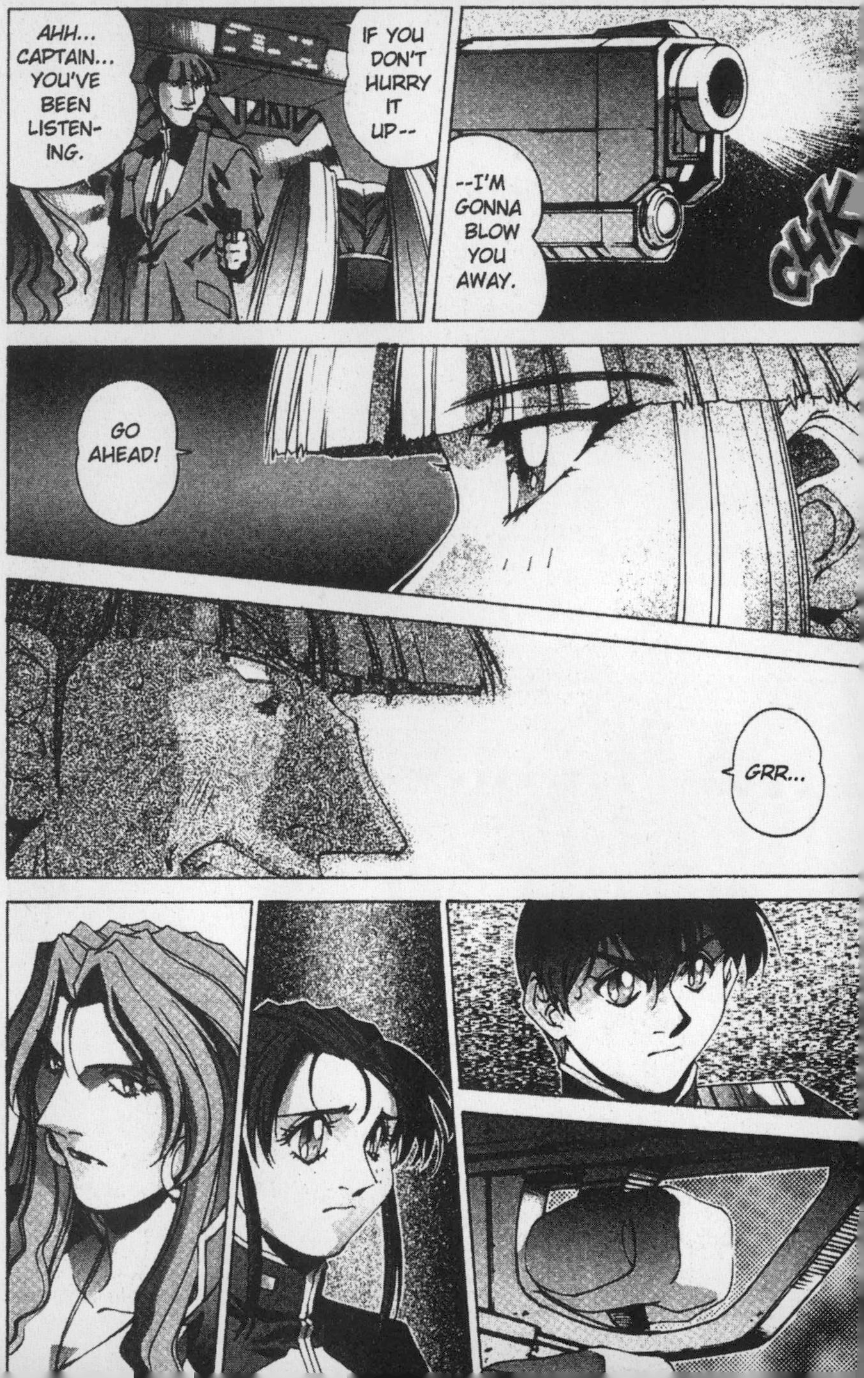
AHH... CAPTAIN... YOU'VE BEEN LISTEN-ING.
IF YOU DON'T HURRY IT UP--
--I'M GONNA BLOW YOU AWAY.
CLIK
GO AHEAD!
GRR...

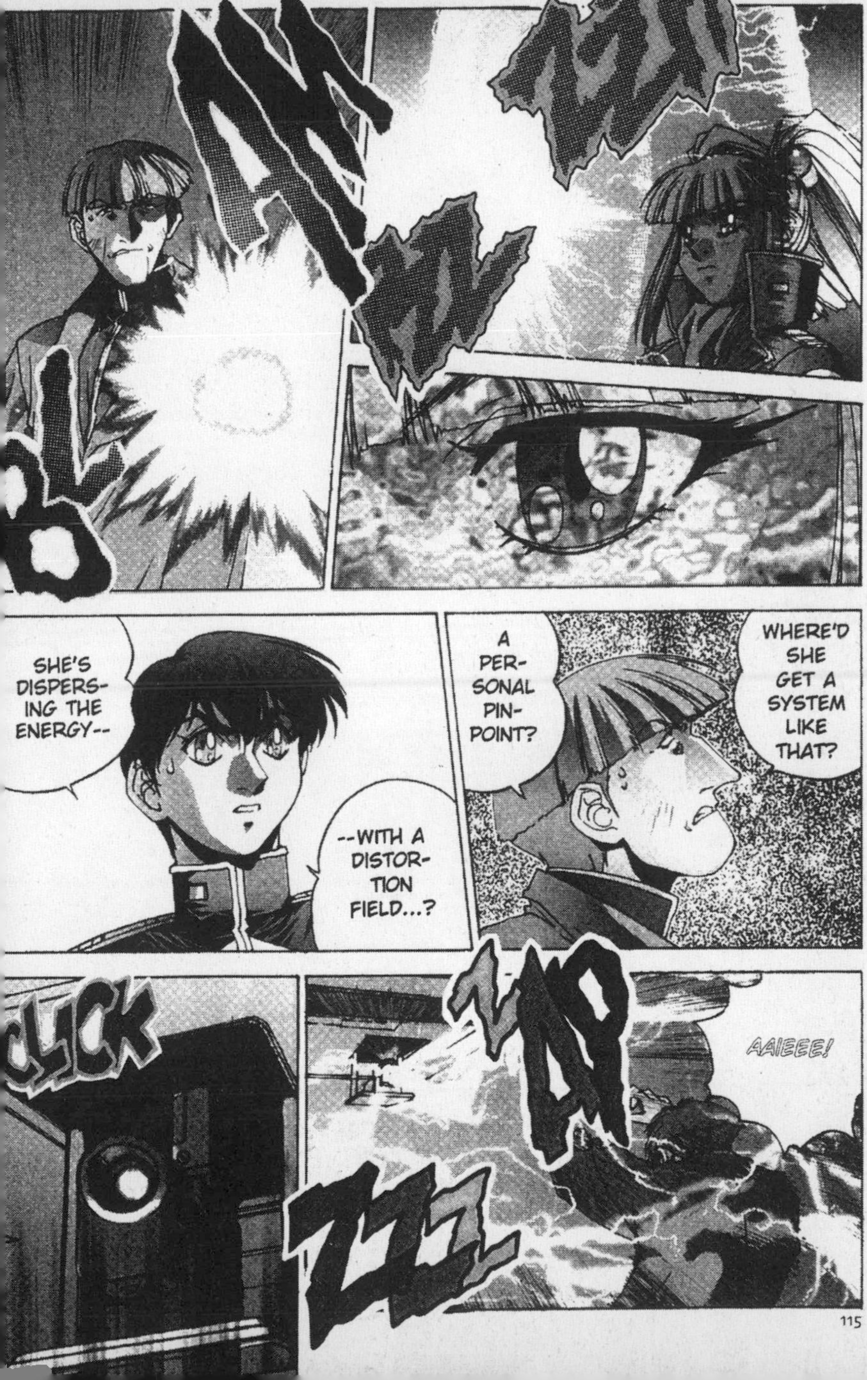

SHE'S DISPERSING THE ENERGY--
--WITH A DISTORTION FIELD...?
A PERSONAL PINPOINT?
WHERE'D SHE GET A SYSTEM LIKE THAT?
CLICK
AAIEEE!

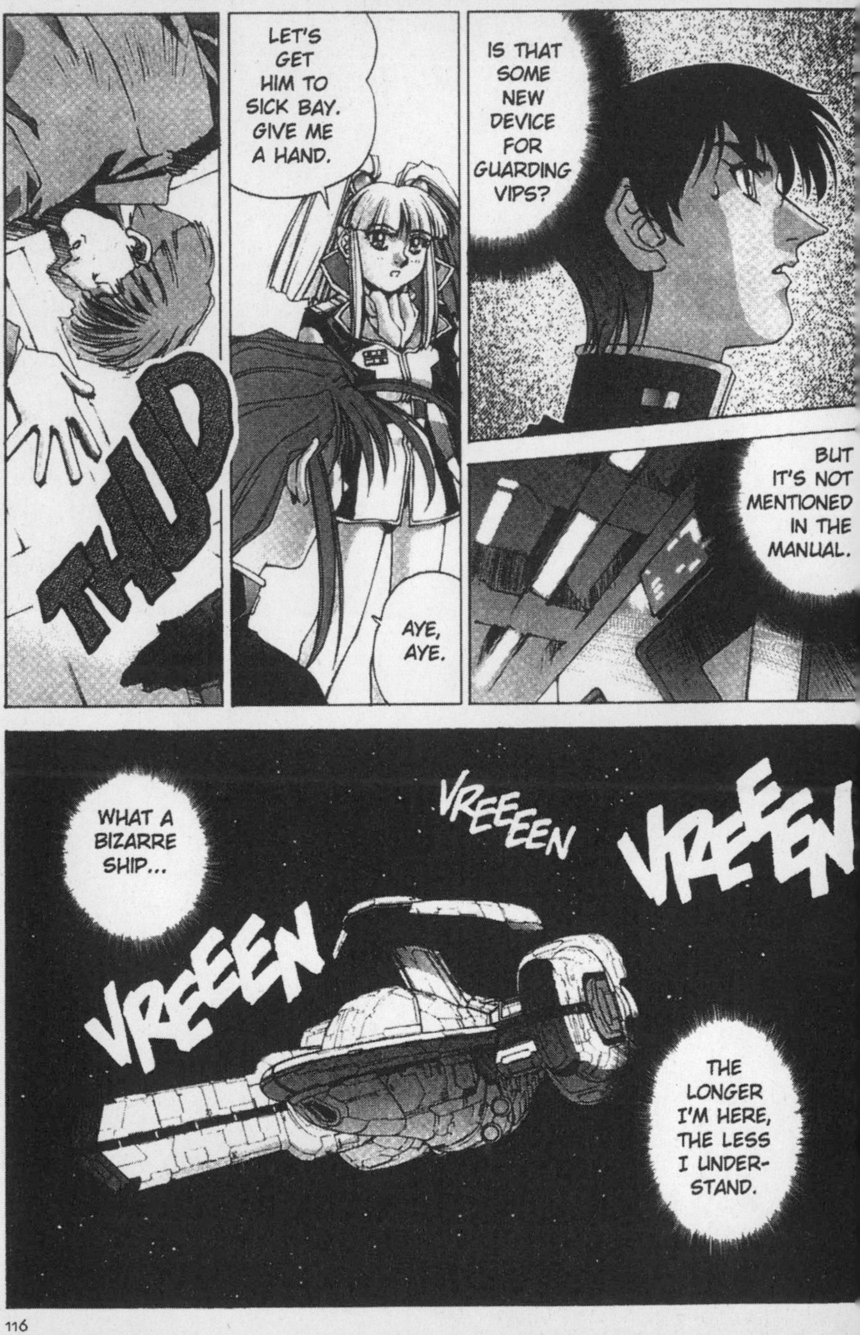
THUD
LET'S GET HIM TO SICK BAY. GIVE ME A HAND.
AYE, AYE.
IS THAT SOME NEW DEVICE FOR GUARDING VIPS?
BUT IT'S NOT MENTIONED IN THE MANUAL.
WHAT A BIZARRE SHIP...
VREEEEN
VREEEN
VREEEN
THE LONGER I'M HERE, THE LESS I UNDER-STAND.

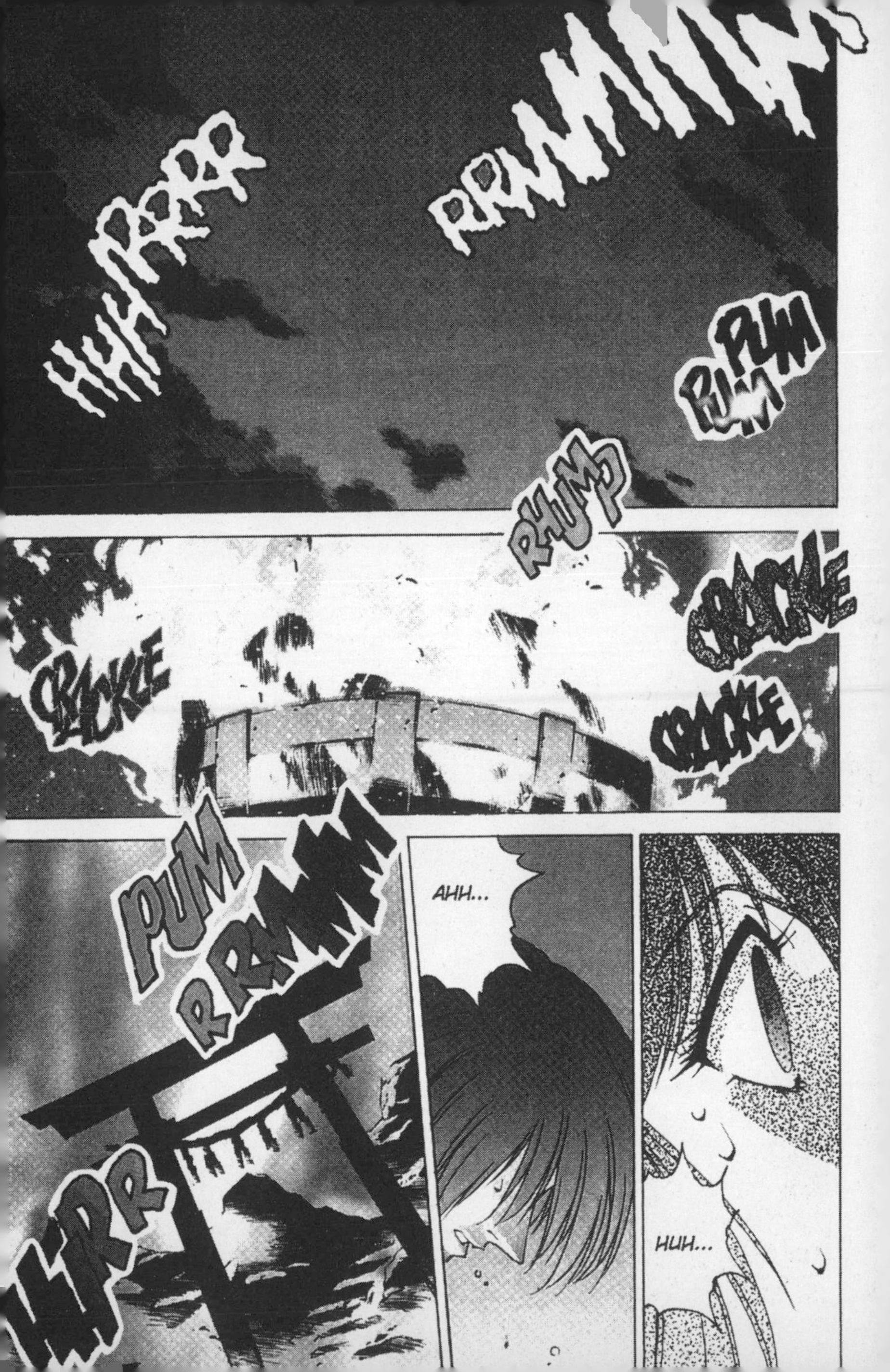

HUHRRRR
RRRMMMM
PUM PUM
RHUMP
CRACKLE
CRACKLE
CRACKLE
PUM
RRMMM
HURR
AHH...
HUH...

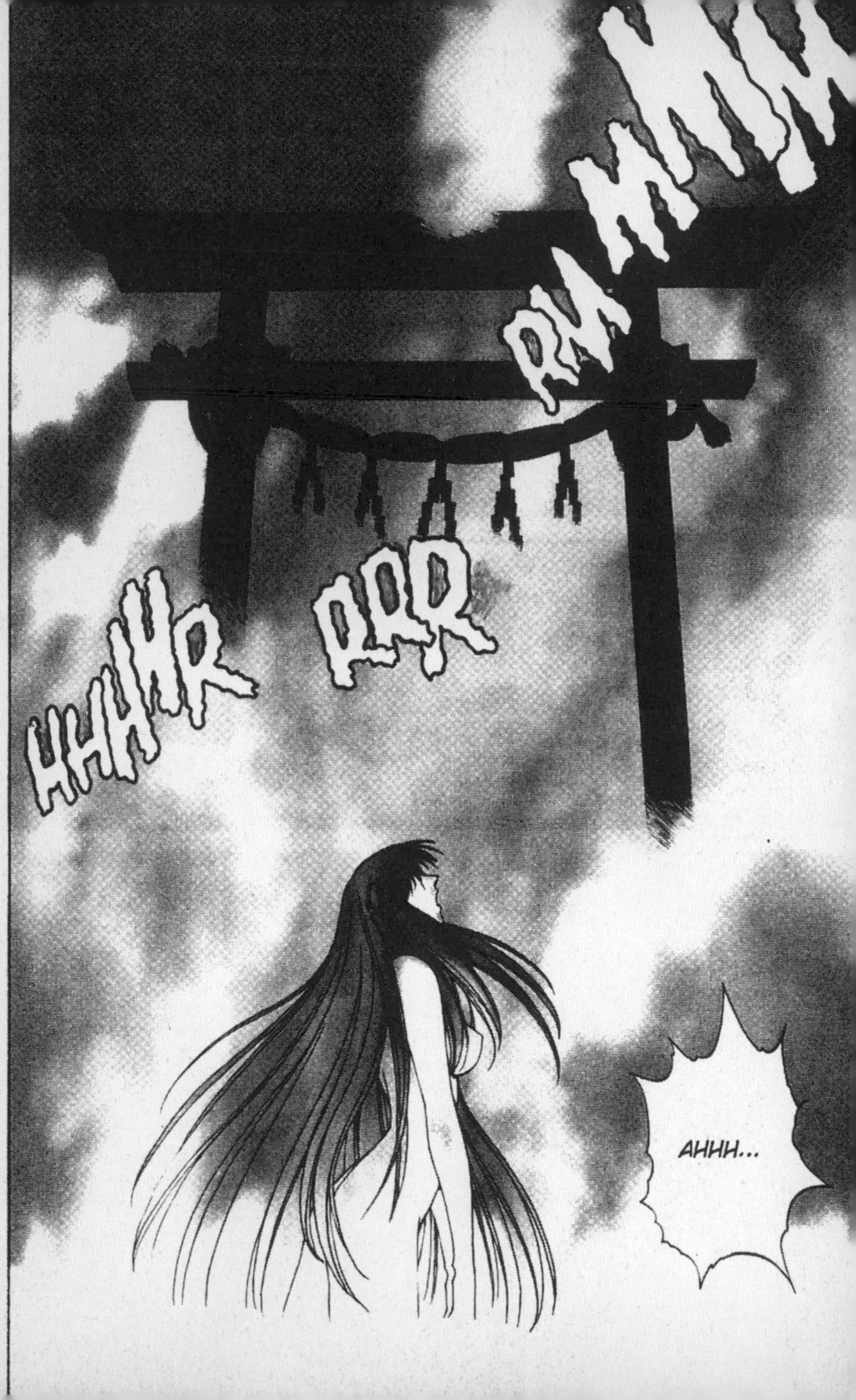
HHHR
RRR
AHHH...

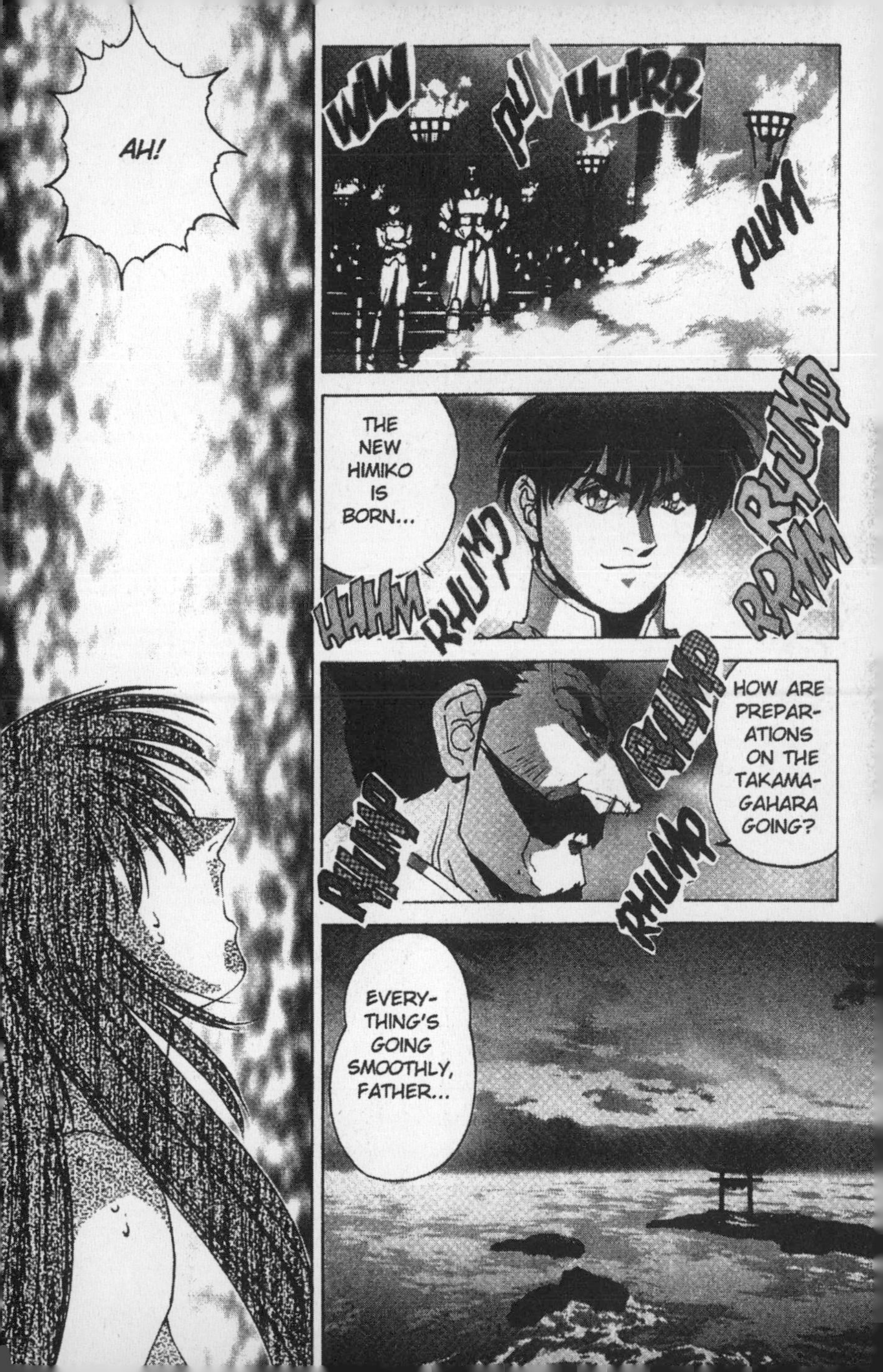
AH!
WHIRR
PUM
PUM
THE NEW HIMIKO IS BORN...
HHHM
RHUMP
RHUMP
RHUMP
HOW ARE PREPARATIONS ON THE TAKAMA-GAHARA GOING?
RHUMP
EVERYTHING'S GOING SMOOTHLY, FATHER...

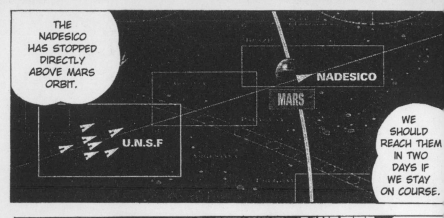

THE NADESICO HAS STOPPED DIRECTLY ABOVE MARS ORBIT.

NADESICO

MARS

U.N.S.F

WE SHOULD REACH THEM IN TWO DAYS IF WE STAY ON COURSE.

FORGET ABOUT THE NADESICO. OUR DESTINATION IS THE ASTEROID BELT.

PROCEED STRAIGHT AHEAD!

VREEEN

VREEEN

VREEEN

VR EEEEN

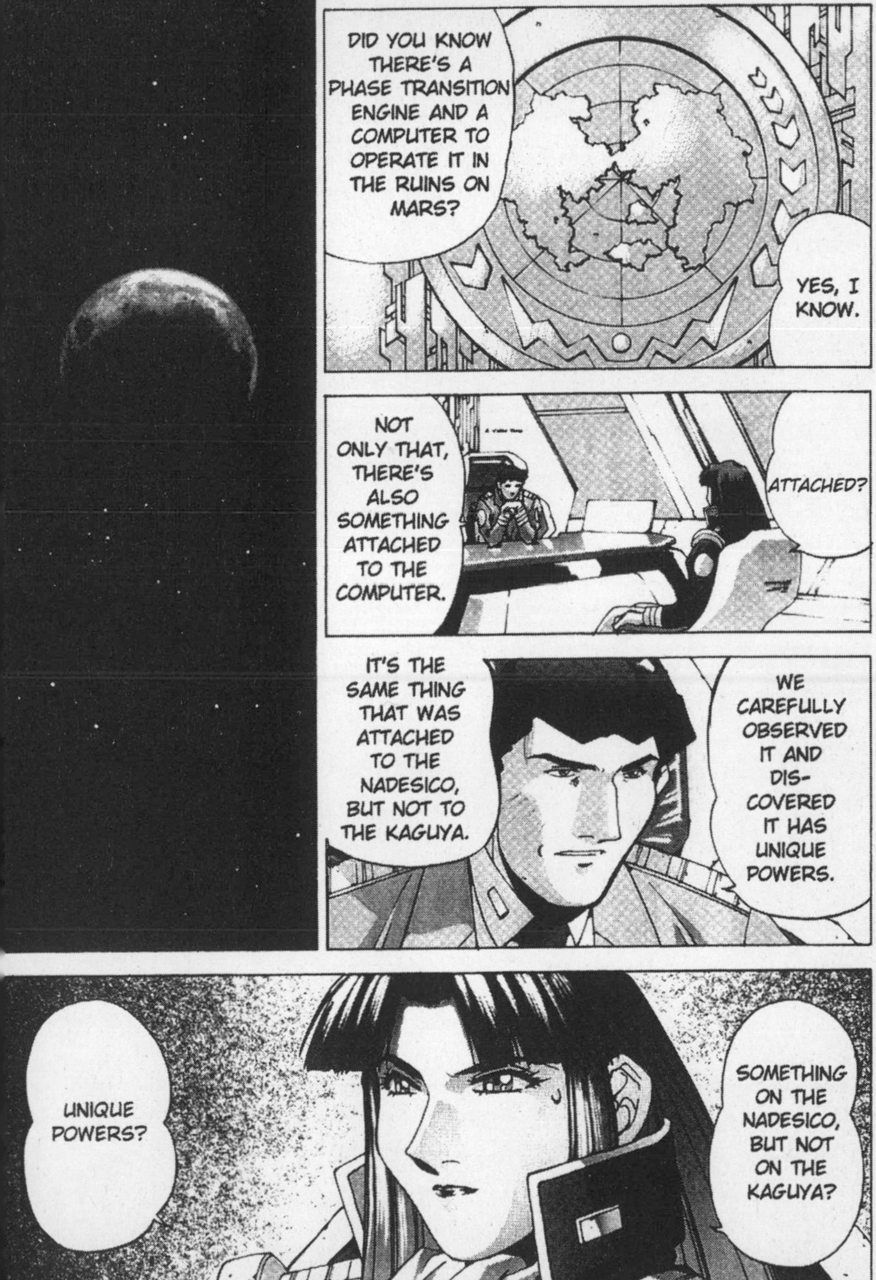
DID YOU KNOW THERE'S A PHASE TRANSITION ENGINE AND A COMPUTER TO OPERATE IT IN THE RUINS ON MARS?
YES, I KNOW.
NOT ONLY THAT, THERE'S ALSO SOMETHING ATTACHED TO THE COMPUTER.
ATTACHED?
IT'S THE SAME THING THAT WAS ATTACHED TO THE NADESICO, BUT NOT TO THE KAGUYA.
WE CAREFULLY OBSERVED IT AND DIS-COVERED IT HAS UNIQUE POWERS.
UNIQUE POWERS?
SOMETHING ON THE NADESICO, BUT NOT ON THE KAGUYA?

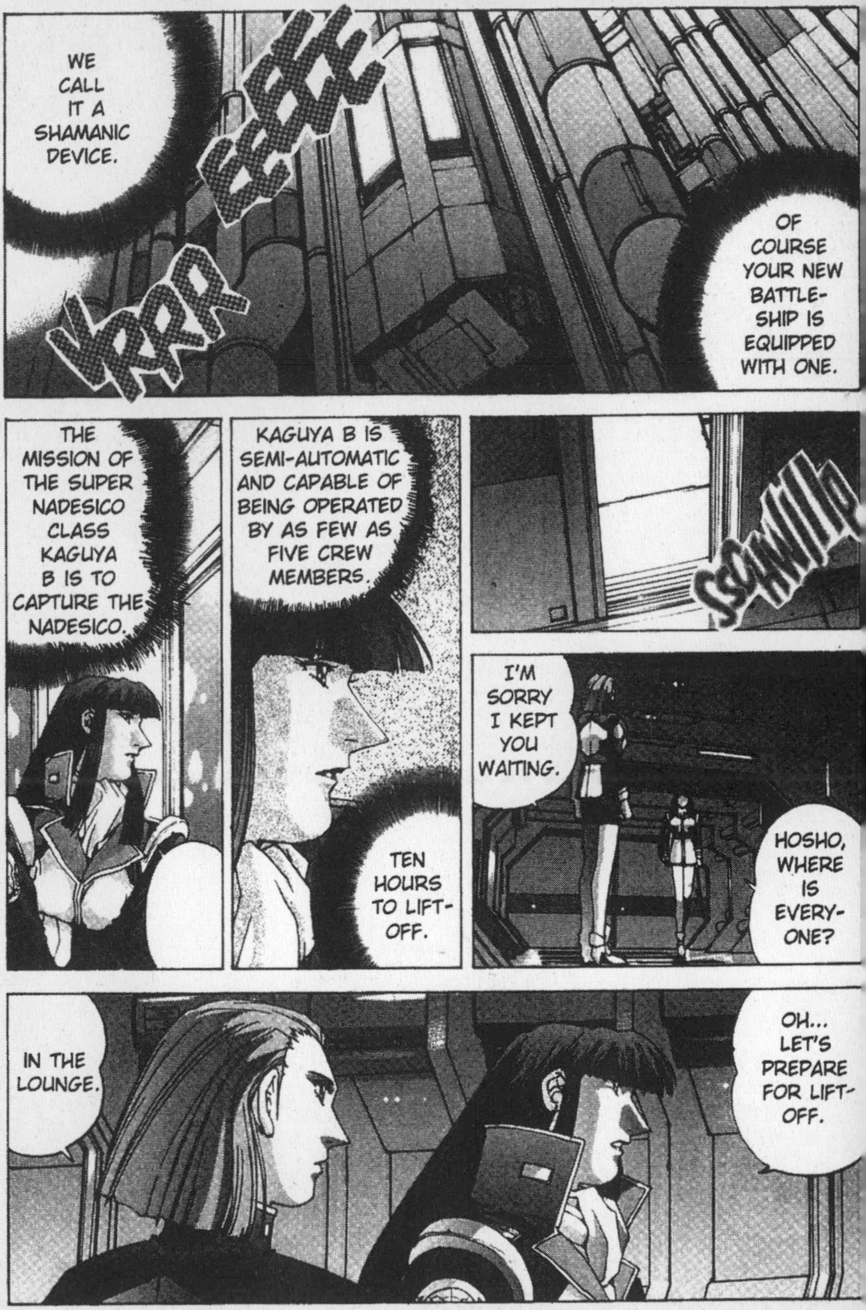
WE CALL IT A SHAMANIC DEVICE.
KRRR
OF COURSE YOUR NEW BATTLE-SHIP IS EQUIPPED WITH ONE.
THE MISSION OF THE SUPER NADESICO CLASS KAGUYA B IS TO CAPTURE THE NADESICO.
KAGUYA B IS SEMI-AUTOMATIC AND CAPABLE OF BEING OPERATED BY AS FEW AS FIVE CREW MEMBERS.
TEN HOURS TO LIFT-OFF.
I'M SORRY I KEPT YOU WAITING.
HOSHO, WHERE IS EVERY-ONE?
IN THE LOUNGE.
OH... LET'S PREPARE FOR LIFT-OFF.

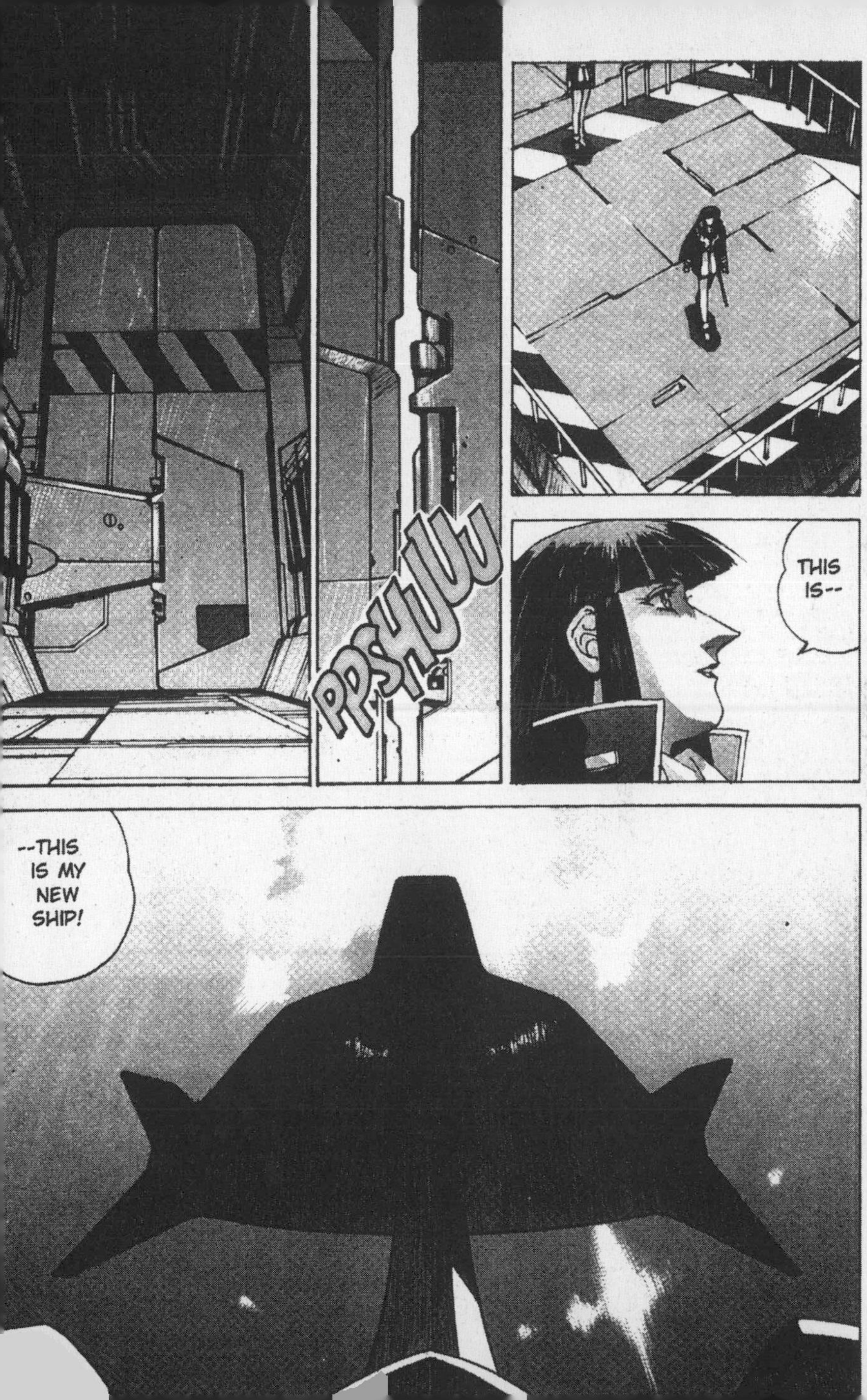
PPSHUUU
THIS IS--
--THIS IS MY NEW SHIP!

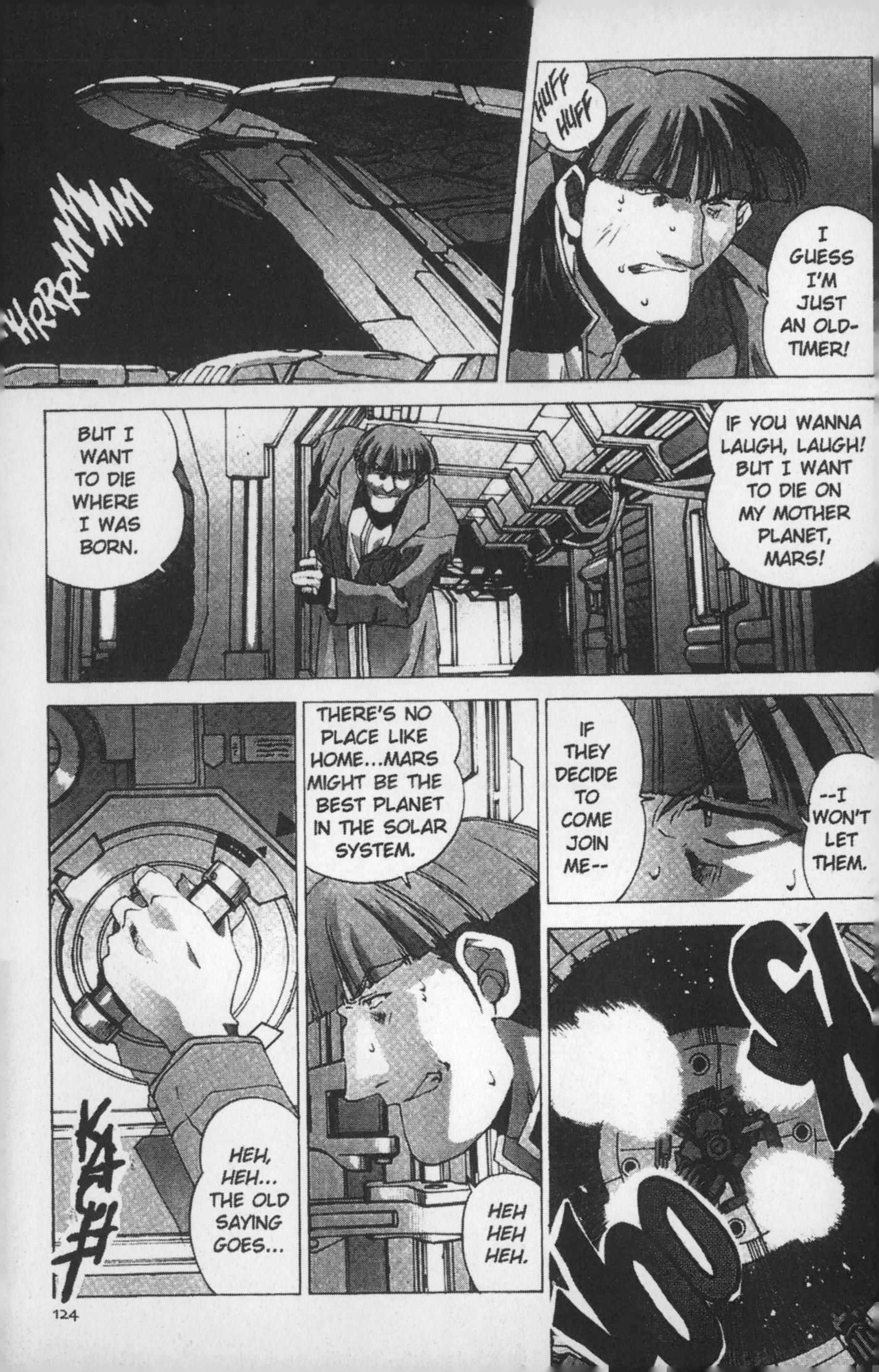
HUFF HUFF
I GUESS I'M JUST AN OLD-TIMER!
BUT I WANT TO DIE WHERE I WAS BORN.
IF YOU WANNA LAUGH, LAUGH! BUT I WANT TO DIE ON MY MOTHER PLANET, MARS!
HEH, HEH... THE OLD SAYING GOES...
THERE'S NO PLACE LIKE HOME...MARS MIGHT BE THE BEST PLANET IN THE SOLAR SYSTEM.
HEH HEH HEH.
IF THEY DECIDE TO COME JOIN ME--
--I WON'T LET THEM.

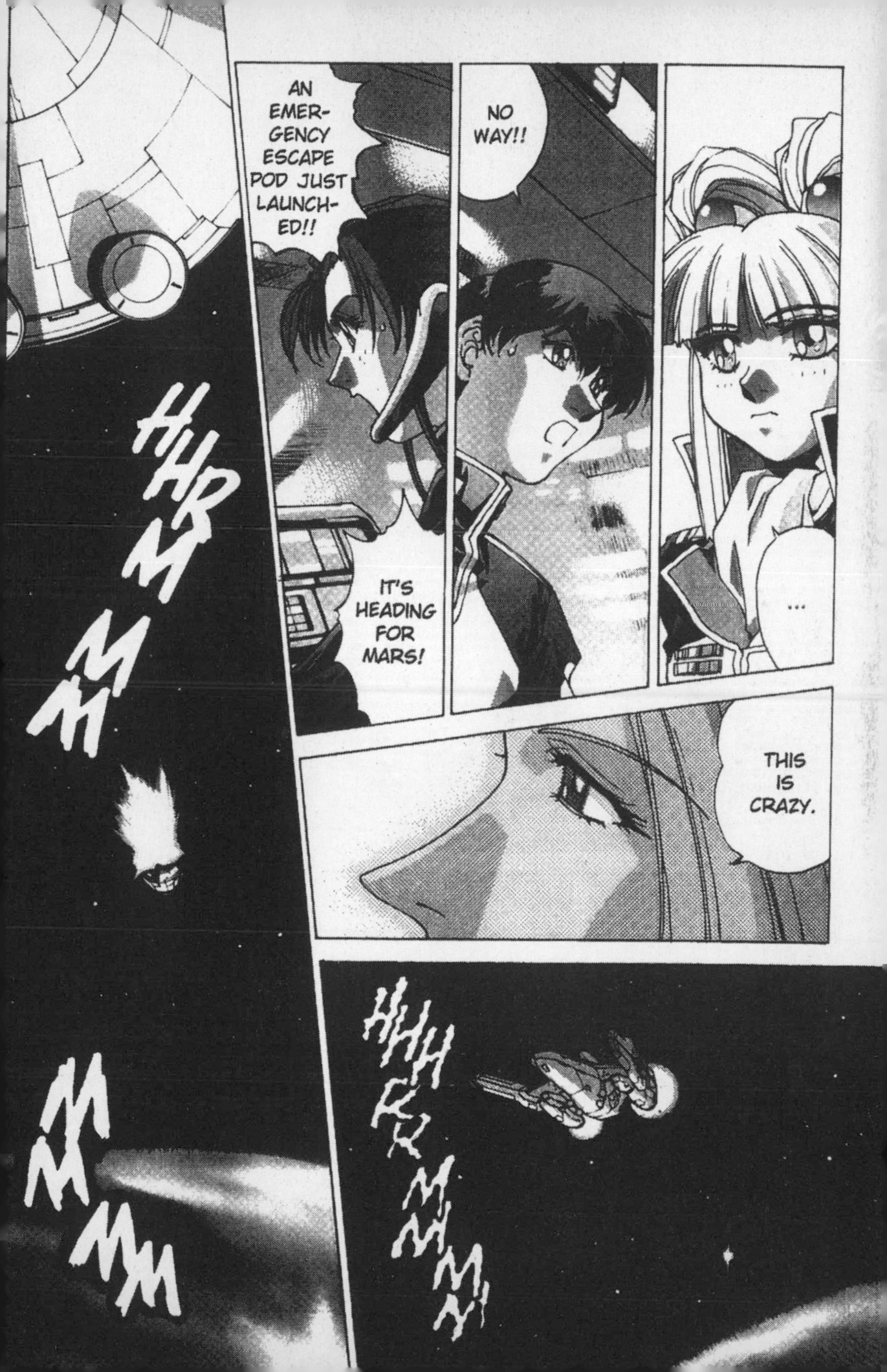
HHRMMMM
AN EMERGENCY ESCAPE POD JUST LAUNCHED!!
NO WAY!!
IT'S HEADING FOR MARS!
...
THIS IS CRAZY.
HHHRMMMMM

...

LOOKS LIKE RYOKO LOST AGAIN.

WE HAVEN'T WON ONE YET.

HE'S BEEN DOING MORE THAN READING MANGA IN THERE.

SIGH.

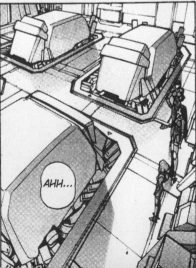

AHH...

THAT'S THIRTY-FOUR OUT OF THIRTY-FOUR.

HEH HEH HEH.

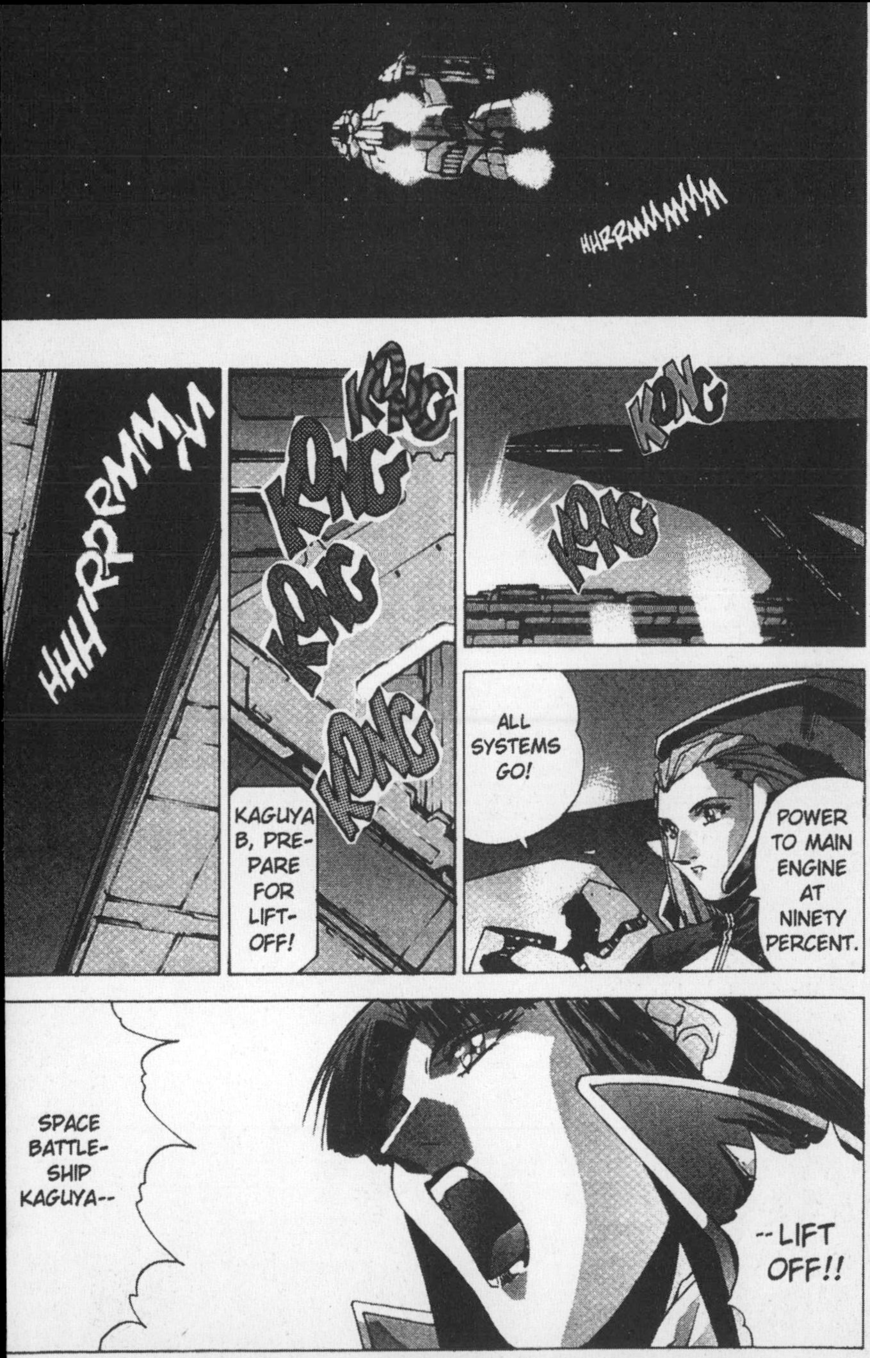
HHRRMMMMMM
HHHRRRMMMM
KONG
KONG
KONG
KONG
KAGUYA B, PRE-PARE FOR LIFT-OFF!
KONG
KONG
ALL SYSTEMS GO!
POWER TO MAIN ENGINE AT NINETY PERCENT.
SPACE BATTLE-SHIP KAGUYA--
--LIFT OFF!!

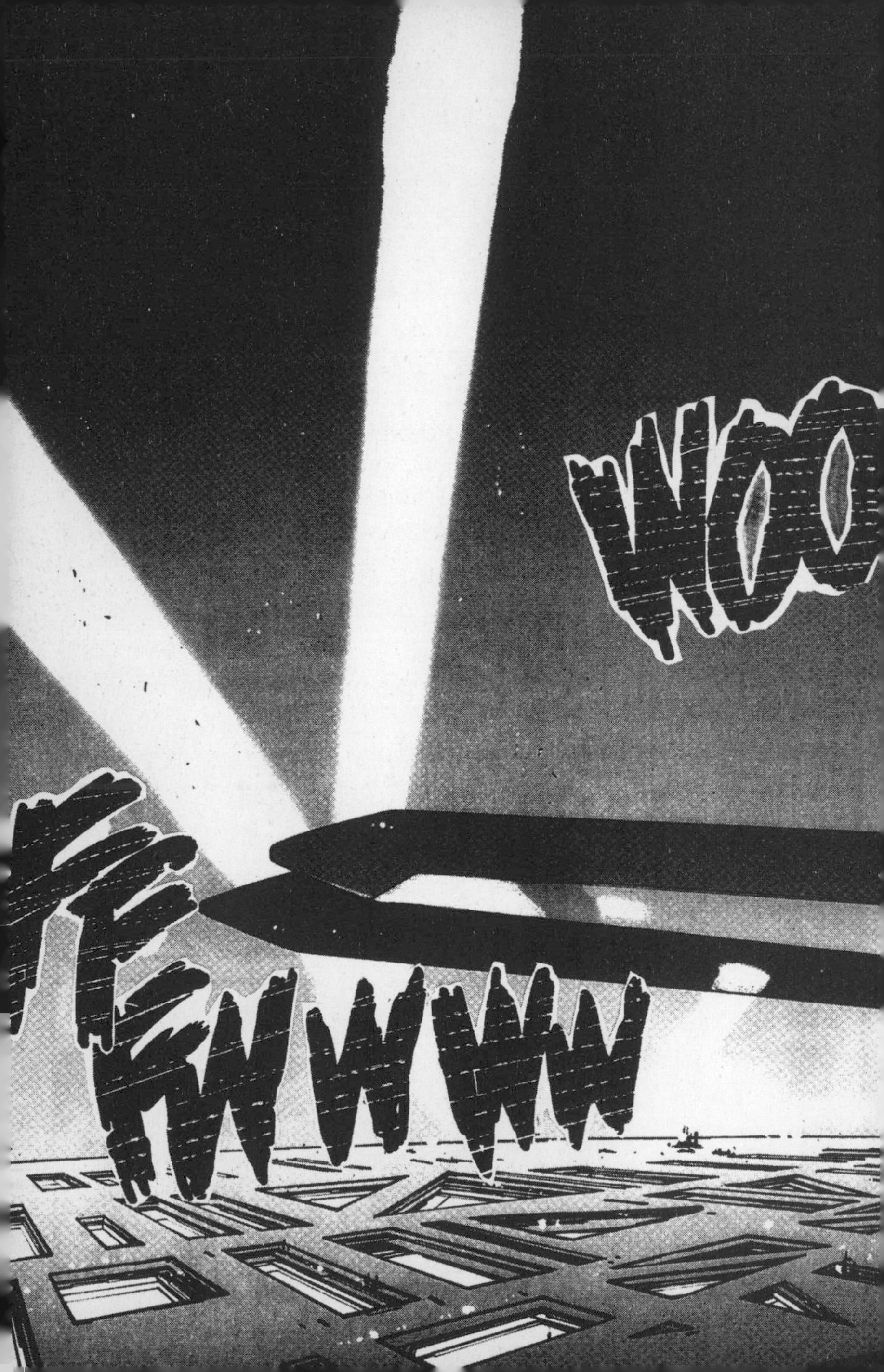
WOO

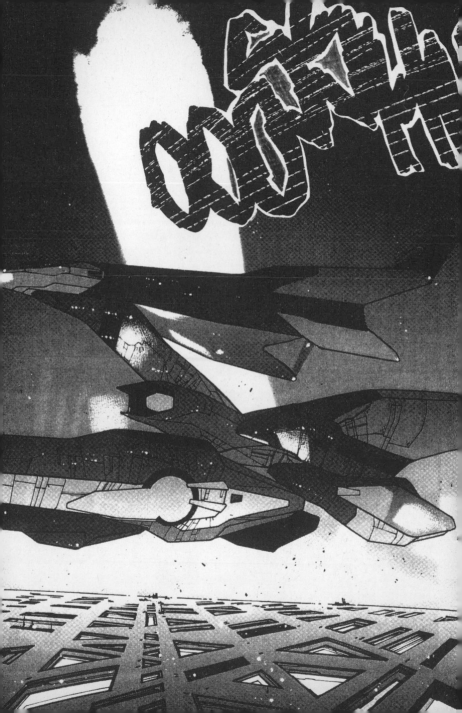

SUPER NADESICO CLASS KAGUYA. DESIGNED BY MIKA AKI.

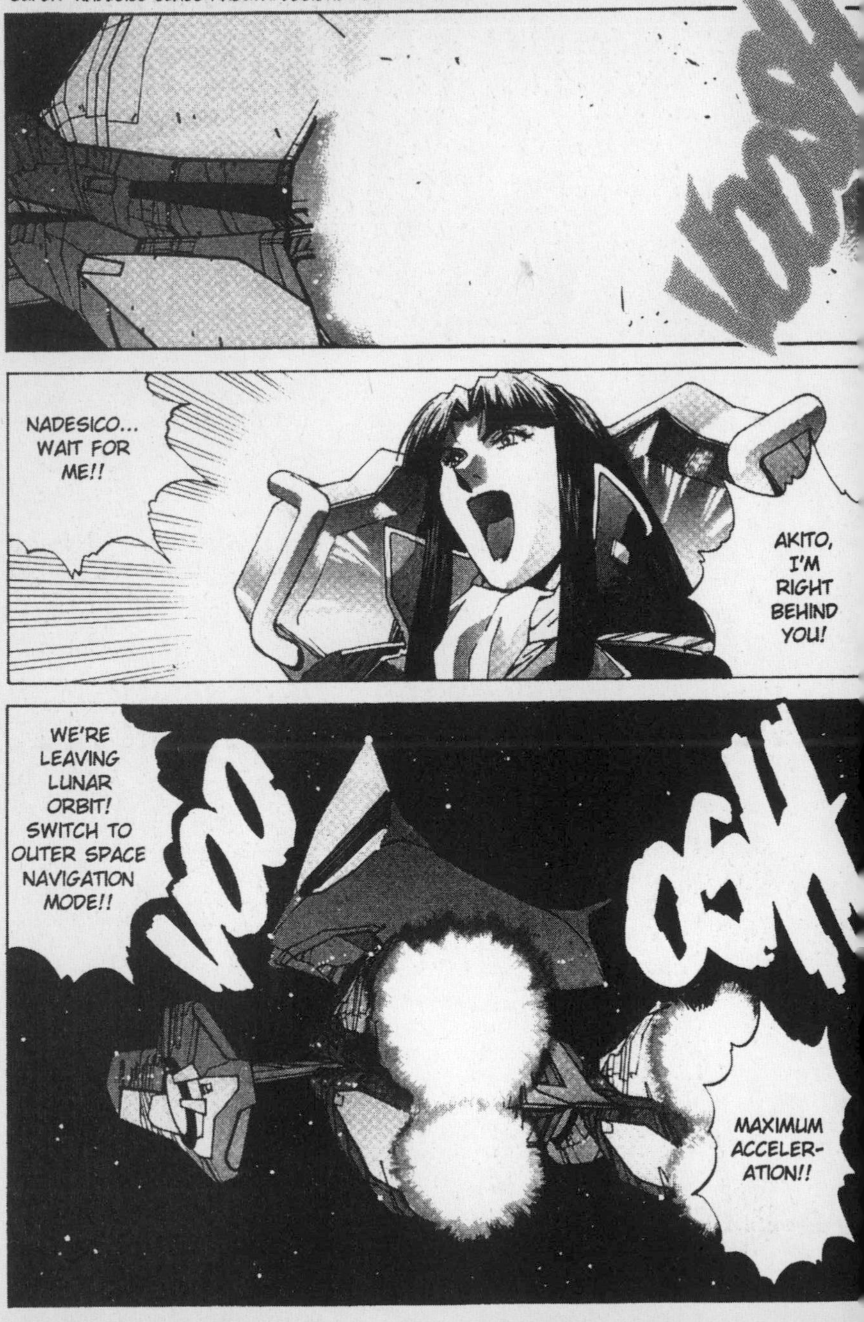
VOOSH
NADESICO... WAIT FOR ME!!
AKITO, I'M RIGHT BEHIND YOU!
WE'RE LEAVING LUNAR ORBIT! SWITCH TO OUTER SPACE NAVIGATION MODE!!
VOO
OSH
MAXIMUM ACCELER-ATION!!

CONFIRMING ENEMY PRESENCE!! 135,000 JUPITERIANS!!

WE'LL BE ENTERING ENEMY TERRITORY IN SIX HUNDRED SECONDS.

BATTALION ONE, PREPARE FOR ATTACK!! ANTIFIELD SHIPS IN LINE FORMATION!!

BATTALIONS TWO AND THREE, CONTINUE PREPARATIONS.

THEY'RE JUST GUARDIANS.

THIS BETTER NOT LAST LONG.

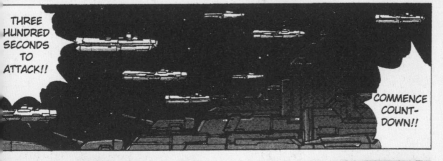

THREE HUNDRED SECONDS TO ATTACK!!

COMMENCE COUNTDOWN!!

EARTH FORCES ARE IN ATTACK FORMATION.

I SEE.

第18話 決戦は木星で

DECISIVE BATTLE OF JUPITER

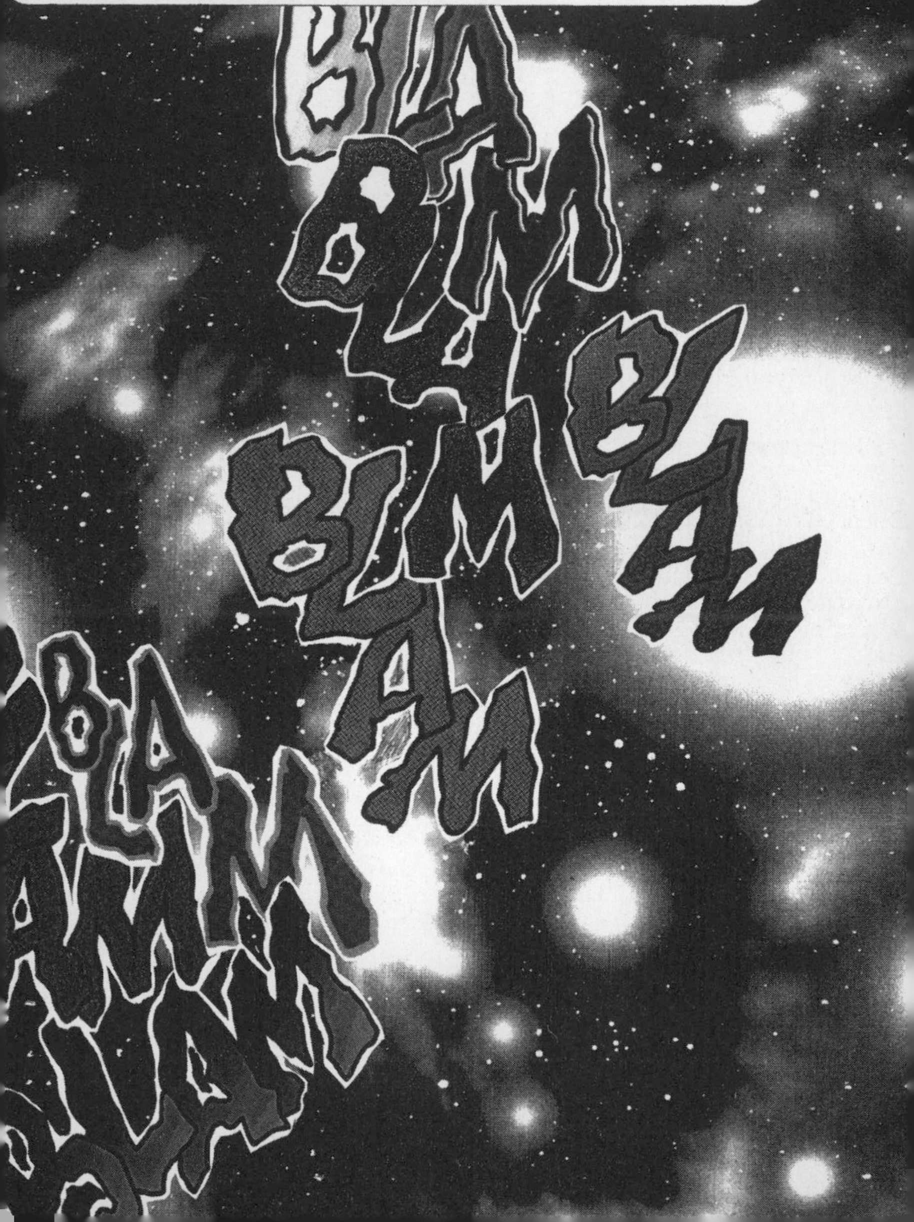
BLAM
BLAM
BLAM
BLAM
BLAM

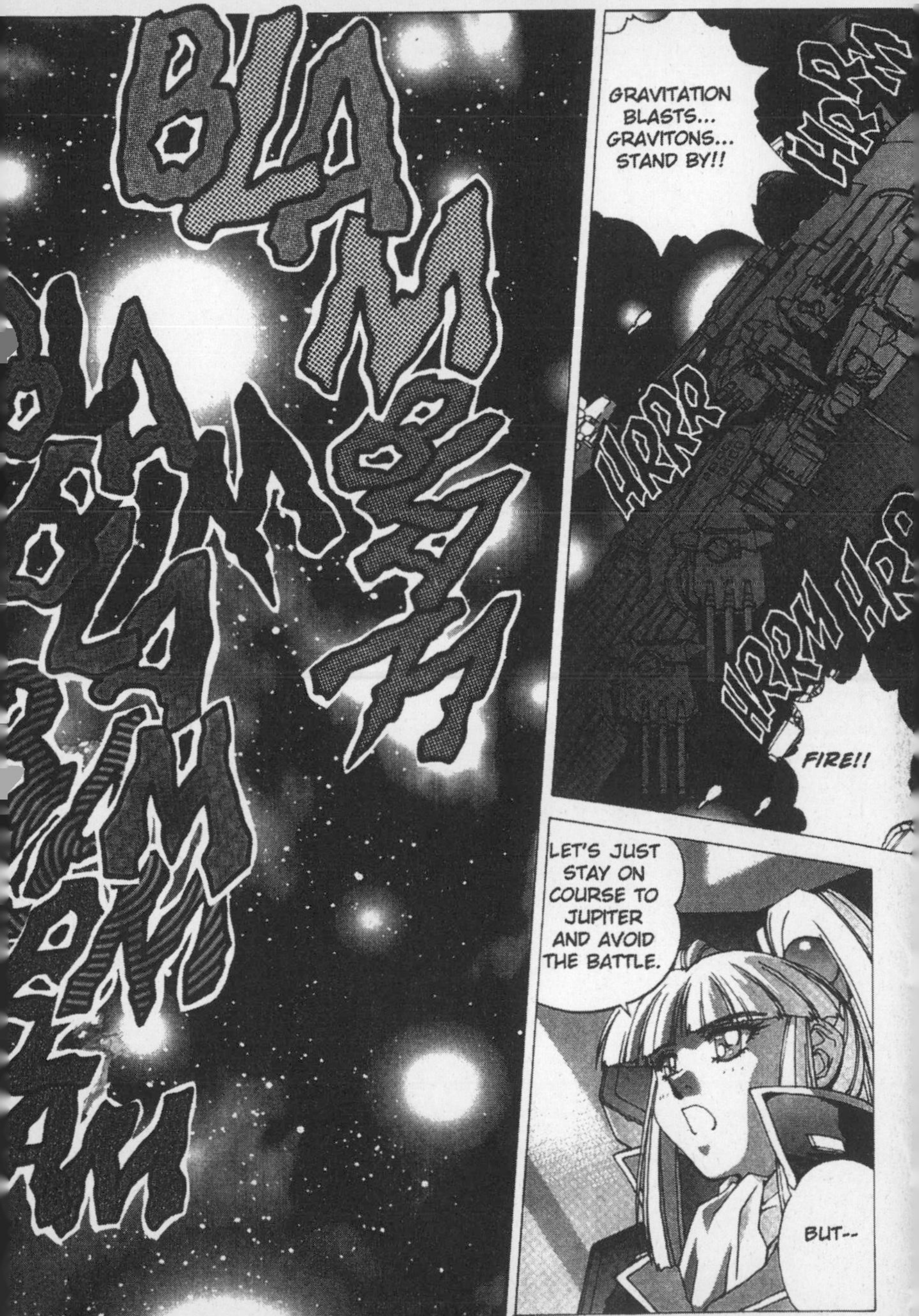
BLAM
GRAVITATION BLASTS... GRAVITONS... STAND BY!!
HRRM
HRRR
HRRM HRR
FIRE!!
LET'S JUST STAY ON COURSE TO JUPITER AND AVOID THE BATTLE.
BUT--

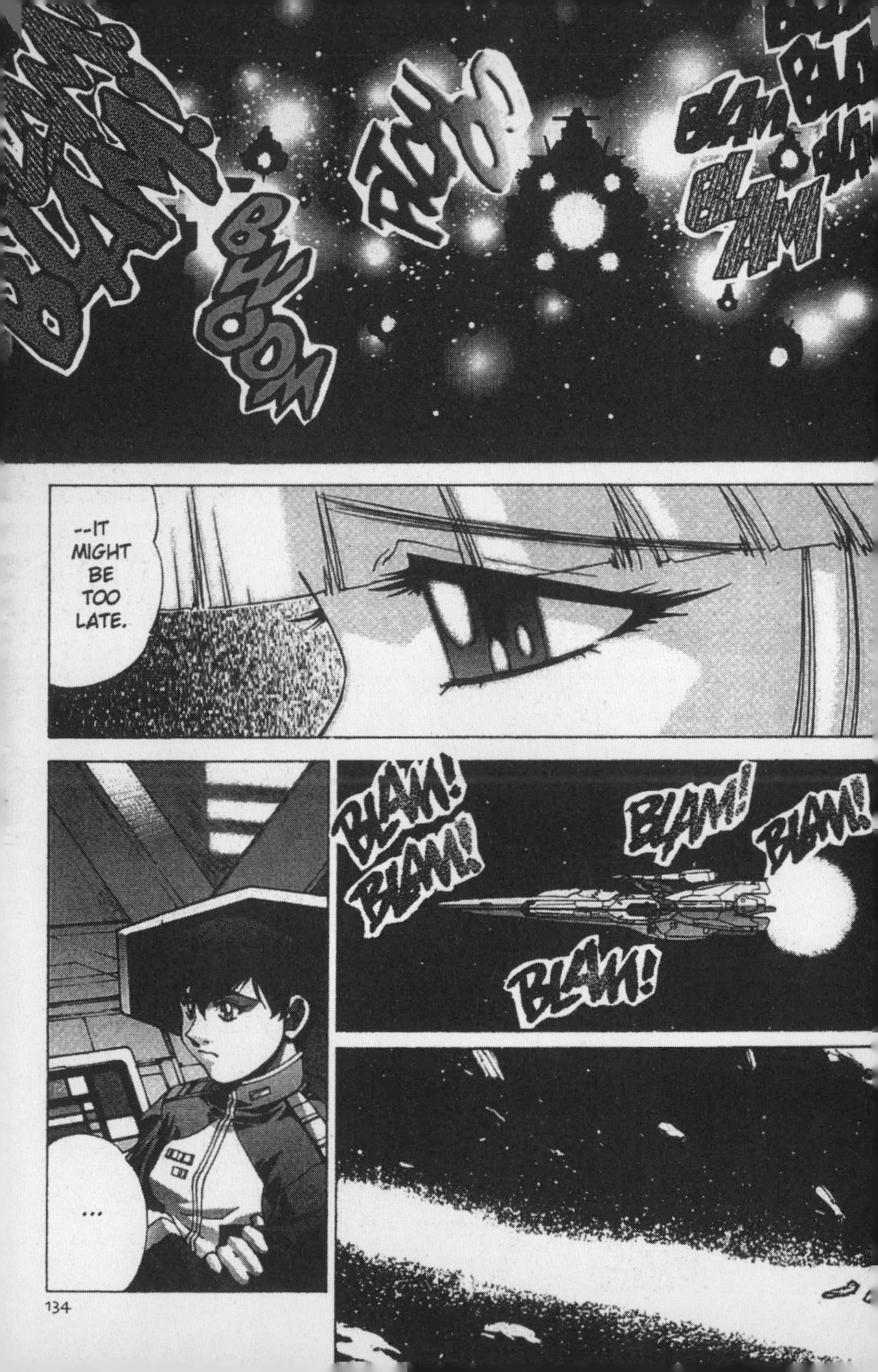
BLAM BLAM
BLAM
BLAM
BLAM
RUSH
BLAM!
BLAM!
BWOOM
--IT MIGHT BE TOO LATE.
BLAM!
BLAM!
BLAM!
BLAM!
BLAM!
...

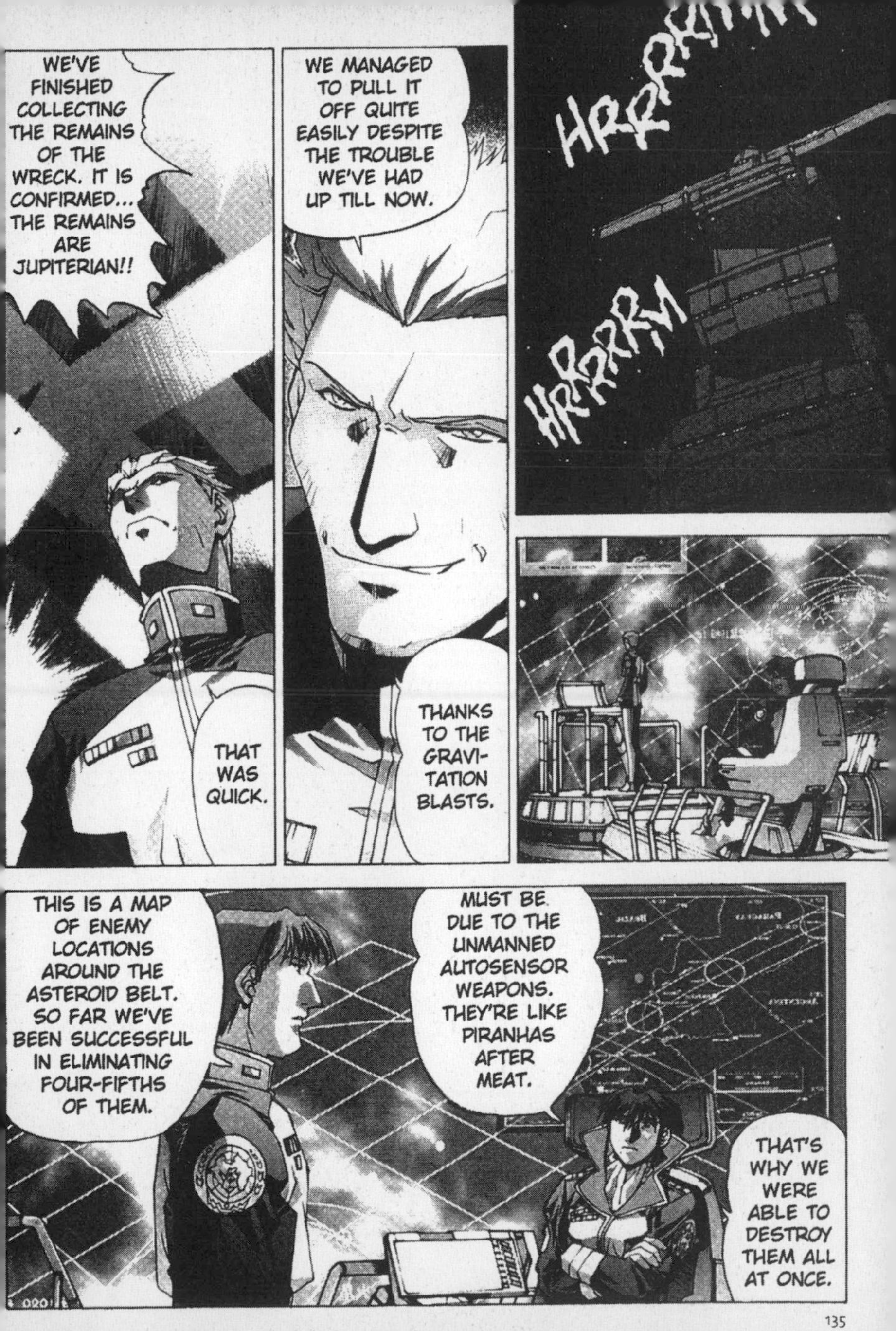
WE'VE FINISHED COLLECTING THE REMAINS OF THE WRECK. IT IS CONFIRMED... THE REMAINS ARE JUPITERIAN!!
THAT WAS QUICK.
WE MANAGED TO PULL IT OFF QUITE EASILY DESPITE THE TROUBLE WE'VE HAD UP TILL NOW.
THANKS TO THE GRAVI-TATION BLASTS.
HRRRRM
HRRRRM
THIS IS A MAP OF ENEMY LOCATIONS AROUND THE ASTEROID BELT. SO FAR WE'VE BEEN SUCCESSFUL IN ELIMINATING FOUR-FIFTHS OF THEM.
MUST BE DUE TO THE UNMANNED AUTOSENSOR WEAPONS. THEY'RE LIKE PIRANHAS AFTER MEAT.
THAT'S WHY WE WERE ABLE TO DESTROY THEM ALL AT ONCE.

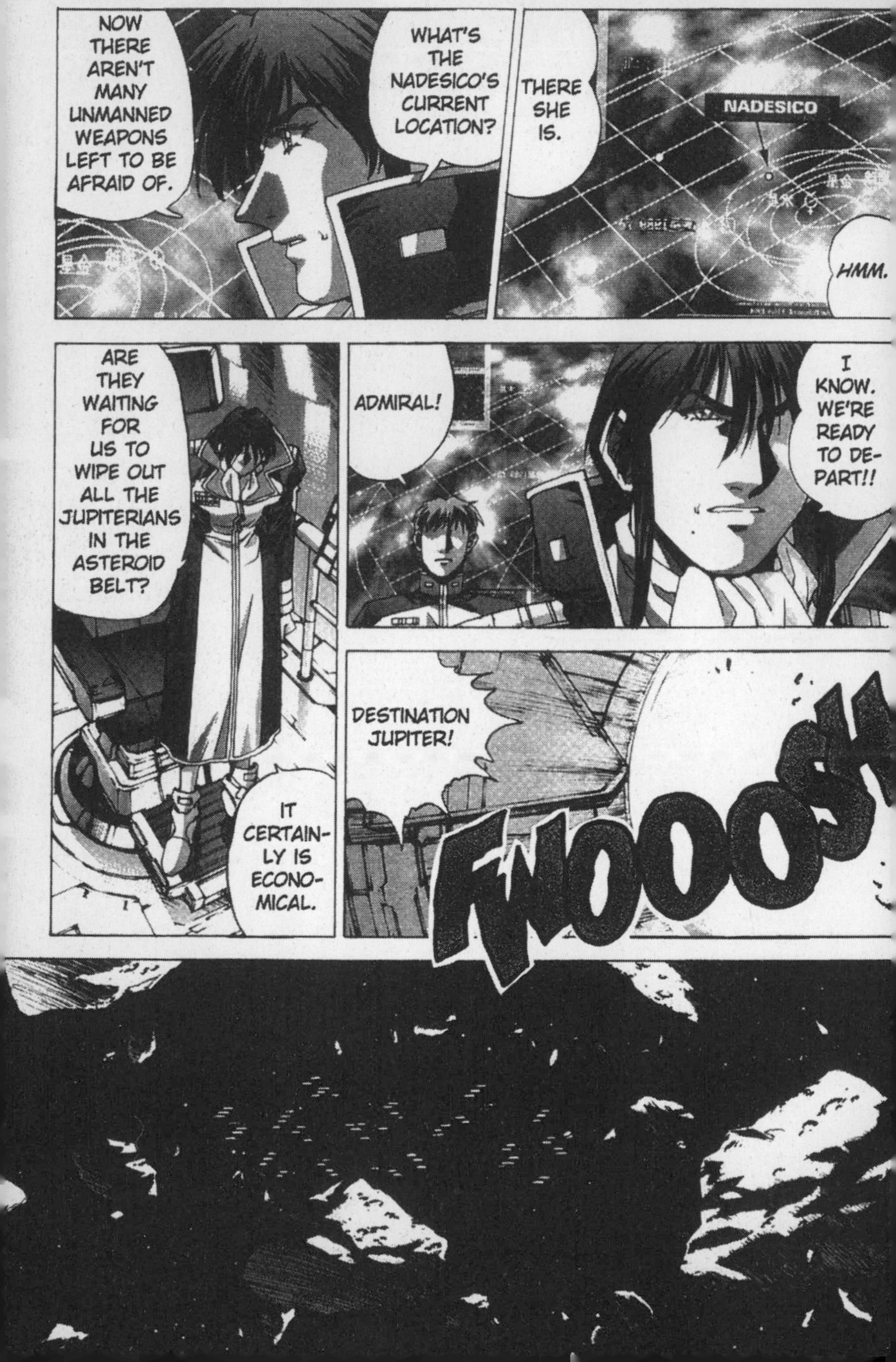
NOW THERE AREN'T MANY UNMANNED WEAPONS LEFT TO BE AFRAID OF.
WHAT'S THE NADESICO'S CURRENT LOCATION?
THERE SHE IS.
NADESICO
HMM.
ARE THEY WAITING FOR US TO WIPE OUT ALL THE JUPITERIANS IN THE ASTEROID BELT?
IT CERTAIN-LY IS ECONO-MICAL.
ADMIRAL!
I KNOW. WE'RE READY TO DE-PART!!
DESTINATION JUPITER!
FWOOOSH

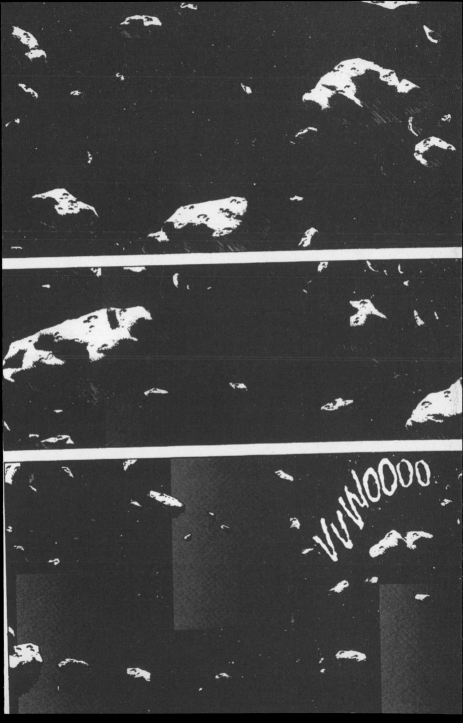

VUWOOOO

FWOOSH

CAPTAIN, WE'RE CURRENTLY IN OUTER SPACE NAVIGATION MODE B.

AT THIS RATE WE SHOULD REACH THE NADESICO IN THREE DAYS.

I SEE. PLEASE MAINTAIN THIS SPEED, HOSHO.

MURASAME, CHECK CURRENT ENEMY STATUS. ARE THERE ANY IN OUR PATH?

I DON'T SEE ANY. IF WE STAY ON COURSE WE SHOULD BE OKAY.

GOT IT.

TAKACHIHO, GET READY FOR OFFENSIVE FORMATION AND STAND BY.

AYE, AYE.

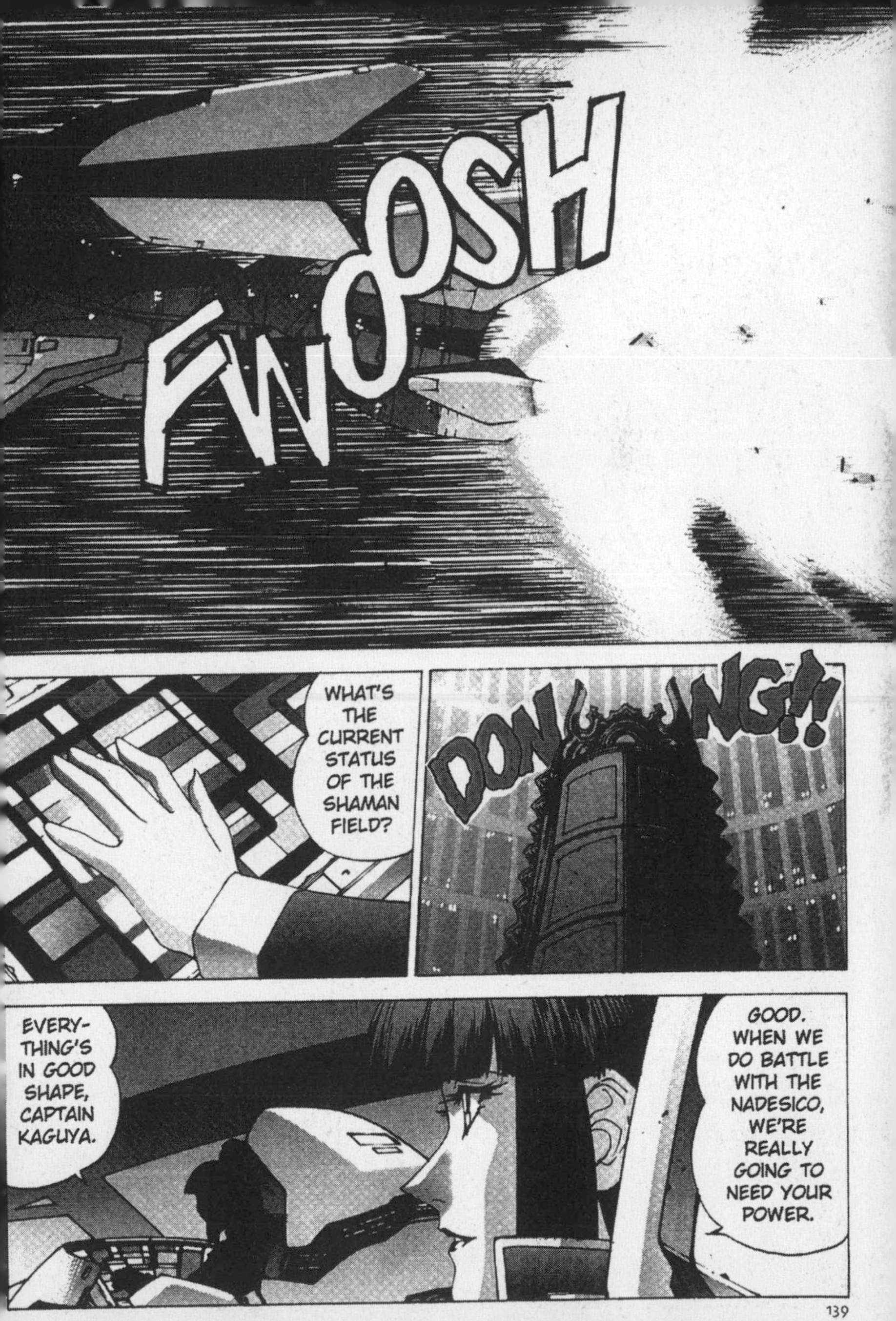
FWOOSH
WHAT'S THE CURRENT STATUS OF THE SHAMAN FIELD?
DON
NG!!
EVERY-THING'S IN GOOD SHAPE, CAPTAIN KAGUYA.
GOOD. WHEN WE DO BATTLE WITH THE NADESICO, WE'RE REALLY GOING TO NEED YOUR POWER.

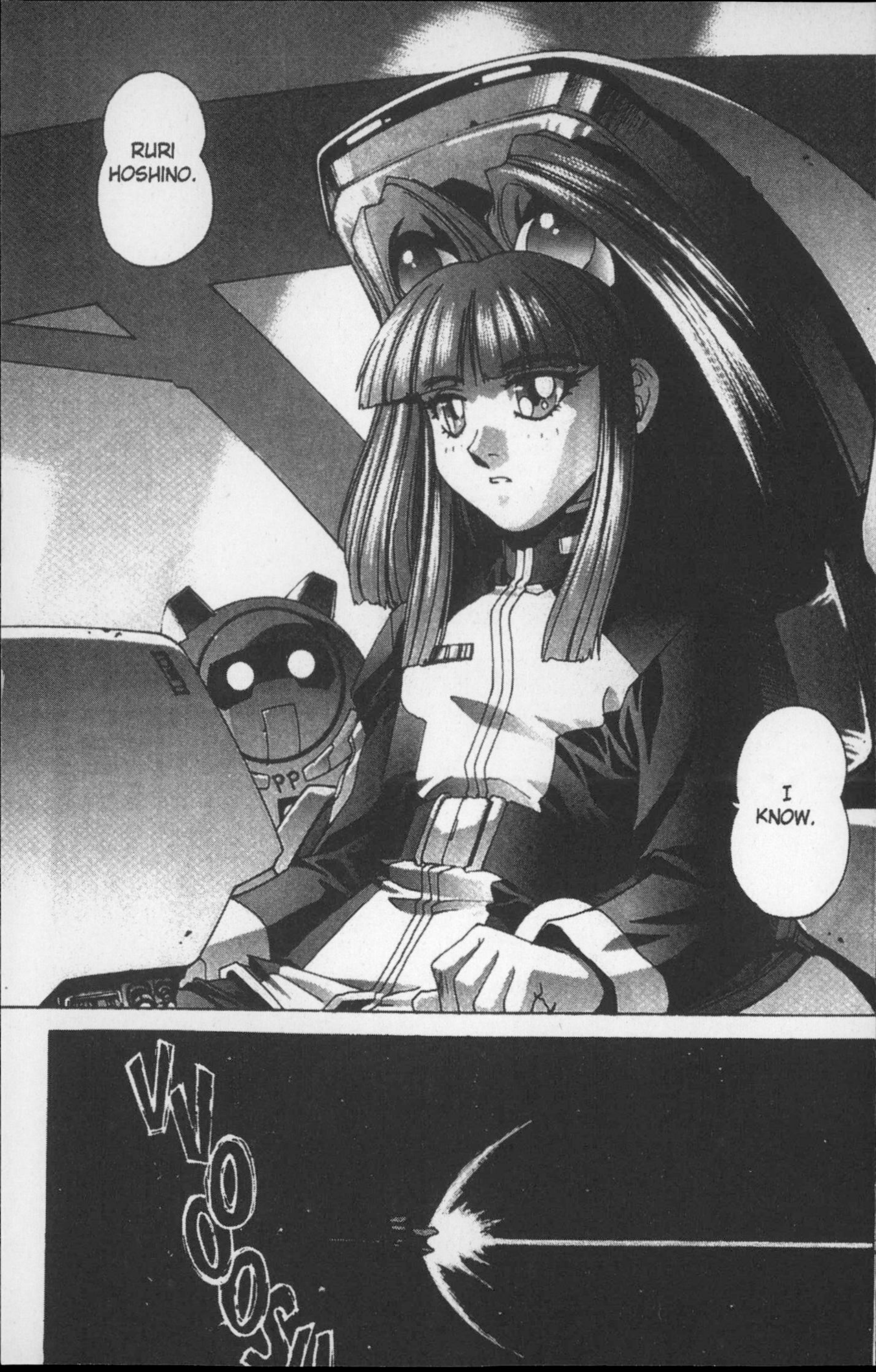
RURI HOSHINO.
I KNOW.
VVOOOSH

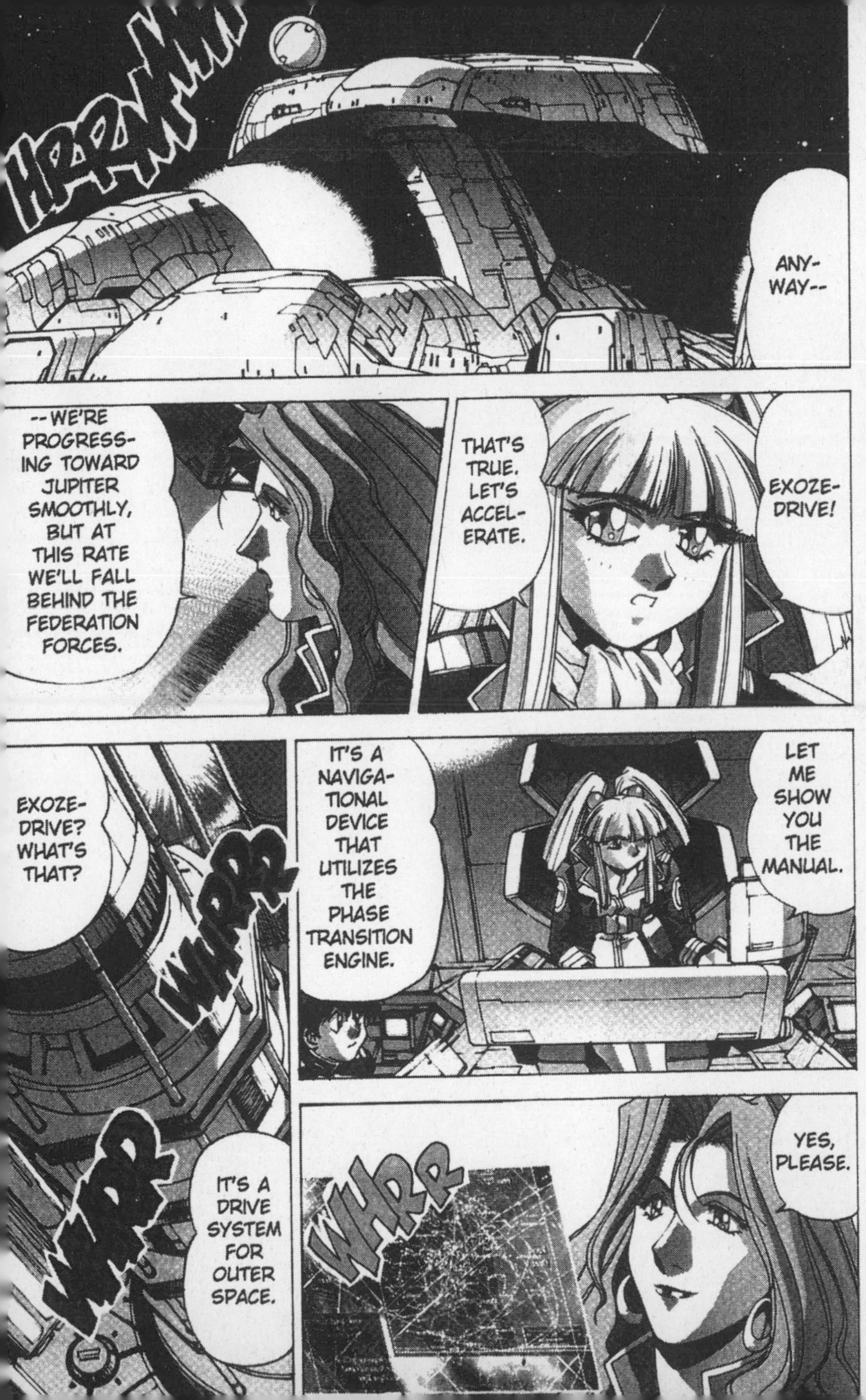
HRRNNNN
ANY-WAY--
--WE'RE PROGRESSING TOWARD JUPITER SMOOTHLY, BUT AT THIS RATE WE'LL FALL BEHIND THE FEDERATION FORCES.
THAT'S TRUE. LET'S ACCELERATE.
EXOZE-DRIVE!
EXOZE-DRIVE? WHAT'S THAT?
WHRR
WHRR
IT'S A DRIVE SYSTEM FOR OUTER SPACE.
IT'S A NAVIGATIONAL DEVICE THAT UTILIZES THE PHASE TRANSITION ENGINE.
LET ME SHOW YOU THE MANUAL.
WHRR
YES, PLEASE.

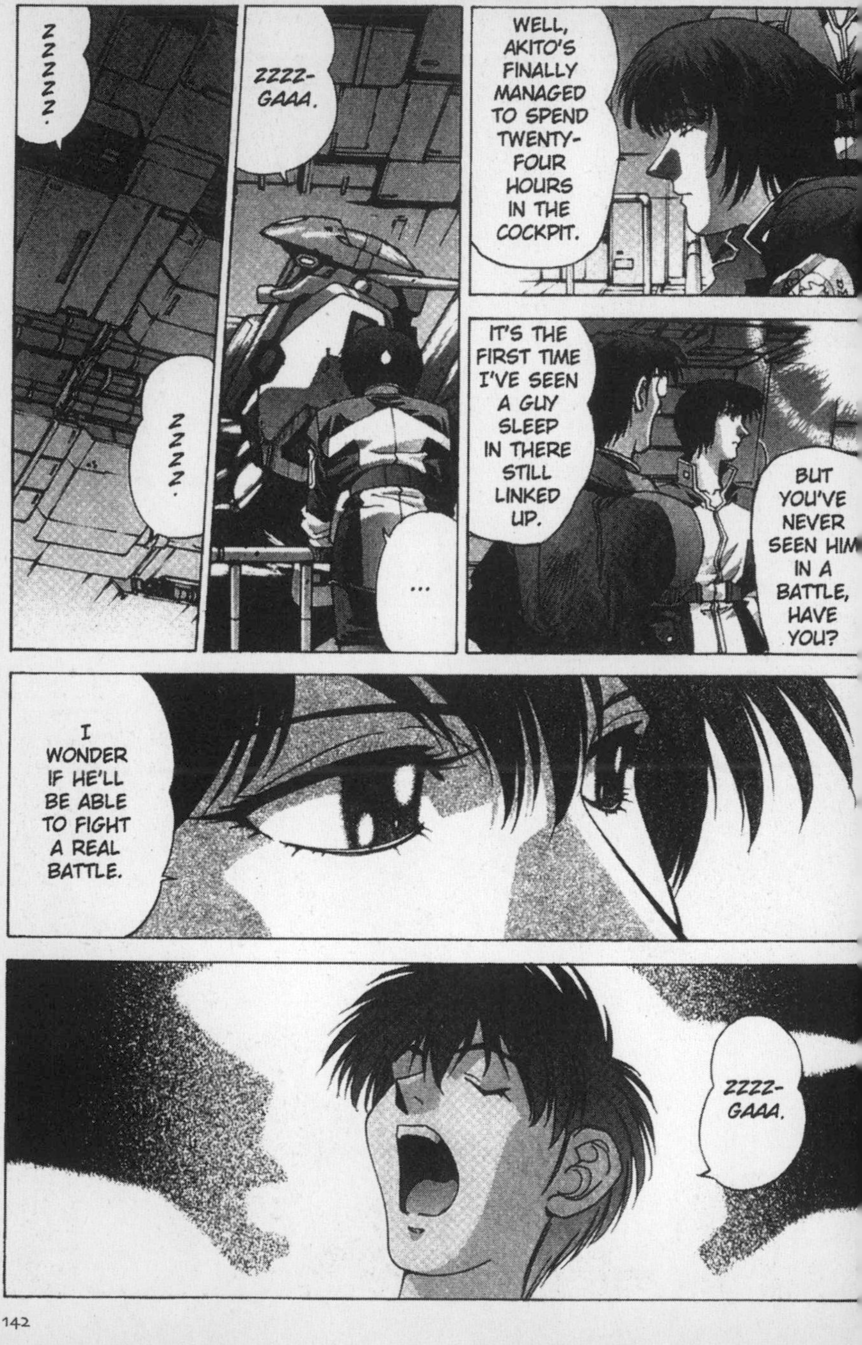
ZZZZZ.
ZZZZ.
ZZZZ-GAAA.
...
WELL, AKITO'S FINALLY MANAGED TO SPEND TWENTY-FOUR HOURS IN THE COCKPIT.
IT'S THE FIRST TIME I'VE SEEN A GUY SLEEP IN THERE STILL LINKED UP.
BUT YOU'VE NEVER SEEN HIM IN A BATTLE, HAVE YOU?
I WONDER IF HE'LL BE ABLE TO FIGHT A REAL BATTLE.
ZZZZ-GAAA.

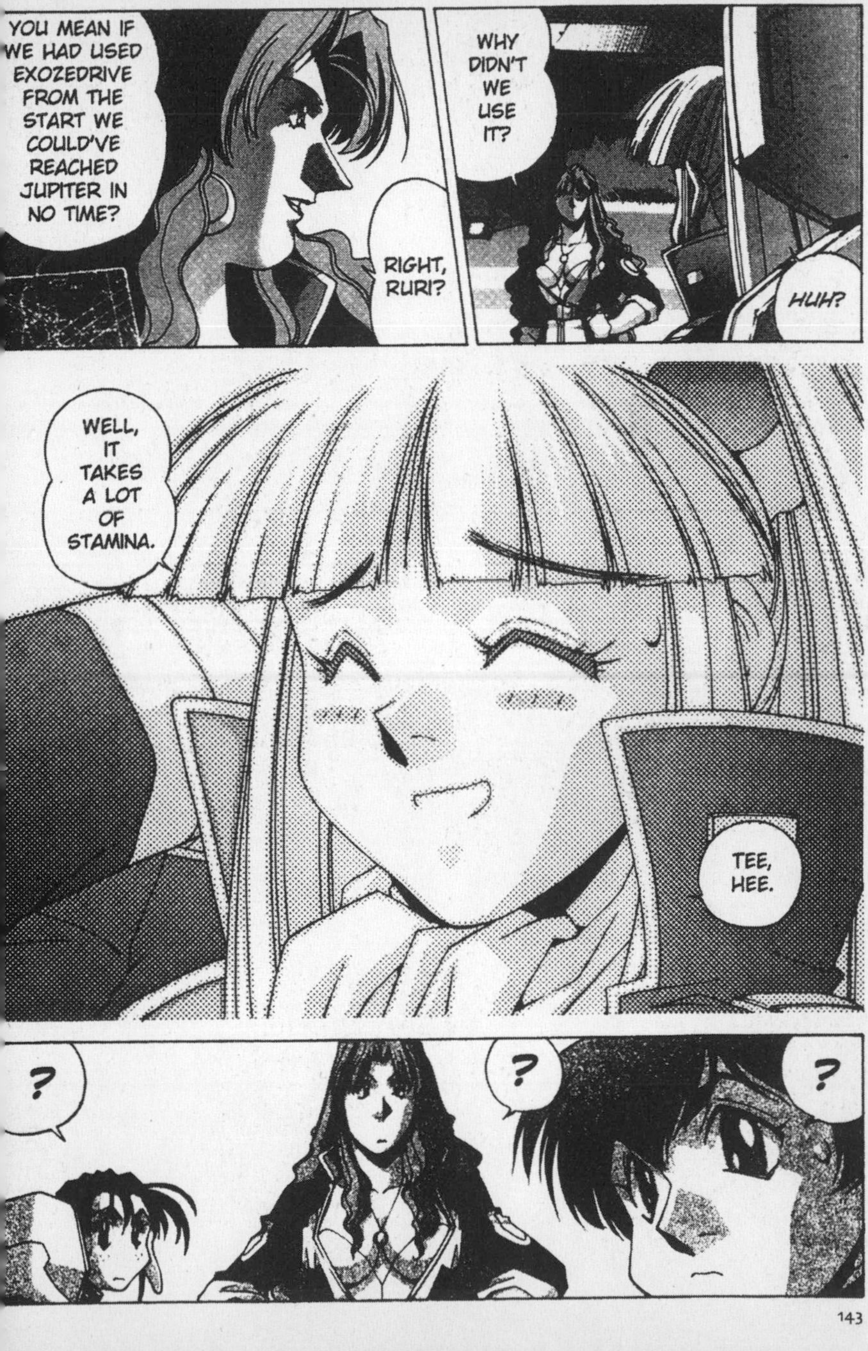
YOU MEAN IF WE HAD USED EXOZEDRIVE FROM THE START WE COULD'VE REACHED JUPITER IN NO TIME?
RIGHT, RURI?
WHY DIDN'T WE USE IT?
HUH?
WELL, IT TAKES A LOT OF STAMINA.
TEE, HEE.
?
?
?

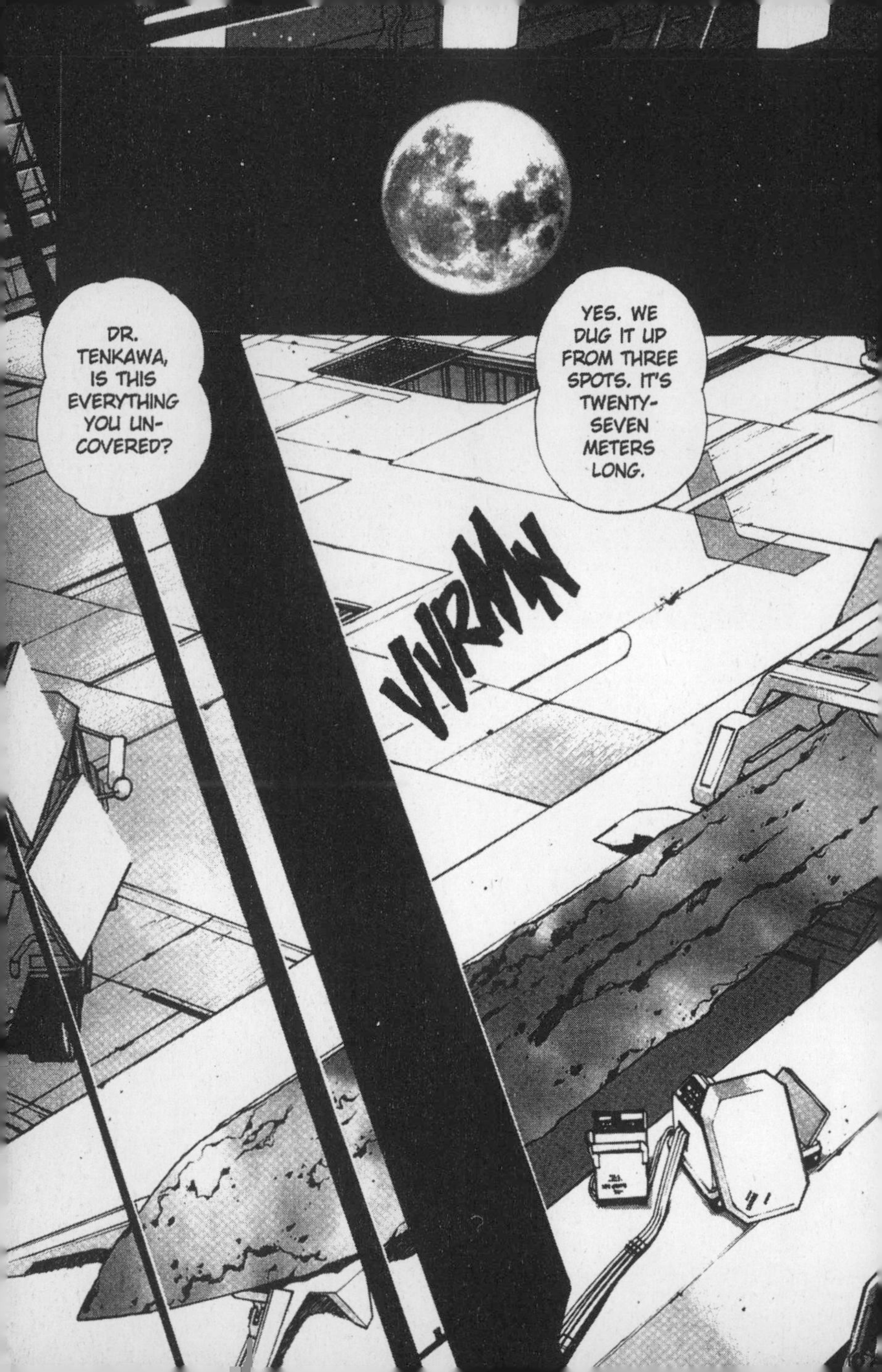
DR. TENKAWA, IS THIS EVERYTHING YOU UN-COVERED?
YES. WE DUG IT UP FROM THREE SPOTS. IT'S TWENTY-SEVEN METERS LONG.
VVRMM

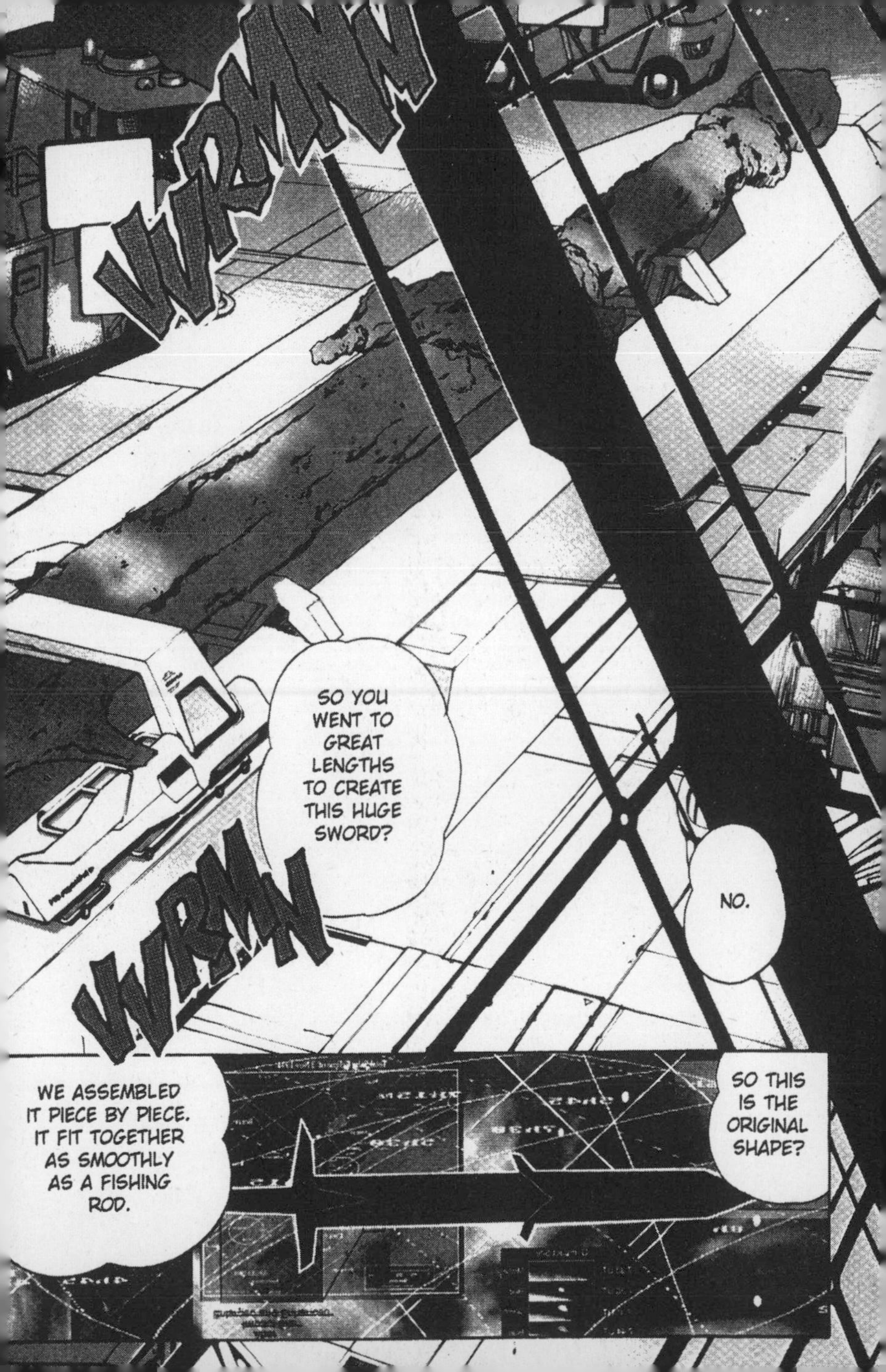
VVRMMN
SO YOU WENT TO GREAT LENGTHS TO CREATE THIS HUGE SWORD?
NO.
VVRMN
WE ASSEMBLED IT PIECE BY PIECE. IT FIT TOGETHER AS SMOOTHLY AS A FISHING ROD.
SO THIS IS THE ORIGINAL SHAPE?

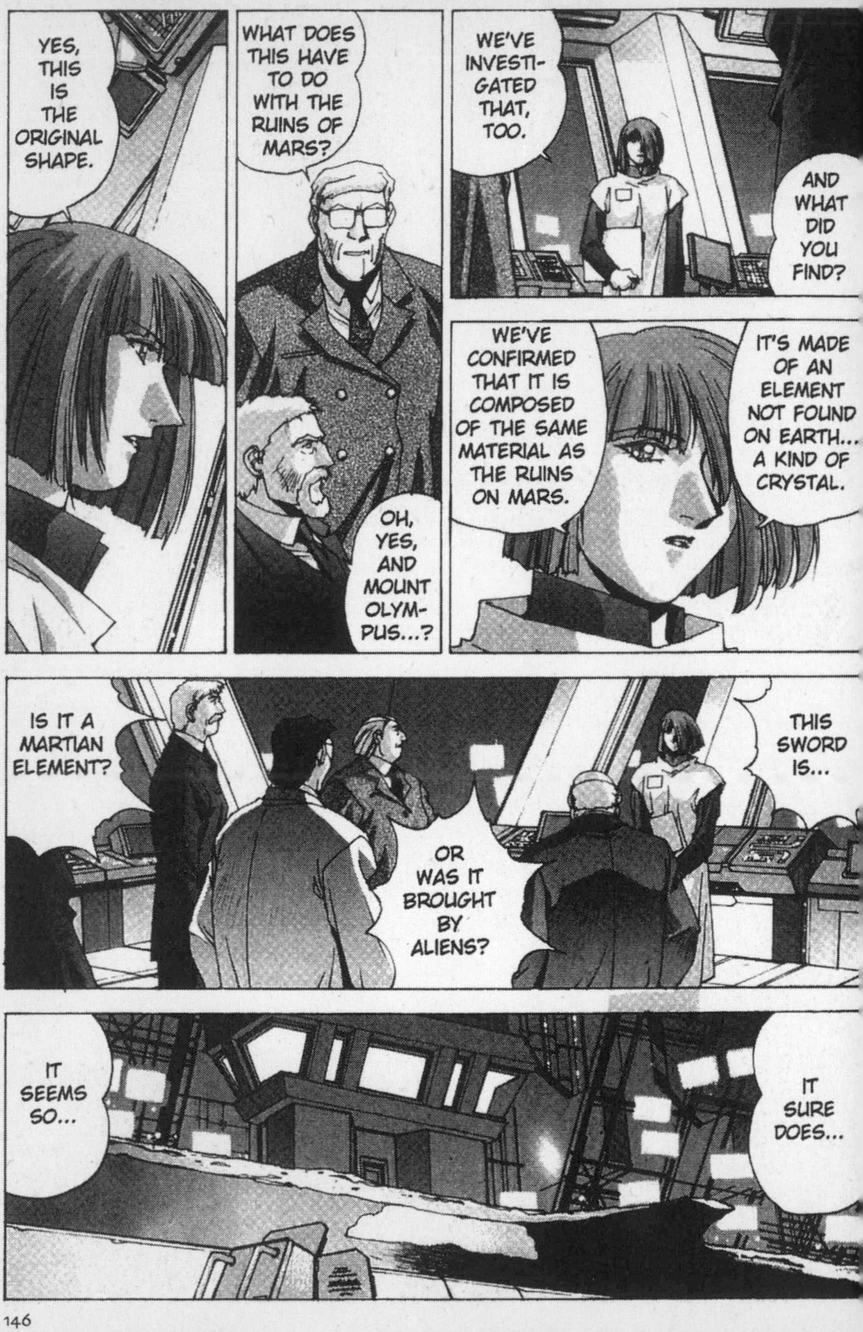
YES, THIS IS THE ORIGINAL SHAPE.
WHAT DOES THIS HAVE TO DO WITH THE RUINS OF MARS?
OH, YES, AND MOUNT OLYMPUS...?
WE'VE INVESTIGATED THAT, TOO.
AND WHAT DID YOU FIND?
WE'VE CONFIRMED THAT IT IS COMPOSED OF THE SAME MATERIAL AS THE RUINS ON MARS.
IT'S MADE OF AN ELEMENT NOT FOUND ON EARTH... A KIND OF CRYSTAL.
IS IT A MARTIAN ELEMENT?
OR WAS IT BROUGHT BY ALIENS?
THIS SWORD IS...
IT SEEMS SO...
IT SURE DOES...

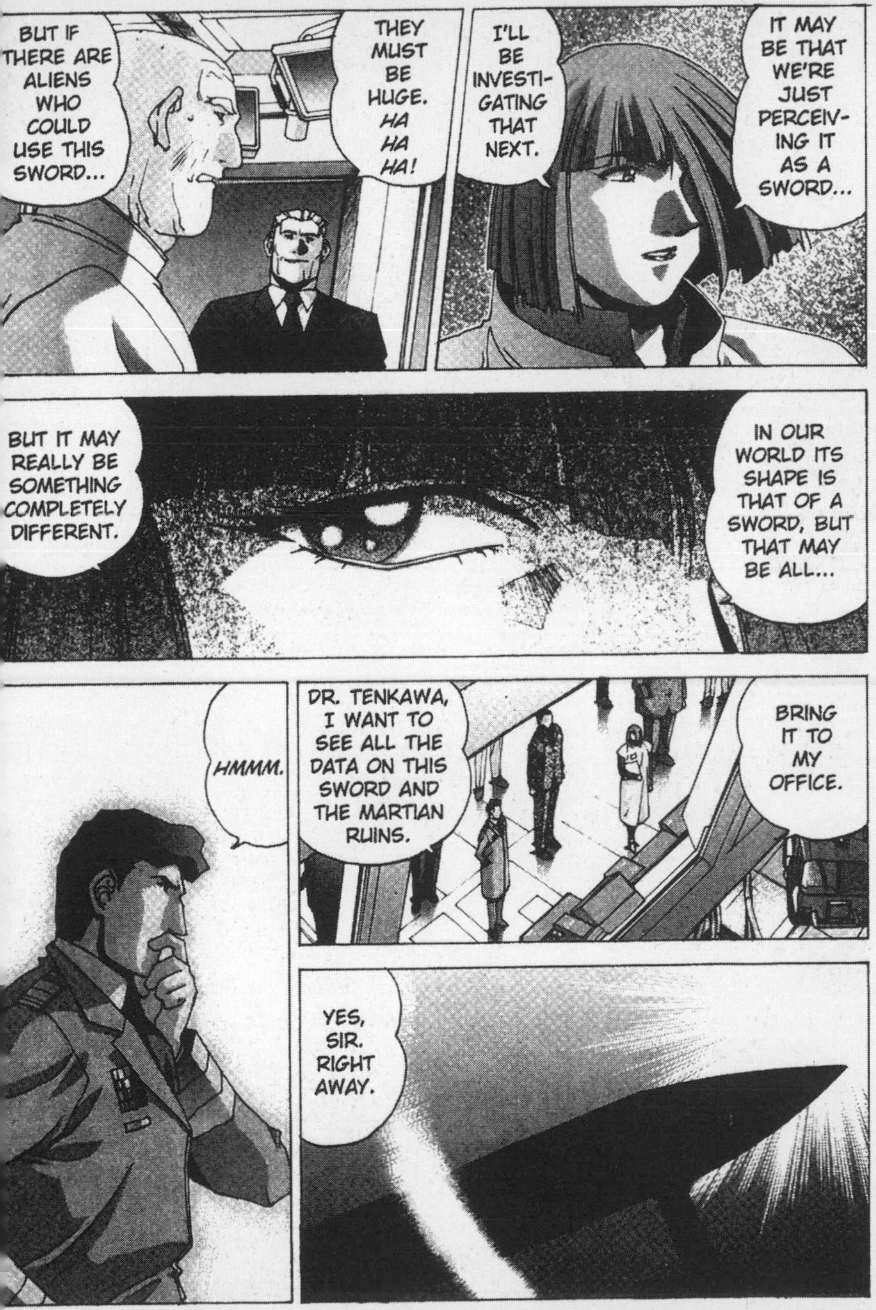

BUT IF THERE ARE ALIENS WHO COULD USE THIS SWORD...
THEY MUST BE HUGE. HA HA HA!
I'LL BE INVESTIGATING THAT NEXT.
IT MAY BE THAT WE'RE JUST PERCEIVING IT AS A SWORD...
BUT IT MAY REALLY BE SOMETHING COMPLETELY DIFFERENT.
IN OUR WORLD ITS SHAPE IS THAT OF A SWORD, BUT THAT MAY BE ALL...
HMMM.
DR. TENKAWA, I WANT TO SEE ALL THE DATA ON THIS SWORD AND THE MARTIAN RUINS.
BRING IT TO MY OFFICE.
YES, SIR. RIGHT AWAY.

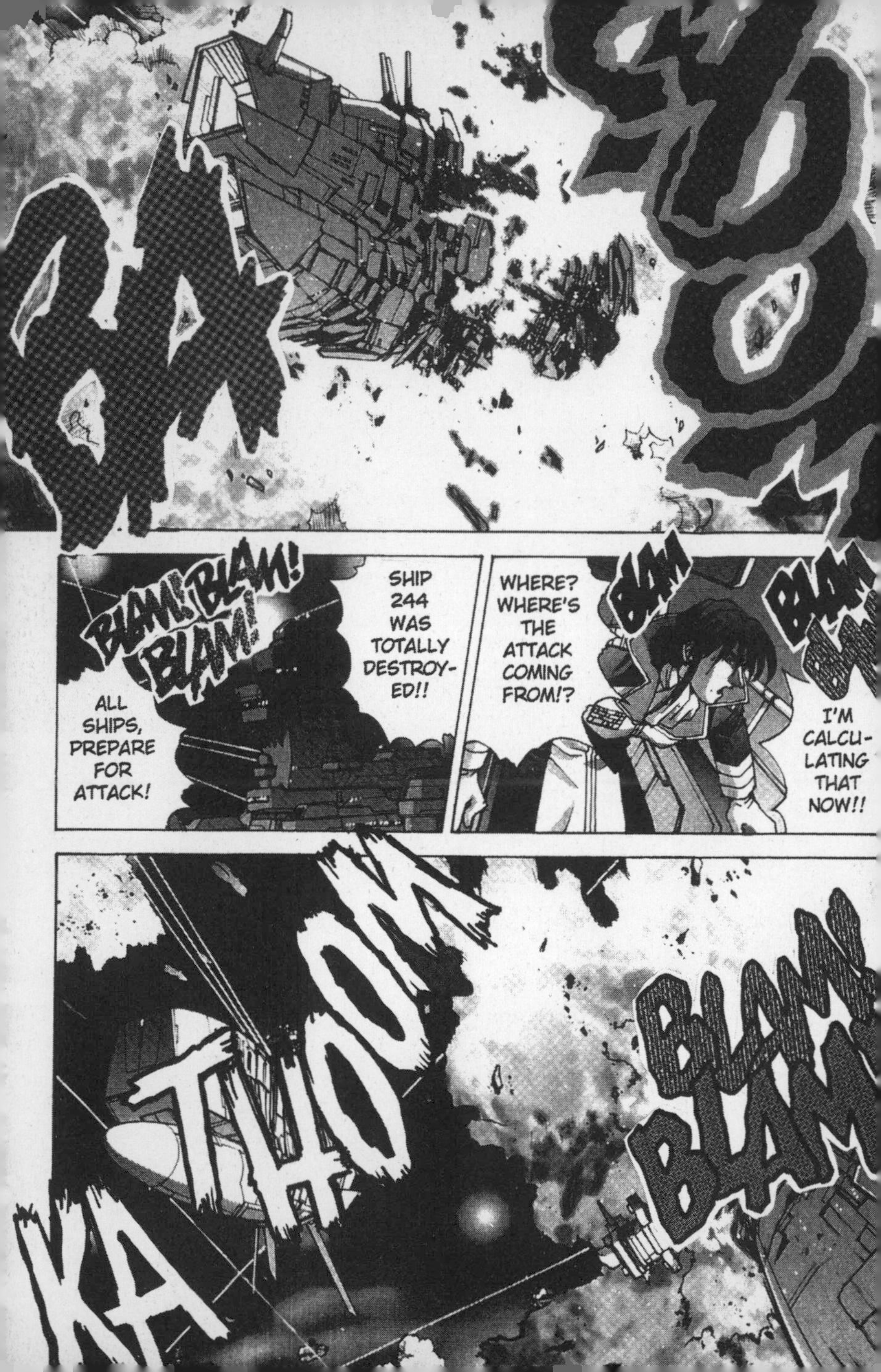
BAM
BLAM! BLAM! BLAM!
ALL SHIPS, PREPARE FOR ATTACK!
SHIP 244 WAS TOTALLY DESTROY-ED!!
BLAM
WHERE? WHERE'S THE ATTACK COMING FROM!?
I'M CALCU-LATING THAT NOW!!
KATHOOM
BLAM! BLAM!

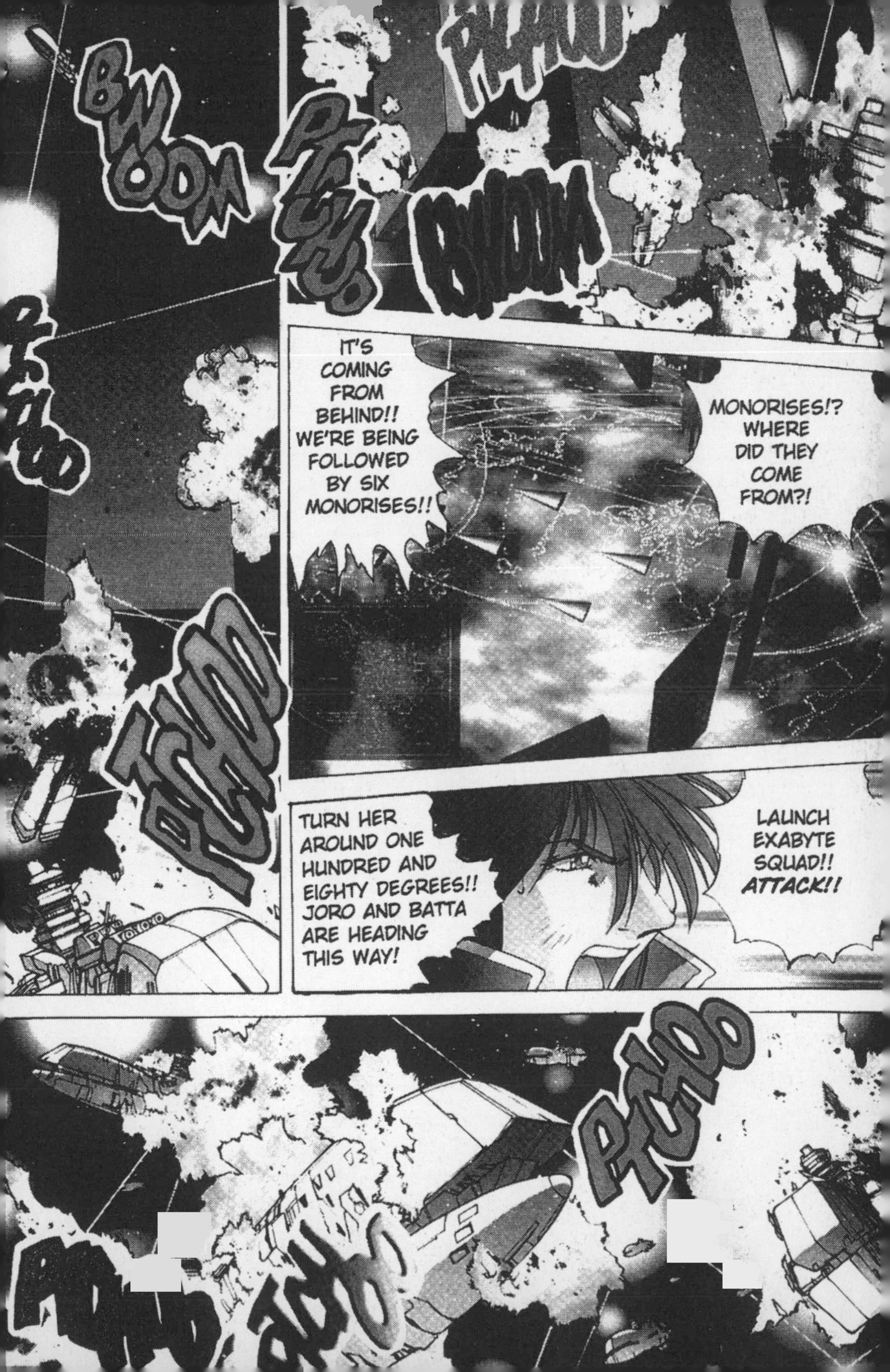
BWOOM
PTCHOO
BWOOM
IT'S COMING FROM BEHIND!! WE'RE BEING FOLLOWED BY SIX MONORISES!!
MONORISES!? WHERE DID THEY COME FROM?!
TURN HER AROUND ONE HUNDRED AND EIGHTY DEGREES!! JORO AND BATTA ARE HEADING THIS WAY!
LAUNCH EXABYTE SQUAD!! ATTACK!!
PTCHOO

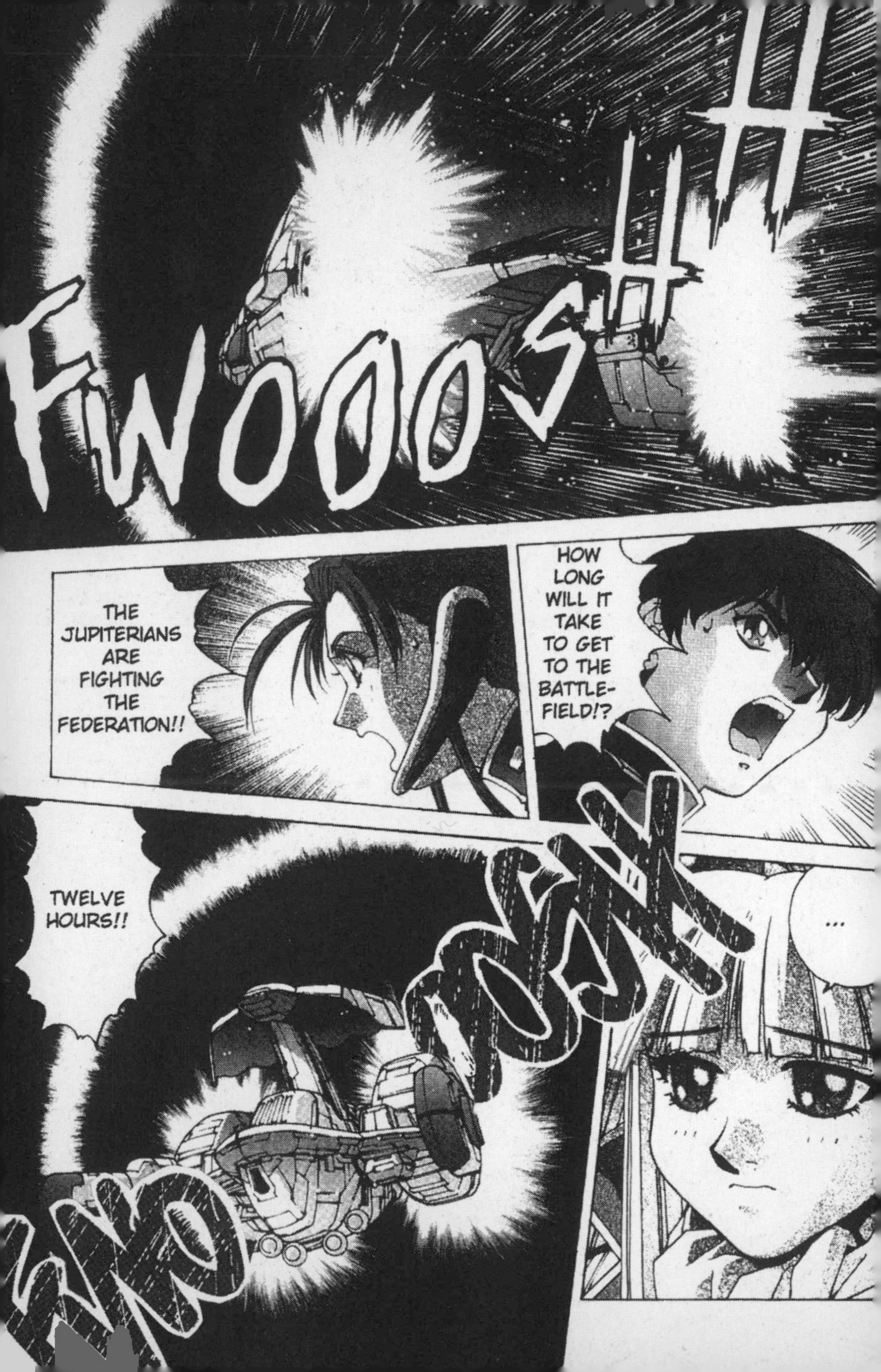
FWOOOSH
THE JUPITERIANS ARE FIGHTING THE FEDERATION!!
HOW LONG WILL IT TAKE TO GET TO THE BATTLE-FIELD!?
TWELVE HOURS!!
...

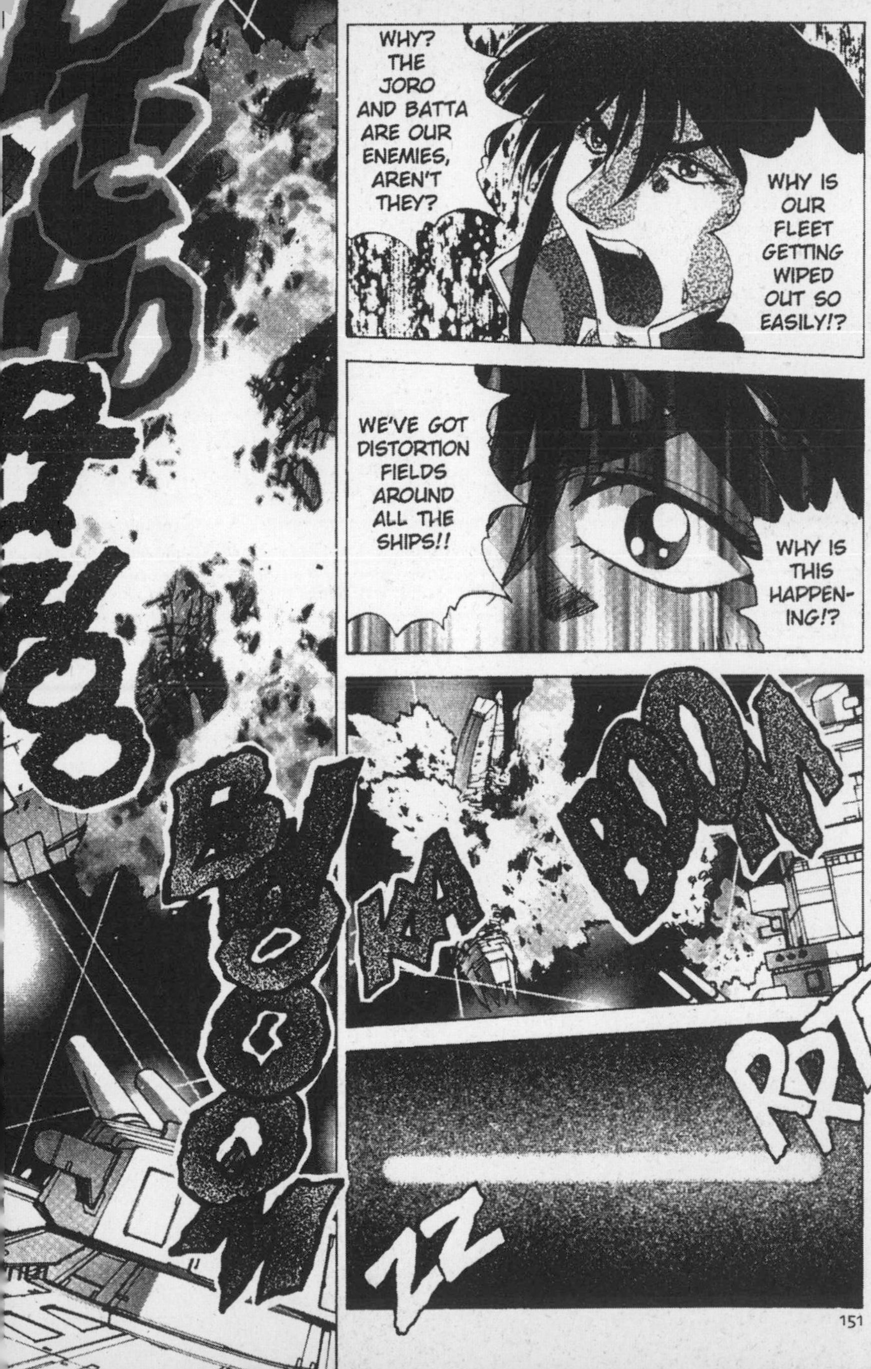
WHY? THE JORO AND BATTA ARE OUR ENEMIES, AREN'T THEY?
WHY IS OUR FLEET GETTING WIPED OUT SO EASILY!?
WE'VE GOT DISTORTION FIELDS AROUND ALL THE SHIPS!!
WHY IS THIS HAPPEN-ING!?
KA BOOM
RRT
ZZ

ASUKA
INDUSTRY CO., LTD.,

IT'S SARASHINA, I'M COMING IN.

GO AHEAD.

COMMANDER YAHATA, WHEN DID YOU ARRIVE ON THE MOON?

SARASHINA, I LOOKED OVER YOUR REPORT.

IT'S VERY INTERESTING.

NADESICO, KAGUYA, THE RUINS OF MARS, AND THE SWORD...

DO YOU THINK THIS WARRANTS KNOCKING OUT NERGAL?

THREE HOURS AGO.

OF COURSE.

BY THE WAY--

-- HOW LONG DO YOU INTEND TO REFER TO THE ENEMY AS JUPITERIAN?

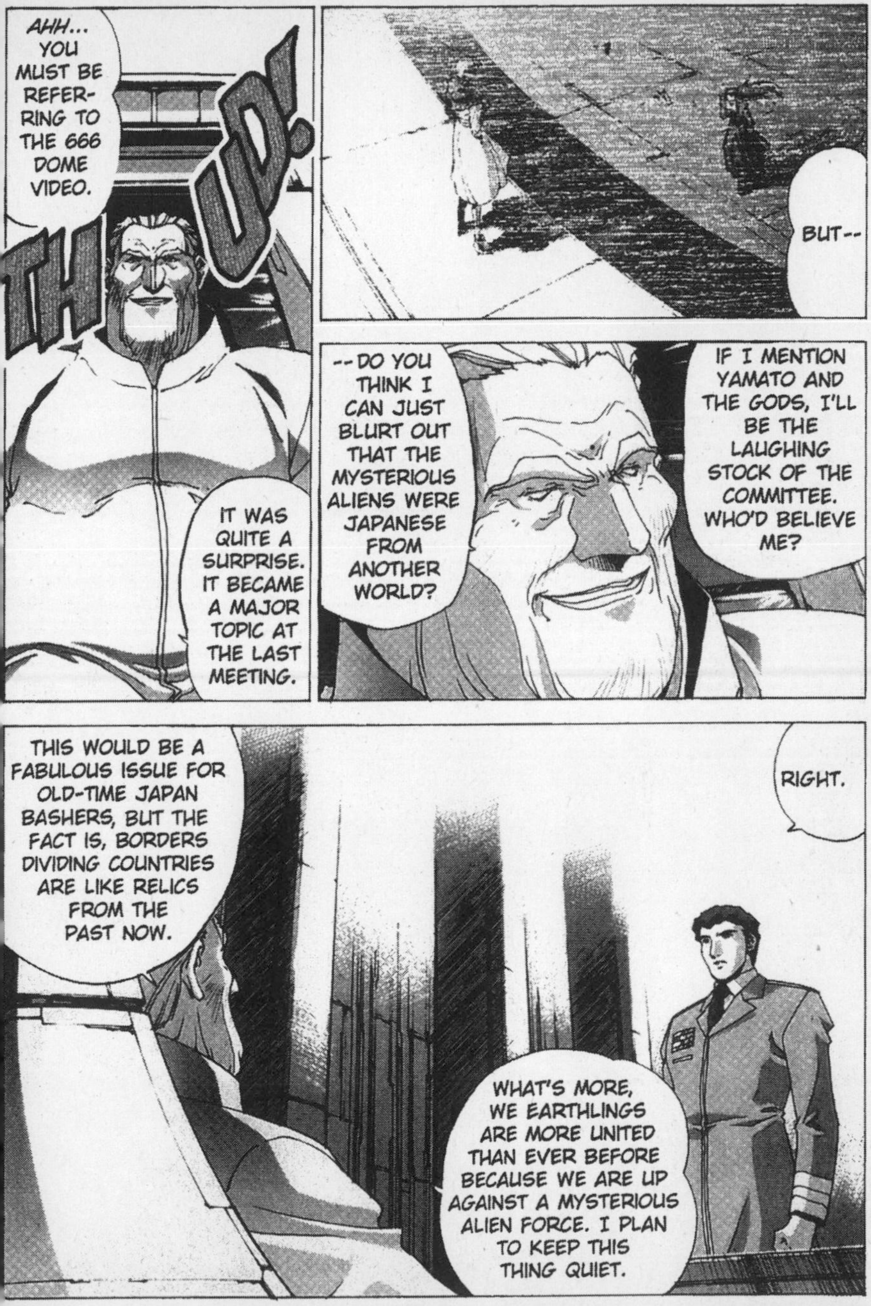
AHH... YOU MUST BE REFERRING TO THE 666 DOME VIDEO.
THUD!
IT WAS QUITE A SURPRISE. IT BECAME A MAJOR TOPIC AT THE LAST MEETING.
BUT--
--DO YOU THINK I CAN JUST BLURT OUT THAT THE MYSTERIOUS ALIENS WERE JAPANESE FROM ANOTHER WORLD?
IF I MENTION YAMATO AND THE GODS, I'LL BE THE LAUGHING STOCK OF THE COMMITTEE. WHO'D BELIEVE ME?
THIS WOULD BE A FABULOUS ISSUE FOR OLD-TIME JAPAN BASHERS, BUT THE FACT IS, BORDERS DIVIDING COUNTRIES ARE LIKE RELICS FROM THE PAST NOW.
RIGHT.
WHAT'S MORE, WE EARTHLINGS ARE MORE UNITED THAN EVER BEFORE BECAUSE WE ARE UP AGAINST A MYSTERIOUS ALIEN FORCE. I PLAN TO KEEP THIS THING QUIET.

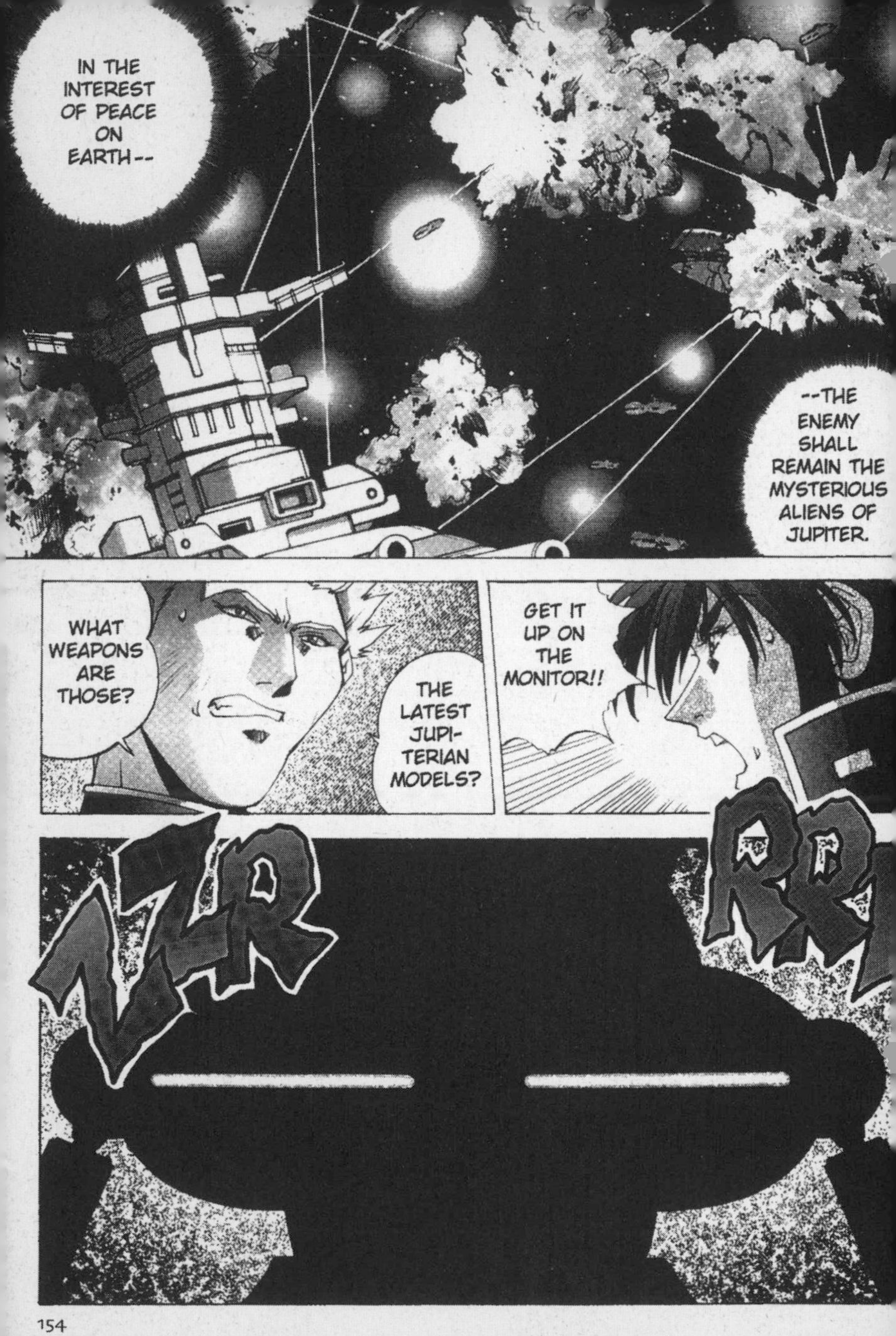
IN THE INTEREST OF PEACE ON EARTH--
--THE ENEMY SHALL REMAIN THE MYSTERIOUS ALIENS OF JUPITER.
WHAT WEAPONS ARE THOSE?
THE LATEST JUPI-TERIAN MODELS?
GET IT UP ON THE MONITOR!!

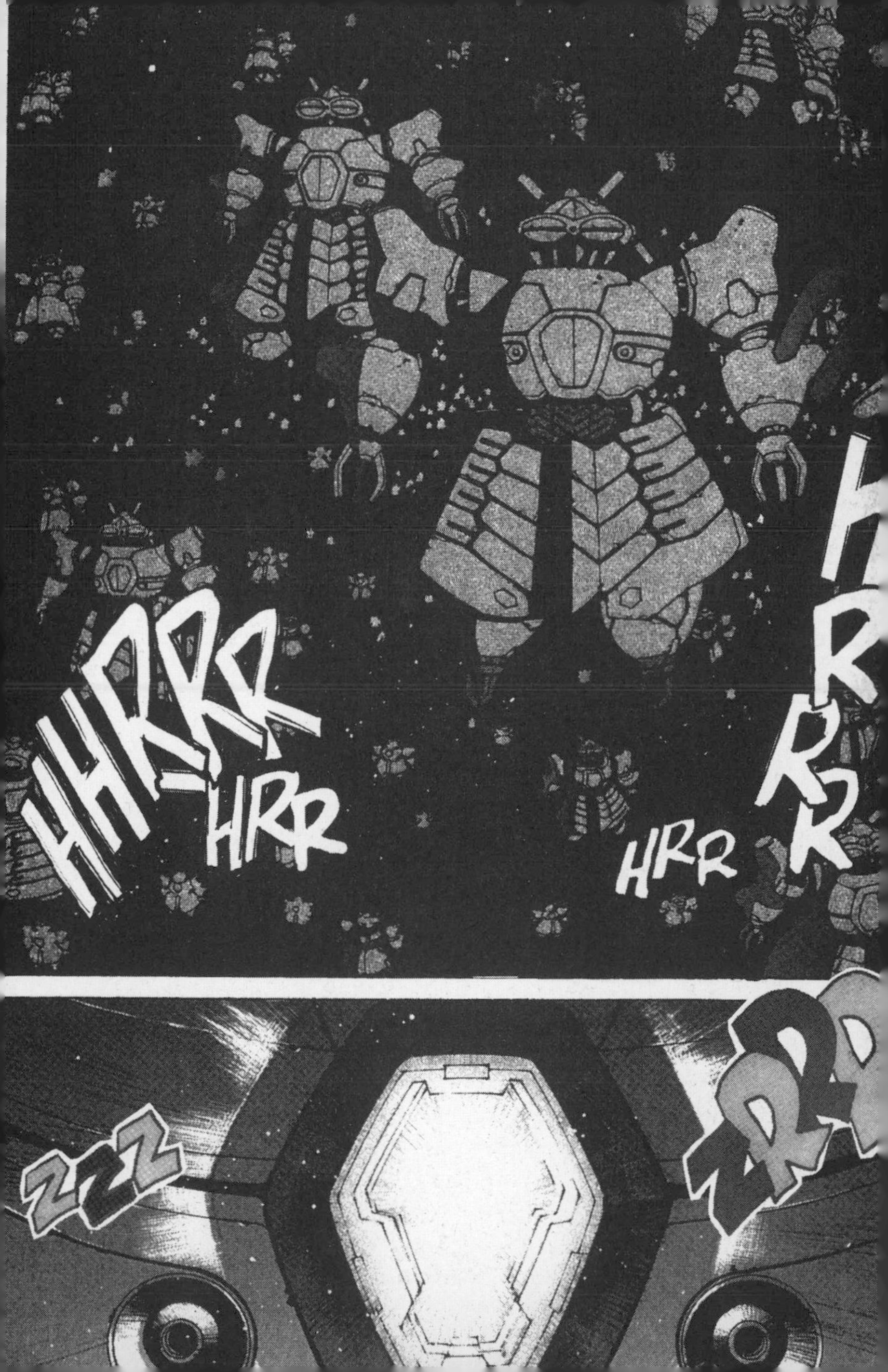
HHRRR-HRR
HRR
HRRRR
ZZZ
ZRRR

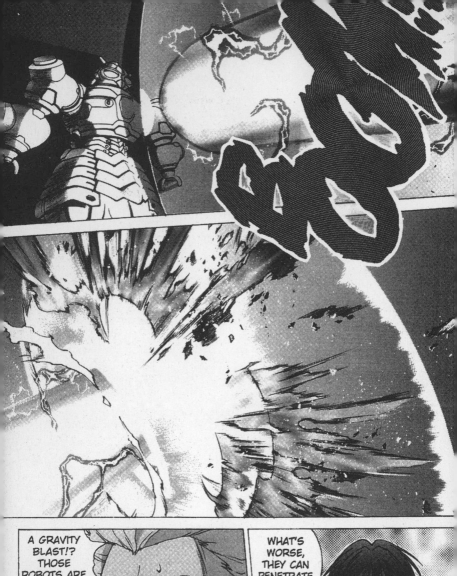

A GRAVITY BLAST!? THOSE ROBOTS ARE EQUIPPED WITH GRAVITY BLASTERS!

THAT'S WHY!! THAT'S HOW THEY DID IT!!

WHAT'S WORSE, THEY CAN PENETRATE OUR DISTORTION FIELDS--

--SO THEY HAVE A NEW WEAPON!!

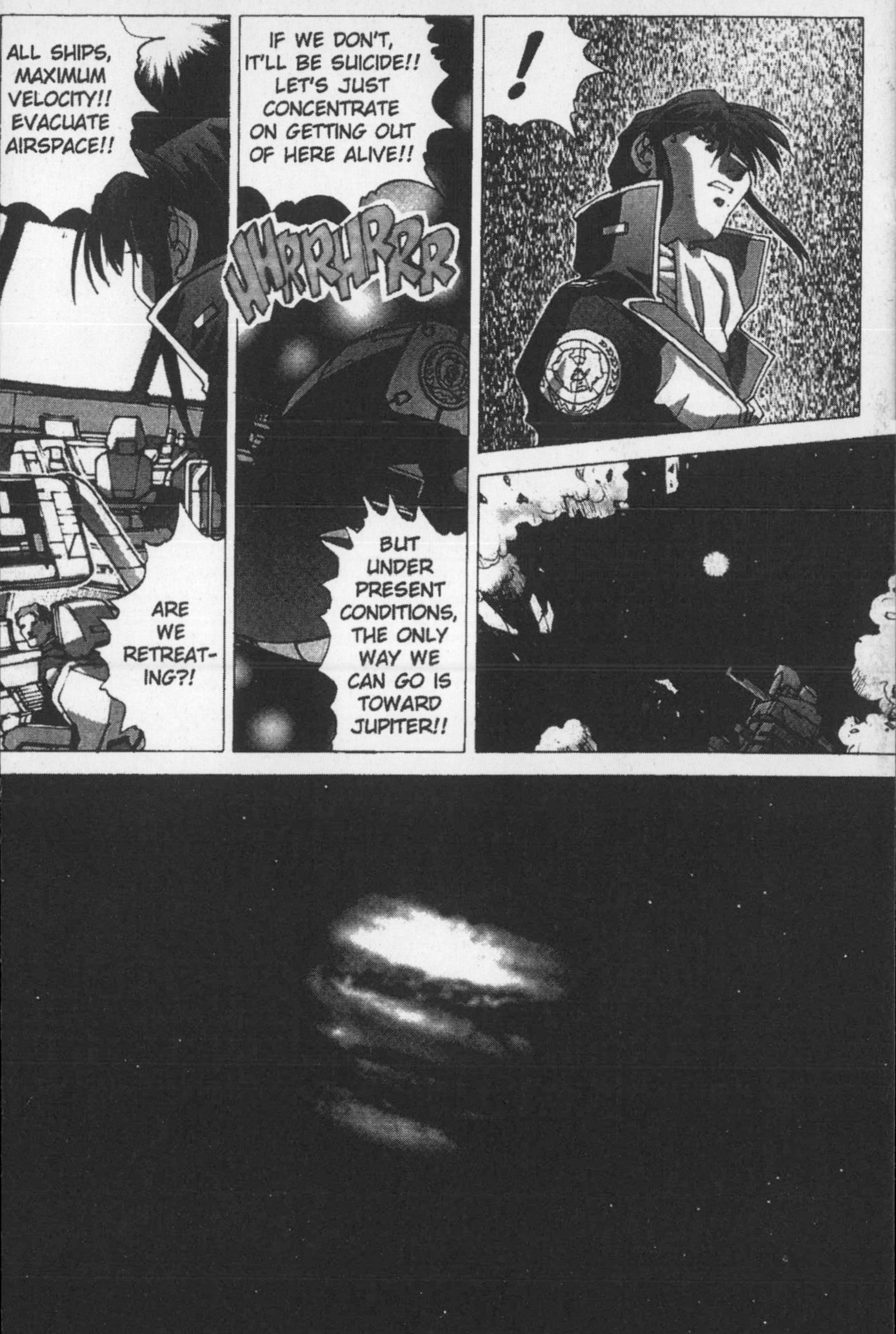
ALL SHIPS, MAXIMUM VELOCITY!! EVACUATE AIRSPACE!!
ARE WE RETREATING?!
IF WE DON'T, IT'LL BE SUICIDE!! LET'S JUST CONCENTRATE ON GETTING OUT OF HERE ALIVE!!
WHRRWRRR
BUT UNDER PRESENT CONDITIONS, THE ONLY WAY WE CAN GO IS TOWARD JUPITER!!
!

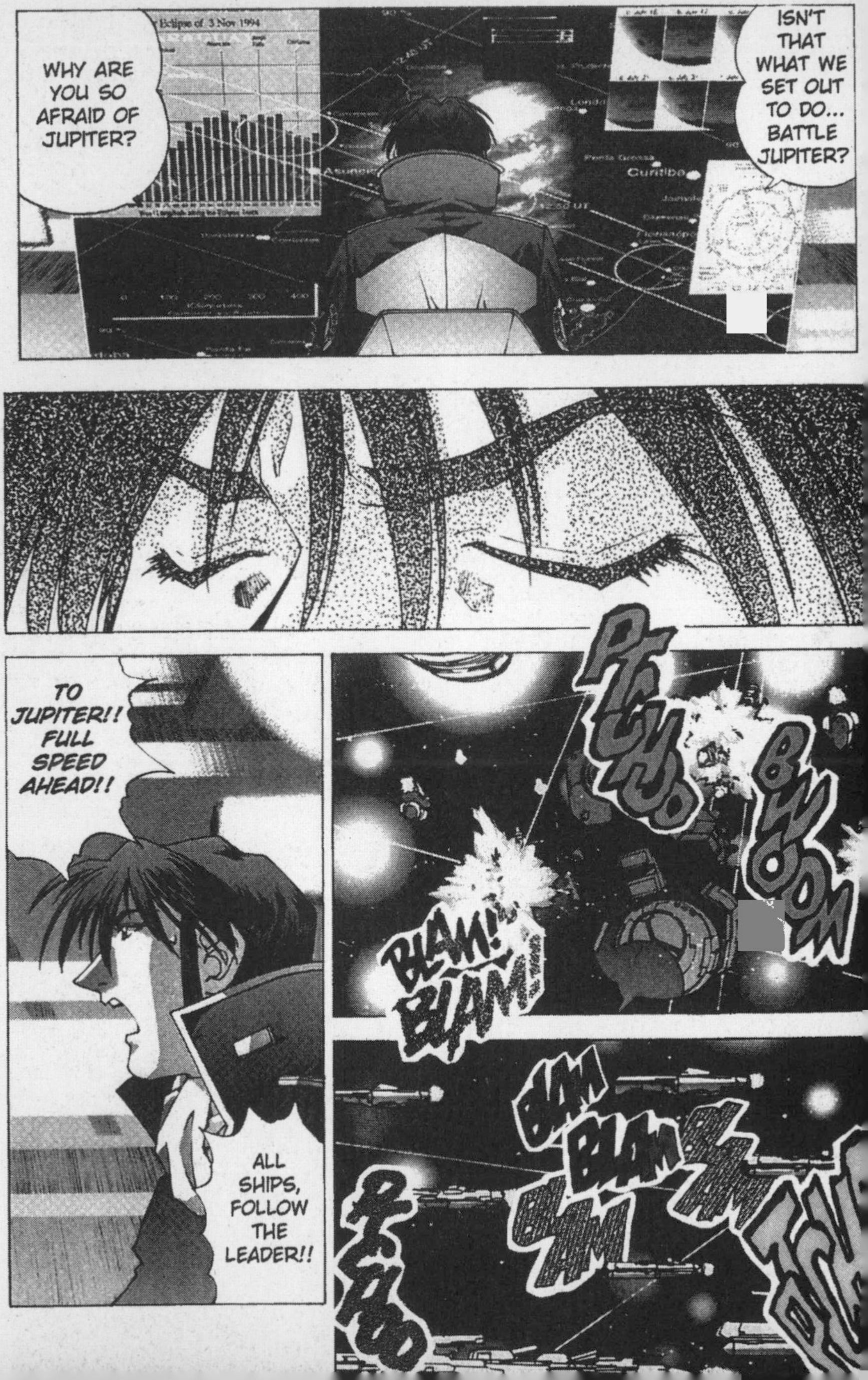
WHY ARE YOU SO AFRAID OF JUPITER?
ISN'T THAT WHAT WE SET OUT TO DO... BATTLE JUPITER?
TO JUPITER!! FULL SPEED AHEAD!!
ALL SHIPS, FOLLOW THE LEADER!!
PTCHOO
BWOOM
BLAM! BLAM!
BLAM
BLAM

THE FEDERATION FORCES ARE HEADING TOWARD JUPITER!!

JUPITER

U.N.S.F

JUPITLIEN

IT LOOKS LIKE THEY'RE EVADING THEIR ENEMY.

RETREAT-ING FROM BATTLE... THE UNITED EARTH FEDER-ATION FORCES...

BUT WHY?

ACCORDING TO THE MONITOR, THE EARTH'S FEDERATION FORCES SHOULD BE ABLE TO OVERPOWER THEM--

--BASED ON THE NUM-BERS.

ON

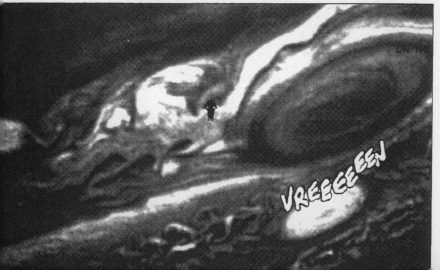

VREEEEEN

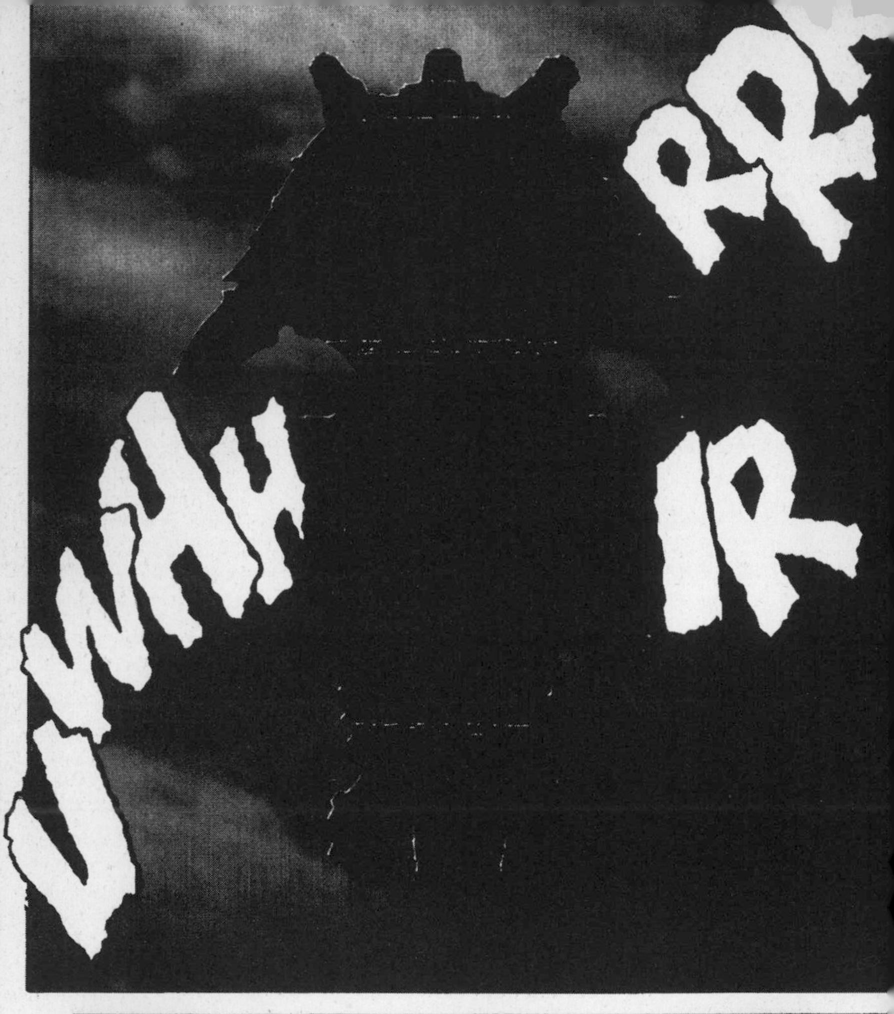

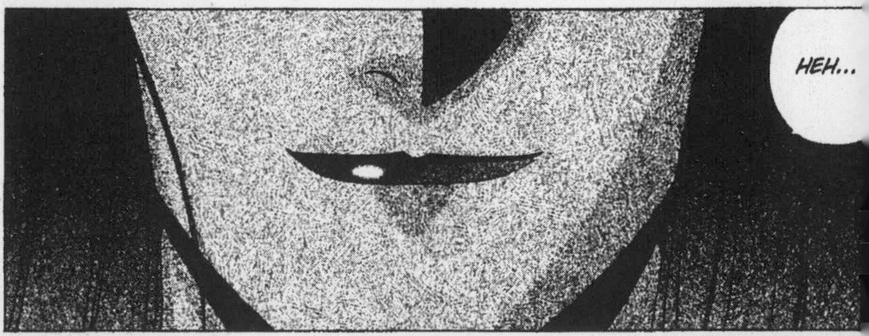
HEH...

To Be Continued
In Book Four

About Kia Asamiya

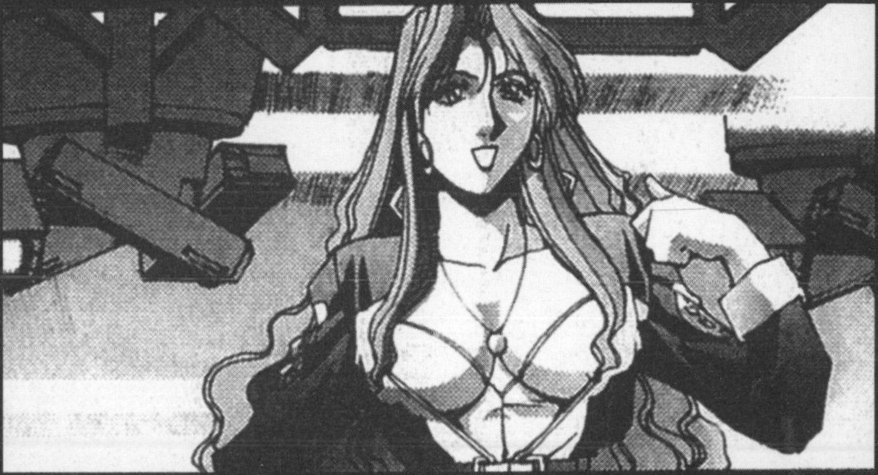

Kia Asamiya is a world-famous master of manga. He has created several series, including *Silent Möbius, Dark Angel, Gunhed* and *Nadesico,* which have been the basis for many popular motion pictures and anime. His titles define entire genres within Japanese popular culture, and fans and creators alike respect him.

A fan of American comic books, he has done manga adaptations of *Star Wars,* and was the artist for *Uncanny X-Men* and *Batman: Child of Dreams.*

A frequent visitor to the United States and a popular American convention guest, he is the founder of his own manga workshop, Studio Tron.

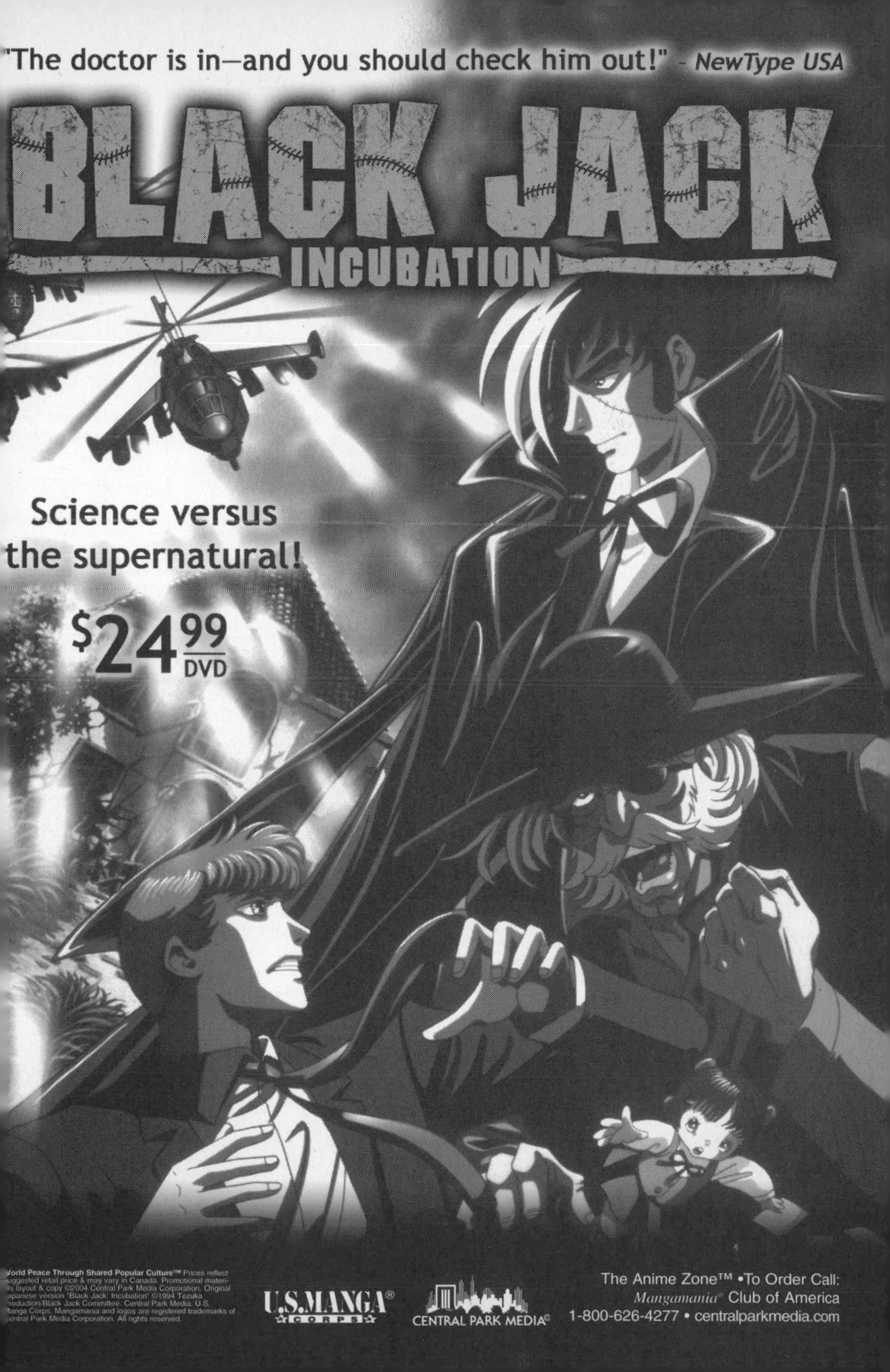

"The doctor is in—and you should check him out!" - NewType USA
BLACK JACK
INCUBATION
Science versus the supernatural!
$24.99 DVD
World Peace Through Shared Popular Culture™ Prices reflect suggested retail price & may vary in Canada. Promotional materials layout & copy ©2004 Central Park Media Corporation. Original Japanese version "Black Jack: Incubation" ©1994 Tezuka Production/Black Jack Committee. Central Park Media, U.S. Manga Corps, Mangamania and logos are registered trademarks of Central Park Media Corporation. All rights reserved.
U.S.MANGA CORPS
CENTRAL PARK MEDIA
The Anime Zone™ •To Order Call:
Mangamania® Club of America
1-800-626-4277 • centralparkmedia.com

The WORLD'S FIRST *ALIEN NINE*
DVD and MANGA BOXED SET!

ALIENNINE
ULTIMATE COLLECTION

"one seriously mind-bending trip" —*Anime Insider*
"entertaining adventure" —*Sci-Fi Magazine*
"good weird fun" —*Comics Buyer's Guide*
"bold and effective" —*Publisher's Weekly*

672 PAGES
and
100 MINUTES
of **SCI-FI**
ACTION!

Only
$59⁹⁹

The Anime Zone™
To Order Call:
Mangamania Club of America
1-800-626-4277
centralparkmedia.com
cpmmanga.com

CENTRAL PARK MEDIA®

CPM®
MANGA

U.S.MANGA
CORPS

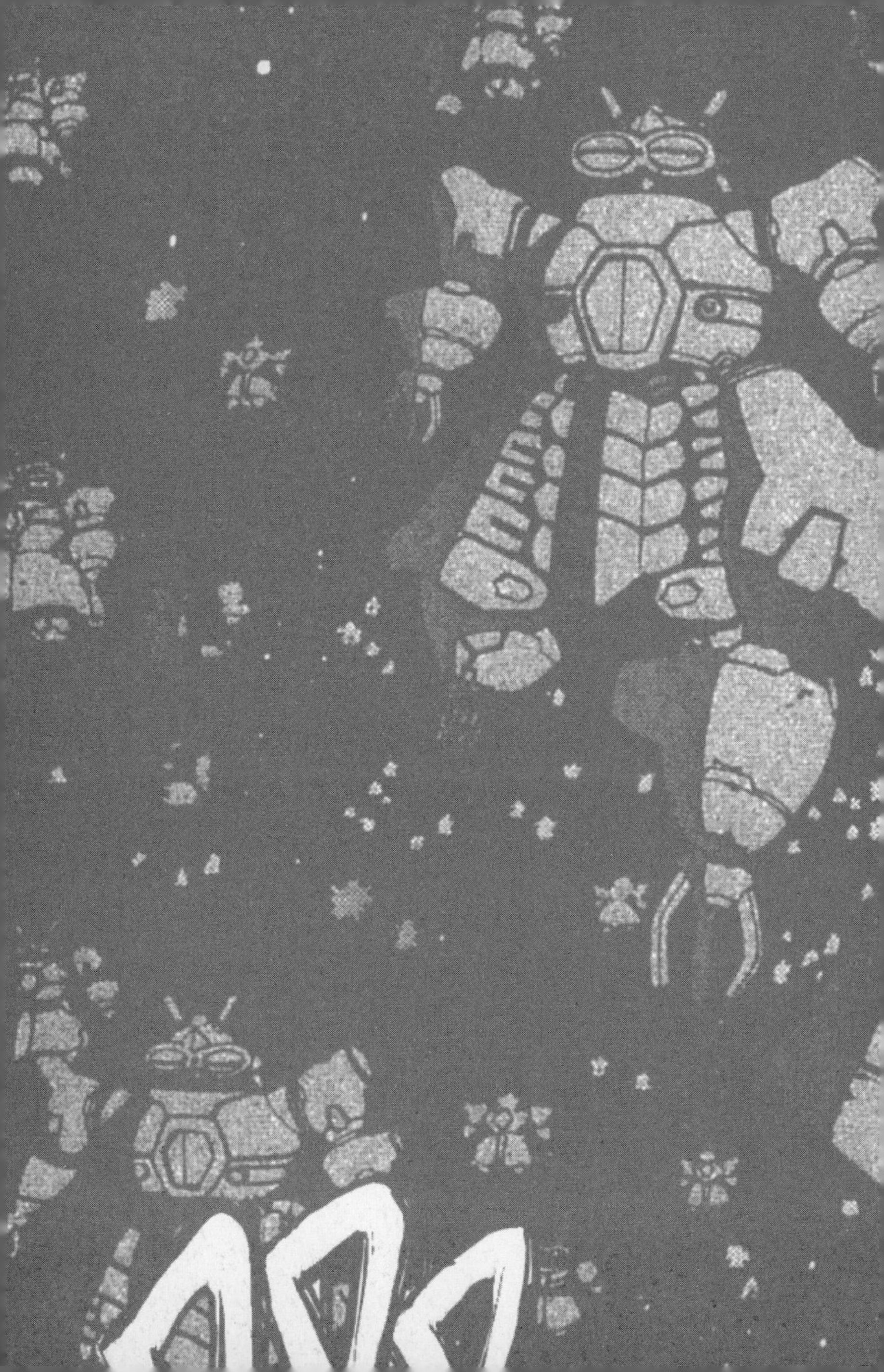